Diary of a Shipping Clerk
VOLUME I

Diary of a Shipping Clerk
VOLUME I

David Miles-Hanschell

DIARY OF A SHIPPING CLERK ~ Volume 1
by David Miles-Hanschell

First published 2022

Copyright © David Miles-Hanschell 2022

The right of David Miles-Hanschell to be identified as
the author of this work has been asserted by him
in accordance with the Copyright, Designs
and Patents Act 1988.

All rights reserved.
No part of this book may be reproduced in any form
or by any electronic or mechanical means, including information
storage and retrieval systems, without written permission from
the author, except for the use of brief quotations in a book review.

Copyedited by Northern Editorial
Cover design by Red Axe Design
Book interior by Eleanor Abraham

Typeset in Adobe Garamond Pro and Proxima Nova

ISBN: 978-1-7391426-0-5

Contents

Introduction	7
Chapter One – How it all Began	13
Chapter Two – I Make Arrangements to Deliver More Educational Resources to Grand Roy Government School	56
Chapter Three – Back to the Port School	74
Chapter Four – The Shipping Clerk Purchases a 40-foot Ocean Freight Container	86
Chapter Five – The Fact-Finding Trip to the Isle of Spices	115
Chapter Six – My Attempt to Solve the Wasteful Disposal of Educational Resources	139
Chapter Seven – The Family Visit Grenada	246
Chapter Eight – I Persevere With My Project	265
Acknowledgements	366

Dedication

To Marion, Amy, David and Johanna –
who bore the cost without complaint – and all
those who made the shipments a reality.

Introduction

Let me introduce myself. I was once a teacher at North Bute Primary School, Port Bannatyne, Isle of Bute. I am someone whose preferred form of travel, apart from walking on this tiny island, has been riding a bicycle. If you were a sailor with a yacht at anchor in Kames Bay, you might have noticed me. I was the chap in blue overalls who worked at the 20-foot Gray Adams reefer that was parked inside the gates at the boatyard from 2005–2008.

I was born on the island of Barbados in the West Indies. On my father's side, the family came from Puerto Rico and Denmark, in the middle of the nineteenth century, to settle eventually on the island of Barbados, where they opened a ship chandlery business, Hanschell & Co, in the capital of Bridgetown. On my mother's side of the family I had grandparents who had emigrated from the British Isles to western Canada, some of whom had settled in the town of Rothesay in New Brunswick. When I was seven, in 1950, my family moved to Trinidad where I completed my primary education. I returned to Barbados in 1955 to attend a boarding school for my secondary education.

I was not happy at this school and dreamt of escape to the great North American outdoors and the freedom, I then believed it offered, to create a life based one's own efforts. I thought that I, too, could settle somewhere in Canada and begin my working life. However, on arriving in Canada for a family holiday in the summer of 1961, the immigration authorities informed my parents that I did not qualify for permanent residence, and the only basis on which I could remain in their country was to obtain a student visa and complete my secondary education, which I felt I had already done. I did this by attending Rothesay Collegiate School. After the

Introduction

completion of a Canadian secondary school education, two years later, I was to learn from the Canadian immigration authorities that I still did not qualify for permanent resident status.

I was determined to remain in the country and I decided reluctantly to extend my student visa status. I had gained the necessary qualifications to attend Dalhousie University in Halifax, Nova Scotia, thanks to the long-suffering generosity of my dear parents. And after several wandering gap years in Europe and across Canada I eventually graduated with a Bachelor of Arts degree in 1970 and on that I was granted landed immigrant status. I obtained several temporary teaching posts with the Halifax City School Board and was later offered a permanent teaching post at King's College School in Windsor, Nova Scotia. As it turned out I was unsuited for that post and in November of that year I resigned and returned to live in the city of Halifax.

I soon found employment as a cleaner on the night shift at the National Sea Products fish processing plant at the dockside. Here I was to work alongside retired deep sea trawlermen. It took me a while to get accustomed to the monotonous and demanding physical routine of the fish skinning machinery and filleting tables and to meet the eagle-eyed foreman's satisfaction. I was determined that I would meet the standard of work required from this Cape Breton islander. Here, in this factory, I was to cut my manual labouring teeth never having previously held down a manual labourer's job. It would have been unthinkable for someone in the Caribbean, from the social milieu into which I had been born, to have ended up doing this type of work. I worked away steadily at the fish plant until the spring of 1971.

I still had vague notions of self-realisation, of somehow achieving the dream that I had arrived with from Barbados, way back in July 1961. It was a hard decision to hand in my notice as I liked and respected my workmates. They had stuck with me until I was able to carry out the job properly. I would never have completed my section were it not for their help. So, one morning, I said

INTRODUCTION

goodbye to my friends at the boarding house and began to hitch-hike my way across the country.

I am unable to recall precisely my journeying over the next two years. I wandered all over the continent of Canada from Halifax to Vancouver, never settling anywhere, or at anything worthwhile for very long. However a number of places and temporary employments stand out during the ensuing months of 1971. For example, Prince Rupert, British Columbia. On arrival in the town I set out on an old salmon trawler whose owner and skipper had come from a Dutch immigrant family and who had a butcher shop downtown. There was no more salmon to be caught, as the pulp and paper mills had polluted the rivers, but there were still large shoals of tuna fish, which could be caught in large numbers off the Queen Charlotte Islands. On our return to dock after a week out on the Pacific Ocean I was paid off with more money than I had been paid since I had ended my teaching career, with which I was well pleased, but with regret that these wonderful fish were being used to keep the once busy salmon cannery in production to feed cats.

Sometime that year I landed up working with Mexican labourers in a large pear orchard outside the town of Walnut Grove on the banks of the Sacramento River. I made my way back across the border, thumbed my way back to Winnipeg, Manitoba, and found work with Dutch tree nurserymen who were creating a tree nursery outside the town of Selkirk.

I decided sometime the following year to visit my mother in Barbados. She had returned to live with my aunt Jean after the death of my father while they were on holiday in Barbados in June 1970. For a brief period I worked as an overseer on a sugar plantation in the parish of St Lucy, and for a longer period as an agricultural field labourer growing vegetables on what had once been a sugar plantation in the parish of St Peter. I realised that since I now had achieved permanent residence status in Canada that was where I had to make something of my life. I was able to work my passage back to that country on board a Norwegian bulk carrier. I made my way to the city of Quebec where I found a job as a kitchen porter at Chez Rabelais, where I worked until the Spring of 1973.

In May 1973 I arrived at Prestwick en route for Prestatyn in Wales to visit my sister Diana, her husband Jim, and their family. My sister had come over to London from Trinidad in the early sixties to study floristry, and had met and married an Englishman in the British Army. I should say that almost immediately I felt a certain affinity with Scotland, which is not surprising given that my maternal grandmother had emigrated to Calgary, Canada, from the Inverlael estate outside Ullapool with her widowed mother, brothers and sisters. I did not know that then, but learnt it some years later. My father, however, had come over from Barbados to attend Edinburgh University in the thirties and had graduated with an honours degree in agricultural botany.

I worked at casual employment for a year in Wales and France. I decided to extend my stay in the United Kingdom and enrol in the Post Graduate Certificate in Education course at Moray House College of Education in Edinburgh. On completion of the course I began my Scottish teaching career in the East End of Glasgow, eventually marrying and coming to teach on the Island of Bute some thirty years ago.

Prior to hurricane Ivan's devastation of Grenada on 7 September 2004, I had had no direct contact with Grenada. However, some of my first chums in Saint Augustine, Trinidad, where we had gone to live on leaving Barbados in 1950, had grandparents who owned a coconut plantation in Grenada. These young friends would often make me envious with tales of the holidays they had spent galloping their horses along the beaches, and shooting wild pigeons in the surrounding rainforest. For my young imagination, it was an island of immense variety and appeal after the sterility and colonial sugar cane monoculture of Barbados. Later, I would board with a Mr and Mrs Alleyne at Newcastle Plantation when I returned to Barbados for my secondary schooling. Mrs Alleyne

INTRODUCTION

came from Grenada and some of my fellow boarders also came from there.

Grenada lies at the southern end of the chain of islands known as the West Indies. It has had a turbulent and unsettled history: colonised for nearly two centuries by the French, and fought over several times by the British until eventually the French Estate owners were replaced by British ones, who continued to grow sugar, coffee and cocoa with slave labour from Africa. It is a beautiful island with a tropical climate and rich vegetation, and attracts holidaymakers throughout the year. The tourist industry now plays a vital part in the islands economy. The island achieved nation status in 1974.

Hurricane Ivan devastated the island on 7 September 2004. I was first informed of the extent of that devastation in a brief report contained in a letter handed to me by a parent of a pupil in my P4/5 class at the Port school and I decided that my class, as part of their enterprise education curriculum, could do something to help a school on that hurricane devastated island. Also at the time, the pupils as part of the environmental studies curriculum were learning about the effects of extreme weather in different parts of the world. I was able to share with them my memories of Hurricane Janet that swept over Barbados and Grenada in 1955 when I was sent from the Alleyene's boarding establishment to stay with my Scottish granny for safety at her small rented flat in the capital, Bridgetown. For me, the experience was of great excitement, watching coconut trees and galvanised roofs flying through the air, though I was unaware of the danger and real damage being done not only to buildings, but also to people's lives.

The letter detailing the devastation of Hurricane Ivan was to change my life. It began the start of an epic journey of self-discovery, where my desire to help the people of Grenada was to consume my waking life.

The shipping clerk at the entrance to the Caribbean Hurricane Relief Depot.

Chapter One

How it all Began

Friday 11/02/2005 Isle of Bute

I am surfing the web reading an article by Peter Goldring, Canadian Member of Parliament for Edmonton East, Alberta, the opposition MP for Foreign Affairs, who has an interest in the Caribbean. As it would happen so do I, who was born and brought up to the age of 18 on the island of Barbados in the West Indies.

'A Paradise in Hell's Grip', written 21 July 2004. I copy some quotes from that article.

> The parliament buildings, major churches, schools, the jail and the Governor's residence are all suffering from some hurricane bomb blast damage as are homes and businesses. Two weeks after the disaster the population is stranded in absolute shock and squalor. Canada should contribute by helping to rebuild the island schools. The children must return to school, away from their damaged homes while their parents rebuild their lives.

Monday 14/02/2005

11 a.m. A parent is in the classroom at the moment making models with two pupils. I sent the 'To Whom it May Concern' letter from the principal of Grand Roy Government School, Grenada, (GRGS) to someone who I thought might be interested in helping the reforesting of Grenada post Hurricane Ivan. The class Enterprise Education project had a bring-and-buy sale of their unwanted toys and books at a Soup and Warmer Parent-Teacher Association fundraiser on Saturday 27 November 2004, which raised £57. I will open a bank account on their behalf at a bank in the town. Pupils later made and sold Christmas cards, and now, this morning, they are making plaster of Paris picture frames – a product to sell for their class 'Educate And Keep a Child Alive P4/5 Enterprises Unlimited' project, at gala day in May.

7:30 p.m. I am now attending a school board meeting: councillor for the local ward; the head teacher; three parents; a retired teacher, and myself, the teacher representative. To each I gave a copy of the letter from the principal of GRGS. The retired teacher thought it was a good idea for the school to support the reconstruction of this Hurricane Ivan-devastated Grenada government school, providing that that there was a bona fide need. It was agreed at the meeting that the next step was to await reports to verify that need, and the school board would await a reply to the letter that I had written to the principal of Grand Roy Government School.

Wednesday 16/02/2005

Today I gave copies of the email letter from the principal of GRGS to the school janitor and to my friend at the local stationery shop in the town. So far, I have not received a reply to my letter to the principal of the Grand Roy Government School.

Thursday 17/02/2005

5 p.m. Home. Earlier today, while attending a school in-service at another school on the island, I happened to meet with a teacher who had been out in the Caribbean on holiday. When the cruise ship that she was on was docked in St. George's, the capital of Grenada, the passengers were taken on a brief bus tour of the island. She saw the extensive damage done to the island by Hurricane Ivan and had taken photographs of the devastation. She kindly gave them to me when I told her that I had come from Barbados in the West Indies, and I knew what the experience of a hurricane was like, and that I hoped to involve our school, and possibly the local community of Port Bannatyne, in doing something that would aid in the island of Grenada's recovery. As I was cycling home after the in-service meeting, I stopped in at a local restaurant where the chef told me that he had once been employed in one of Grenada's well-known hotels and he could identify some of the sites where Hurricane Ivan had wrought destruction. He kindly offered to obtain some contacts on the island for me, should my idea of doing something to help Grenada come to fruition.

Friday 18/02/2005

6:30 p.m. I have just come off the telephone to the chief executive officer at the Ministry of Education and Labour in Grenada, telling him about what I hoped to do in some small but meaningful way for his country and its people, and that I was awaiting a reply from the principal of Grand Roy Government School.

Monday 21/02/2005

On the way up the road to school on my bicycle this morning, I stopped to speak to George to tell him about my concerns for a Grenadian school that had been virtually destroyed by Hurricane Ivan, and gave him a copy of the principal of Grand Roy Government Schools reply to my letter. George told me that he was attending a council meeting that day, and would pass on to those present my concerns and suggestions regarding the council's disposal of fit-for-purpose, surplus to requirements, educational resources. Over the summer holidays I was to collect enough good quality, surplus to requirements, educational resources to fill a ocean freight container for our Grenadian school. I have sent a copy the GRGS principal's letter to the councillor.

5:30 p.m. Home. I am not long in from a cycle through the breeze, and on the way home stopped to speak to another councillor, Len Scoullar, who took his gloves off to speak with me. He heard what I had to tell him about my concern for the situation in Grenada and about my Primary 4/5 class Grenada Schools Relief environmental studies project post Hurricane Ivan. He was interested in what I had to say and said he would like to read the principal of Grand Roy Government School's letter to the world. Before cycling out of town I had gone to the local branch of Citizens Advice with the cri de coeur letter from the Grenada school principal and there I met the manager. I told him that I was looking for someone with business/bookkeeping expertise who would volunteer for a couple of hours to help with handling financial accounts of the money raised for this project. He told me that he had also stopped off in Grenada while on a Caribbean Cruise. He listened attentively to what I had to say and I gave him a copy of the letter from the Grenadian school head teacher, and my address should a potential volunteer with double entry bookkeeping skill care to lend a hand. I then went further along the street and stopped in at the local travel agent and gave him a copy also. And cycled on home. Where on arrival I was back on the telephone making another transatlantic telephone call to Grenada to the office of Sylvan McIntyre, and I spoke with Miss Murray who told me he was not available. I then called the Grenada High Commission in London and asked to speak with the High Commissioner. *'How come you in Scotland?'* he asked me, when I told him that I was a Bajan. He was curious and I answered his question at some length, since he seemed interested in what I hoped to accomplish, but he did not commit himself.

Tuesday 22/02/2005

4:30 p.m. Home. In the town I met the librarian of the town's library as I was leaving Woolworth's and gave him a copy of the head teacher's letter. As I cycled out of town I met a teacher from another school, a kindred spirit, who had taught in Brazil and also in the island of Trinidad West Indies, where I once lived from 1950 to 1961. *'We have just ordered The Oxford Reading Tree and I've got over 800 'Reading 360 Scheme' Reading Books. I was going to send them off to Scottish International Relief but they are way over in Kinning Park in Glasgow, and I have no way of getting them over there. Do you want them?'* she asks kindly.

'Oh yes please! Thank you very much,' I reply eagerly, not having a clue as to where I could store them. I told her that I hoped one day, if it were possible, I would try to get a small ocean freight container temporarily sited at the local boatyard, where donated fit-for-purpose, surplus to local schools' requirements, educational resources could be sorted, inventoried, packaged and shipped out to the Hurricane Ivan-devastated island of Grenada in the West Indies.

'Here I go again, with my ebullient enthusiasm, high hopes and daft notions,' I thought to myself. *'You are just blagging.'* What someone in Glasgow once described as 'another of David's zany ideas.' I was always one who was always to run, before he had even learned how to walk. I did not have clue as to where I could hold on to this wonderful gift of school reading books.

'That's a great idea, David. I'll tell you what I will do. I'll keep them for you down at the Red Cross depot, and when you are ready to collect them, let me know,' she said. I gave her copy of Janice Thomas's letter (the principal of Grand Roy Government School), and cycled on.

4:55 p.m. Home. I called the High Commissioner for Grenada in London and we spoke once more. He told me that he had been in touch with the principal of Grand Roy Government School and, though she had not received my letter, she told him that there was a registered letter for her awaiting collection at a post office in another part of the island.

I asked the high commissioner if knew of any Grenadians who happened to be studying in Scotland? He said no, but the question gave him pause for thought. *'We must keep in touch,'* he said. That was a positive response to that call. There's no harm in pushing the envelope.

5:10 p.m. I called the Sabre Foundation in Cambridge Mass. USA and spoke with Ray, who gave me Colin (comes from Ulster and studied in Scotland), their programme manager's, email. This organisation, I learned from her, had previously shipped books to Grenada and I wanted to learn from him how it was done. I thought I would make one more telephone call, not transatlantic this time. I called the travel company Just Grenada based in Somerset, United Kingdom. No answer.

Thursday 24/02/2005

I called the travel company Just Grenada and spoke with Nick, who was helpful. He told me that Gerry was the best informed person in the organisation to speak with and that he would be interested in things of a welfare nature. I then asked Nick if he knew of any absentee owners of property in Grenada resident in the United Kingdom, who might be willing to contribute expertise and time to the reconstruction of Grand Roy Government School. He couldn't tell me of any off hand.

6 p.m. I have just spoken to Gerry. Personable. Easy to talk to. He doesn't know me from Adam, but he is on my wavelength right away and hears me out. Positive. I am greatly encouraged by our conversation. He has asked me to write him a letter, which I will do. He said that he might put me in touch with property owners who may wish to contribute expertise, advice and materials towards getting that devastated school up and functioning. My first supporter. My objective is that I will leave no stone unturned and do everything in my power to help to rebuild and re-equip Grand Roy Government School in Grenada, West Indies.

Friday 25/02/2005

I showed the visiting learning support teacher the councillor Len Scoullar's letter of support and gave him a copy of Principal Janice Thomas's worldwide request for help. I posted a letter to Gerry. I spoke to the visiting speech therapist, who is also the local representative of the Red Cross, who is at present trying to find out through that organisation's representative in the Caribbean the legitimacy of the situation at GRGS. On my return home this afternoon I tried again to telephone the Ministry of Education and Human Development in Grenada. I called the home number of the chief education officer and I was given a number to call in the capital, but still no contact. I then called Government House in the Grenada capital and was asked if I wanted to speak to his secretary, and I said that I would be happy to do so. But no reply. After several minutes I hung up. These telephone calls are costing Hanschell Family Plc a fortune.

Some reflections on what I have taken on. Well, are the Grenadians interested? Should I persist? Are my wheeling and dealing transatlantic telephone calling, philanthropic, entrepreneurial efforts misguided, and, ultimately, will win me no friends this side of the Atlantic Ocean? Pointless? Totally outwith my current employment's job description as a local education authority, unpromoted, primary school teacher. Doubts about my inadequacy, and capacity to take on what I hoped to achieve, even if it is only one, 20-foot ocean freight container shipment of surplus to requirements, fit-for-purpose, educational resources. If it is not

Grenada, it could be somewhere else that could put to good use these huge amounts of fit-for-purpose educational resources that are currently being crushed and trucked to landfill at unnecessary cost to the tax payer. I recall times past when I did not persevere with projects and later regretted not having done so. There were times when I was not prepared to take risks. I am here today because I did take a risk and persevere with the work in hand at the time. I have risen because I made an effort. My purpose is essentially the recycling and salvage of perfectly good, classroom suitable, appropriate, educational resources, which are currently being thrown into a skip because someone in the local council education department has the authority to spend money to order new materials and declare the 'old' no longer fit for purpose. What are my reasons for going full tilt at this initiative, which was until only a short while ago a class topic in the Scottish Education Department environmental studies curriculum? Nostalgia? Perhaps a desire to return to some halcyon, imagined, illusory and out-of-date perception of the Caribbean. I do not think that this is unnatural for me to feel like that.

I was born, brought up and educated in that part of the world – it is where, for short periods, I felt at home. I miss the friendliness of my fellow West Indians. Redemption. If only I could return to the islands to reclaim an unhappy childhood and wasted adolescence. I have a wish to see something of value established somewhere. Why not there, on that beautiful tropical island, wasted by Hurricane Ivan? Altruism. Is mine genuine? I get a buzz, excitement, from creating something and seeing it through to fruition. The ambitious class projects undertaken with previous classes here, and with schools on the mainland, which were all seen to successful completion. The Rose Bowl school projects in Easterhouse in the seventies and Bridgeton in the eighties. The challenge that is presented by this initiative. I wish to prove wrong those who have sat on the sidelines to carp, criticise and diss my efforts and vocational enthusiasm.

Tuesday 01/03/2005

It could be a way of getting even with those who have done me down. Pride has always been a factor in my makeup. 'Pride and Industry' is the motto of Barbados. I enjoy not always, except when duty takes over, pushing my will and powers to the limit to accomplish the objective set at the time. Is it wrong to enjoy being and doing good? My failing is that at some point in that process, I have spoiled the good I have accomplished by going over the score. The trouble with me is, I don't do things by halves. A lack of balance. But when knocked off my perch I have picked myself up and started again. The principal of Grand Roy Government School received my letter? What will be her reaction? I will have to wait and see. I am basing this project, self-directed initiative, a frustrated primary teacher's attempts to break out into a new career, on the fact that there may be a school on the island of Hurricane Ivan-devastated Grenada that may have been overlooked in the distribution of educational resources for different reasons. Perhaps there are already sufficient resources available for the supply of resources for schools and reconstruction of schools by relief agencies. If not, as I write there are dozens of ocean freight containers loaded with educational resources with the Grenada Port Authority, or on the way from Grenada's expatriate communities in North America and elsewhere. And if this is the case, then, if this is the situation my efforts, energy and personal cost will have been superfluous. What I am trying to do?

(I knew it had its risks, which I would learn several years later to my cost.)

Tuesday 01/03/2005

11:30 a.m. Classroom. I have been given a message that there has been a telephone call from Grenada. Later the pupils ask me if I have won a cruise.

12:20 p.m. I spoke with the principal of Grand Roy Government School on a poor connection. My hearing is getting worse. I reiterated what I had said in my letter, that if it were possible I could liaise with a representative of their government based here in the United Kingdom, or on the ground in Grenada's Ministry of Education and Human Development, so that the project could be put on a sound basis. She mentioned that her brother knows the High Commissioner for Grenada in London and that he would liaise with them, which is great news. I asked her if it were possible to send some photographs of the effects of Hurricane Ivan on her school. It was not a good line.

5:45 p.m. Home. Earlier I called Macmillan Caribbean publishers and spoke with someone at reception who was helpful and directed to me their representative but who was not in the office.

Wednesday 02/03/2005

9:30 a.m. Classroom. I have just had a conversation with a parent member of the PTA and gave her a copy of Principal Janice Thomas's letter and a brief account of the sequence of events that lead to me receiving that letter:

Hurricane Ivan strikes the island of Grenada, West Indies; I have lived through the experience of a hurricane (Hurricane Janet struck Barbados in 1955, my home island); the class is doing a weather project and I thought it would be interesting for the class to learn about the extreme weather events due to climate change that are affecting many parts of our Blue Planet; a parent of a class member received a Christian Aid newsletter from one of their representatives in the Caribbean, in which was an eyewitness account by Richard Jones of the Caribbean Policy Development Centre, of the devastation wrought by Hurricane Ivan; on Saturday 27 November 2004 the class set up a stall at the Parent-Teacher Association winter warmer in the village hall; later that afternoon I went to see the owner of the boatyard, who invited me in for a cup of tea and I told him that I wished to purchase a container.

The following week I received a letter from a cousin in Barbados describing her visit to the island as part of a team of insurance adjusters who had gone to the island of Grenada to assess the damage that had been caused by the hurricane; I contacted my fellow Barbadian by telephone and after not a few expensive transatlantic phone calls to Mr Jones at Caribbean Policy Development Centre I received from him, by email, an attached cri de coeur from the principal of Grand Roy Government School; I wrote an airmail recorded-delivery letter to the principal in Grenada in response to the email attached letter, in which I offered my support; in February I contacted the High Commissioner for Grenada in London, who happens to know the principal's brother.

Thursday 03/03/2005

9:10 a.m. Classroom. Earlier, at 8:55 a.m., I spoke with our head teacher in the playground and I asked him if it would be acceptable for me to speak to other school board members at the school board training session weekend on 5 March about the donation of unwanted, fit-for-purpose, educational resources to this Grenadian hurricane-devastated school. I have not figured out yet how I am to collect, let alone store and send, these resources. I also discussed with our school's head teacher whether it was possible to forge a link between our Scottish primary school and its equivalent in the Caribbean? I told him that I hoped to purchase, out of my own funds, a container to temporarily store donated educational resources until such time as it could be shipped to Grenada. My head teacher said the school's PTA could contribute to the cost of this project, which would be brilliant. I told him that once I could be fairly certain that Janice

Thomas's open letter to the World Wide Web crying out for help was genuine, I would let the rest of the staff and parents know about the class project. A whole school effort of some kind would enhance our own P4/5 entrepreneurial philanthropist's plan to aid Grand Roy Government School.

11:10 a.m. At the break I showed the school board chairman the letter I had received from the local councillor letting our secondary school's bandmaster know about our plans to assist this Grenada school. He appeared to approve. I also mentioned to him that I hoped to let the other school board members, from other school boards attending a training day at the weekend, know about our initiative.

10:09 p.m. Home. I have written to a Grenadian living in the United Kingdom who is preparing a calendar to be sold to aid funds for a charity, GRENED, based in Grenada and run by a Grenadian who is a professor of sociology at a university in the United States of America. I ordered 10 of these calendars. This afternoon I called the Sabre Foundation in Boston Mass long distance and managed to speak this time with its chief executive, who gave me the telephone number of the Grenadian academic, Professor Williams, who is Professor of Sociology at Brandeis University. I then called the number only to learn that she was back in the Isle of Spices. *'Where are all these long-distance telephone calls leading?'* I ask myself. On my return from school this afternoon there was a reply to the letter that I had written to the principal of GRGS. I now feel confident that genuine bona fides have been established between me and our two, small, island schools an ocean apart from each other. Providing we can all work together something of value can be accomplished that will aid that Caribbean hurricane-beleaguered school towards recovery.

Friday 04/03/2005

9:14 a.m. I photocopied JT's letter to me and took a copy of it over to the owner of the boatyard and gave another copy to the head teacher. When the visiting learning support teacher came into the class after the break and I showed him the letter from Grenada and discussed what we now hoped to achieve.

9:40 a.m. Classroom. The learning support teacher is working with two pupils at the sink corner making plaster of Paris mould models. They are required to weigh the correct amount of plaster of Paris and use functional language in their discussion with this teacher. The pupils will sell their models later in the year as part of the enterprise project. The visiting teacher has left with a copy of JT's letter to me. I asked him if he could read this letter at the next Community Neighbourhood Watch meeting. I fear that I am getting carried away with my enthusiasm and desire to help, and I must try and keep myself under control, as sooner or later I am going to get folks' backs up.

11:10 a.m. At the morning interval I showed the visiting speech therapist, who is also the local Red Cross representative, and the P6/7 class teacher the letter from the principal of GRGS. I suggested that the other classes in the school could become involved and linked through correspondence with the school in Grenada.

Saturday 05/03/2005

10 a.m. Home I have spoken to a number of folk already. I had a long chat with the school janitor, who is friendly with the owner of the boatyard on the island. Later I was given the opportunity to speak with all those present at the close of the training session. I will arrange for a sub-committee to be formed at the next meeting of our school board to discuss, make arrangements, ways and means, for the possibilities to be become real on the ground in Grenada and here in Scotland, that are tentative, up in the air, that are birling in my head at the moment and are opportunities open for us as a school in Scotland to establish a creative aid link with the Grand Roy Government School in Grenada, West Indies.

Monday 07/03/2005

11 a.m. Classroom. At the morning interval I gave copies of Principal Janice Thomas's email, and the personal reply from her to my letter, to my colleagues. This was in response to her cry for help. I told them briefly about how this whole initiative on my part had come about. And how, why and what I intended to achieve, and the possible form that our school's assistance, help, and relief work effort could take, should the consensus be that it could be a worthwhile school effort. I suggested an idea for a project, which came from my wife Marion, who is also a primary teacher, and which had been implemented successfully in her mainland school. Her idea: pencils, pencil sharpeners, crayons, notebooks, and small useful classroom essentials could be collected regularly in small quantities by the pupils, with the help of their parents, over several months and stored in A4-size plastic wallets for each pupil, or a shoebox, until full. One of the teachers asked how I proposed to get this material to the pupils in Grenada and what form this would take. I told my colleagues that I was not sure about the delivery, but airfreight could be a means.

I was not exactly bowled over by their response to my proposal but I decided there and then that I would press on regardless, as I had done with my earlier class projects with an environmental theme. My replies to their spoken and unspoken queries and doubts, and my brief presentation, running past them my idea, seemed, for the time being, to satisfy them. I mentioned that I had been in contact with the owner of the boatyard, who said that the ocean freight containers that he had in the yard at present were

Monday 07/03/2005

too damp to store donated educational supplies, but he had reassured me on Saturday 5 March that he was trying to locate a suitable container for me to store donated stuff. Towards the end of the break the head teacher said that he had received a long-distance telephone call from the Grenadian Minister of Education, who had hung up. An opportunity missed. I joked and made light of it, as I do, and could have told my fellow teachers that I had already spent enough of my hard-earned salary on transatlantic telephone calls to establish a formal link with a Grenada government school. I was now acting outwith my teacher's remit and sensed there would be trouble ahead. If I were not so determined, pig-headed, and so caught up in this self-appointed project, I would have given up ages ago. *Transport? Not a problem,* I said to myself. Boxes of good stuff loaded into seagoing ocean freight containers aboard ships from Clydeport Ocean Terminal, Greenock. Or a container of ocean freight resources could transported by a road haulier from our island to a port on the mainland that shipped containers with cargoes for the islands in the West Indies. What's the problem? Just do it!

And yet I will continue to spend more time on the phone when I get home from school.

5:30 p.m. Home. I called Linda at Macmillan Caribbean Oxford about the purchase of new textbooks. I called Professor Williams with request for a mobile library and left a message saying that I had been in touch with Juliette (from whom I learned that Holman Williams, a relative of hers, was my dad's boss at the Colonial Office Department of Agriculture, in Port of Spain, Trinidad, when we moved to that island in 1950). She is sending me some calendars which are costing me £5 each. I called the British Council, Grenada High Commission in London and I spoke to Mr Sandy, and also the Minister of Education and Labour in Grenada. I spoke to her secretary and for the second time she hung up on me. No joy there.

6:05 p.m. Home. I call the Caribbean Policy Development Centre, Bridgetown, Barbados. 'Mr Jones is on an overseas call at the moment. Would you mind calling back in a few minutes?' she tells me in Bajan accent, which I warm to immediately.

I have spoken to Mr Jones, who is going to send me lists of textbooks etc. and information on shipping goods to the West Indies. He said a lot of the cargo from Europe for the West Indies is first shipped to Miami in Florida, USA and trans-shipped from there to the islands. He knew of Professor Williams and that GRENED, her organisation, was one that CPDC worked with. When I told him that I had difficulty in establishing a link with the Ministry of Education in Grenada, he said. *'They are hard to get hold of.'* *'They are stone walling me,'* I said to myself. However, talking to my Barbadian compatriot long-distance was a worthwhile call. I must now find out what the textbook needs of GRGS are at present and when the refurbished school buildings are expected to be wind and watertight once more.

Tuesday 08/03/2005

4:45 p.m. Home. I have just come off the phone to Linda of Macmillan Caribbean and told her about what I hope to accomplish. She suggested I write to Michael who is in charge of textbook sales for the Caribbean. As I was leaving the school, I met a parent at the waterfront taking photographs. I had forgotten that some time ago he had mentioned to me that he knew of an American School in Surrey that was going to throw away a whole computer suite of Apple Mac computers, and as they were about to put them into a skip he had offered to take them. I gave him a copy of JT's reply to my letter and he said that this letter rang bells with him and would be glad to let me have the computers and I could drop by and see them any time. As I continued cycling down the road past the sailing club I stopped to speak to another former parent of our school who was out walking their dog. I told her that I had a 'little project' on the go. She asked about the school. *'You have an active PTA,'* she said. I told her that the school roll was now up to 62 pupils. I gave her the two copies of JT's letter and said if she was interested to get back to me. On my arrival back home there was another letter from the helpful councillor that he had written to the music master of the local secondary school seeking support for the P4/5 class assist enterprise project, GRGS efforts and what possibly could become a whole school project. I then sat down and wrote to the manager for Macmillan Oxford, which is now part of a German conglomerate.

Wednesday 09/03/2005

Classroom. This morning I met Michael and partner from the Book People, who were in the school delivering books to be sold to the staff. I gave them a copy of JT's letter, which was well received. Mr Payne the carpet fitter was in the classroom fitting a brand-new carpet, and when I gave him a copy of the letter he told me. *'I go to a lot of schools.'* I also gave a copy of the principal of Grand Roy Government School letter this afternoon to another parent who is an active member of the Parent-Teacher Association, who said. 'We'll have to do something about this.' And her words encouraged me greatly.

Thursday 10/03/2005

Home. I returned this afternoon to find the GRENED calendars sent by Antoinette, Juliette's aunt. We had a long chat on the phone about Trinidad, where the Hanschell family had lived from 1950 to 1970, and our Grenada connections *'Aren't connections wonderful!'* she said, as I chatted with her about the time when my family had lived on Carmody Road across from, as it was then, the Imperial College of Tropical Agriculture at Saint Augustine, Trinidad, now the campus of the University of the West Indies where my dad, David Manning Hanschell, had studied for his postgraduate diploma in tropical agriculture after return from Edinburgh University.

7:10 p.m. I am not long off the telephone to Michael of Grenada School Supplies Ltd. He told me that he knows Grand Roy Government School well and their principal, Janice Thomas. He corroborated her report and letter to me saying that the school had indeed been devastated by Hurricane Ivan. *'The school will have to be completely refurbished,'* he said, and he went on to tell me that GRGS had begun to raise funds to set up the computer lab which had been destroyed, and that it would take a lot to help them. He knew the Macmillan Caribbean manager and, more importantly, he was able to tell me that the school was not on the Grenada government's list to be reconstructed, which means any efforts to help from Scotland might not be misdirected.

So far, I have been casting my net far and wide, which is what the helpful councillor Len Scoullar said I should do. Nothing in the net yet. The problems of storage, transport, and shipping, which are the nuts and bolts of this project, remain to be solved.

10:15 p.m. I received a call from JT in Grenada wanting to know how our efforts were going, and had I received a fax from the Minister of Education and Human Development. No, I had not. Well, I have contributed to the work of the GRENED Foundation. Perhaps one day I will have my own foundation. Dream on.

11:15 p.m. I sent an email to Mr Philbert of Grenada Educational Supplies Ltd. Did he have any advice regarding the refurbishment of surplus school equipment? Did fit-for-purpose, surplus to requirements, educational resources always have to be scrapped, binned, crushed and trucked to landfill in this inexorable and unsustainable process of technological progress of engineered obsolescence? He did not comment on my views regarding the wasteful disposal of fit-for-purpose, surplus to requirements, educational resources.

Friday 11/03/2005

This morning I gave each of the staff at the school a GRENED calendar before Hurricane Ivan had devastated the Isle of Spices, and one to the supportive councillor Len as I passed his door on the way up the road to school.

6:06 p.m. I have just returned from collecting my Raleigh bicycle from the bike repair shop. I had purchased it in August 1990 on arrival here on this island, with funds from my one and only tax rebate. On the way into town from school this afternoon, I stopped in at the Discovery Centre to meet the island's Tourist Board manager, who received me graciously. I gave him copies of JT's correspondence and he said he would run with it. I suggested if that were possible then he could write to GRGS sending the school some information, and brochures about the island – just to let them know that we here on this small island were going to attempt to contribute in some way to their Grenada island school's refurbishment.

11:45 p.m. To do: write to the local haulage firm confirming a request I made a short while ago, about the possibility of their firm transporting, as and when the time came, donations of resources from off the island that had been collected for Grand Roy Government School.

Saturday 12/03/2005

11:21 a.m. Home. I pause to catch my breath and reflect, record log the events of the past few hours that are relevant to this current preoccupation of mine. On the way in to the wee town this morning, on the trusty wi' white-walled tyres and slightly rusting back wheel metal steed, as I was cycling past the Co-op there was a big, spic-and-span, brand-new articulated lorry and trailer: the owner's son was just out the cab and I pulled up beside him and introduced myself. *'Good morning, are you going to be in your office?'* I asked him. *'Yes. And what is it you want?'* he asked. And I told him briefly what I was after. I am becoming quite confident in button-holing the unsuspecting locals out of the blue for what, to me, is a good cause. I met him a little while later at their transport firm's office and he graciously heard me out. I gave him one of remaining GRENED calendars. He appeared to appreciate the great divide that separates the haves and have-nots in the Blue Planet Global Village. I asked him about information regarding the shipping of containers, customs regulations and freight forwarding procedure. I asked him if a 20-foot ocean freight container could be parked in our back yard if necessary. I said I would write him a letter to confirm what I had just said to him.

Later I cycled on up to the local painter and decorator's shop and the helpful sales manager heard me out, and I gave him a calendar. And shortly after I was in to the local library and the librarian got a calendar. Here he told me that there were a large number of withdrawn library books being given away. Throughout the public libraries of Scotland thousands upon thousands of good reading material is discarded, enough to equip many mobile libraries: there is at least one mobile library for Professor Williams, Brandeis University, Sociology department.

Now I am going to take my mind off all that and head out to the garden at the back of the cottage and shift some rocks.

Sunday 13/05/2005

3:34 p.m. One of the very supportive parents of this project has dropped in for a visit. He said he would contact the Council for

Sunday 13/05/2005

Scottish Local Authorities (COSLA) about their policies regarding the redistribution and disposal of fit-for-purpose educational resources, which were coming on stream in vast quantities as a result of school closures due to falling rolls and the building of a new PFI/PPP privately financed school on the island, and colleges on the mainland and that we will need to rent a property from the council's Property Estates Department so that there could be a focal point for collecting materials that were being donated.

He has encouraged me with his good advice. Brief notes from that meeting. The art shop in the town square belongs to the council and is coming up for sale. We, the royal we, will need a focal point. And should it become available it will make all the difference for people to know where they can leave their donations; he tells me that I need to make a priority list and he said he will donate one of his photographs and auction it for cash. They must be pretty good. He tells me that I need to auction stuff at a garden party and get businesses to donate items to be auctioned; he tells me 'I think of ideas all the time.' The form of words. A charity? The constitution? A business? Whatever the vehicle it will be transparent and I shall not be applying for lottery money, or touting for funding. I will need the expertise of a bookkeeper. An accredited freight forwarder. A logistics expert. Where can I source these clever people, and will they come on board my bus?

5:14 p.m. The supporter has just left. He told me that he is going to contact the Scottish Executive at Holyrood and COSLA about the fit-for-purpose, surplus to requirements, educational resources in the 40 plus local education authorities across Scotland – why not the rest of the United Kingdom that are also engaged in this massive rebuilding (Private Finance Initiative and Public Private Property schemes), where schools and colleges are being demolished to make way for the new infrastructure, and where valuable fit-for-purpose educational resources are currently being crushed on site and trucked to landfill. He is supportive and willing to assist, who could be another member of the team. He arrived several hours ago and I made him welcome. Gave him a GRENED calendar. He said that he would also contact the Foreign and Commonwealth Office to determine exactly what are the post Hurricane Ivan educational resources needs of Grand Roy Government School. He mentioned again his 12 Apple Macs, which he rescued from a skip from an American School down south and which are stored in his caravan and that they might be refurbished and be most useful somewhere.

Monday 14/03/2005

9:15 a.m. School classroom P4/5. On the way up the road I met a kindred spirit and gave her the principal of GRGS's letter to me, and I said that as far as I was concerned this was all the bona fides necessary for those interested in doing something, however small, to get her school in Grenada back on its feet. On arrival earlier at 8:55 a.m. I went downstairs to see the head teacher and gave him the three best fundraising ideas Marion had given me, in which her classes had raised funds with which to purchase resources of a different kind for Bulgaria. And here they were:

1. P4/5 Entrepreneurial Philanthropists speak to the PTA about their project.
2. The school pupils send out a letter with the school's logo asking firms/suppliers of educational products for donations, in which they describe their project to help Grand Roy Government School rise from the rubble of devastation etc.
3. The school purchases an A4 size plastic wallet in which each pupil is responsible for putting a pencil one week, crayons, rulers, plastic scissors, sharpener etc. another week until full and the wallets are ready to be sent to their fellow students in Grenada.

5:45 p.m. I arrived home to find a reply from Juliette Smith of

Wednesday 16/03/2005

the (UK) GRENED Support. On the way home I stopped off at the local travel agency and had another word with the owner, and asked him if he could supply me with the names of any of the hotel owners on the island of Grenada. I must contact the Glasgow University Department of Development Studies to see if they have any information on the effects of Hurricane Ivan on Grenada and what the various aid agencies are doing to assist Post Hurricane Grenada. The Chinese government are not wasting any time in their soft-power initiatives to assist Grenada post Hurricane Ivan – they are constructing a brand-new stadium in the capital, St George's, for the World Cricket championship matches.

Tuesday 15/03/2005

11:30 a.m. School classroom. I assist the Primary 4/5 philanthropic entrepreneurs to draft their letters to the pupils of Grand Roy Government School, along with their self-portrait and the school logo. Today I received a letter from Professor Williams, who has returned to her home in Grenada, along with a gift of pre-Hurricane Ivan, organically grown, nutmegs (*Myristica fragrans*). A wonderful gift, which has brought the Isle of Spices into the classroom. I shared information about the class project with the visiting learning needs teacher, who was in the class this morning. I gave a nutmeg each to the head teacher, janitor and the rest of the staff.

Wednesday 16/03/2005

10:10 p.m. Home. On the way home I stopped off at the office of the local recycling organisation to speak with the manager, to tell him what I intended to do regarding my plans to help a school in Grenada that had been destroyed by Hurricane Ivan, and shared with him the principal of Grand Roy Government

School's letters seeking help for her school. I resent the email to Professor Williams thanking her for the gift of nutmegs. I have given a number of these precious fruit away and I wonder how much their value is appreciated since most of the nutmeg trees in Grenada were destroyed by Hurricane Ivan.

Thursday 17/03/2005

11 a.m. Classroom. Here comes the classroom assistant, this will give me a little time to myself to write up my daily diary. At the break I flagged up the fundraising ideas, adapted from a shoe box of baby things to an A4 see-through plastic envelope into which each child contributes on a weekly basis an item of stationery e.g. a pen, crayons, rubber, pencil etc. At the end of the month the children will have created some 'Tools for School Classrooms' for each student at the Grand Roy Government School. The general consensus at that table were in agreement that such a means of raising funds to send aid to that school in Grenada would be feasible and a worthwhile effort. A wee project. A small token of support from children this side of the Atlantic Ocean. We'll have to wait and see what happens. One of my colleagues mentioned the gala day when I had told them about our curriculum-based enterprise project of making plaster of Paris models to sell, which had been instigated by the parent present at that meeting: these models she said that the event committee might let my class have a stall.

5:30 p.m. Home. I stopped off at the bank and had a fruitful discussion with the young bank manager, who is as ever positive, enthusiastic and open to new ideas. He has suggested making changes to the pending application for a Scottish National Heritage grant to the creation of a garden in the school tarmacadam playground to include the Grenada project.

Friday 18/03/2005

3:55 p.m. Classroom. I have now before me, from each member of the class, their letter redrafted – a revised letter of their rough draft, with spelling corrections, to be posted to their fellow pupils at Grand Roy Government School, along with self-portraits which require no revision whatsoever: sheer creative, artistic, self-expression they are, every single one. A formal letter went out from the school to parents requesting, if possible, weekly donations of stationery items along with their plastic wallet which will be air freighted out to Grenada.

5:27 p.m. Home. I have just come off the phone to Jane, who is the group commercial director for J&J Denholm Shipping Ltd in Glasgow. Denholm Logistics. She was very helpful, switched on right away. *'We often send salted white fish from Whitby, and sometimes cargo, gratis, if its charitable, out to the Caribbean. Please write to me and I will get back to you,'* she said. These words from her encouraged me no end. On my return earlier there was a telephone call with a message from Franklin in London, Principal Thomas's brother, to call back at 7 p.m. I called Chester Portable Offices and spoke with Ian who suggested I call Eldapoint and speak to Neil. He in turn said to get in touch with their depot in Grangemouth, Scotland and speak to Jim. *'We create space and deliver it to your doorstep.'*

This morning the speech therapist kindly offered to let us have some chairs being flung out of a church hall, and said that her husband's painter and decorators shop will donate some paint to smarten them up.

7:30 p.m. I am talking to Franklin. *'West Indian people in de islands selfish, selfish man.' 'Not just in the islands, Franklin, that is why we all live in an ill-divided world,'* I replied.

9:30 p.m. I have just finished a short letter to Jane of J&J Denholm Ltd, Shipping in Glasgow, outlining how their firm can help with delivery of some larger boxes of aid which would not be feasible to go airfreight. Nothing ventured, nothing gained. I am now going to get on the bike and pedal up the road to the town post office, and with first-class post the letter should be received on Monday morning.

Saturday 19/03/2005

6:45 p.m. Home. This morning on the ferry over to the main island I saw the former head teacher of the secondary school and I gave him JT's letter and told him briefly what I was trying to accomplish. I asked him if he was still in the head teachers' conference. He told me that he was no longer a member, but he kindly said he would pass the letter on and mentioned that the council had a procurement department. While at Glasgow University's Faculty of Education I met two of the course tutors for the next set of hoops that I have imposed on myself. I pinned their ears back on what has now become the 'Surplus to Requirements Educational Resources Relief Project for Grenada'. I gave them copies of JT's letter. All donations of surplus-to-requirements educational resources will be gratefully received. On the way home off the 4 o'clock boat I met the supportive councillor Len Scoullar, who was about to turn into his driveway. He told me to continue to cast my net wide; those helpful words of his brought to mind the Bajan fisherman I once saw many years ago casting his huge, hand-knitted, net over the blue Caribbean Sea. I mentioned to Len the conversation I had had yesterday afternoon with the shipping supremo, and he was pleased that I had made that contact. On my return home I found a copy of a letter he had written to the current head teacher of the local secondary school, and he thanked me for the calendar. He is an ally. I will just have to await developments. I await responses that are constructive to my requests. I gave my remaining calendar to the neighbours through the wall and I am just off the phone to my supportive businessman parent, I left my message on his answer machine.

Sunday 20/03/2005

3:15 p.m. Home. The supportive businessman is here to touch base. Notes of our meeting. *'We need working capital to cover running costs and premises; this is what we are doing and this is how you can help us,'* he said. I am uncertain, in fact reluctant to ask anyone for money. I'll play it by ear from now on. Remember to call the other local primary school to find out when I can come and collect their unwanted Apple Macs and make an appointment to see their head teacher.

Monday 21/03/2005

1:40 p.m. Classroom. On the way up the road to school this morning I stopped opposite the home of the local government officer for the council, George, as he was about to leave his house. He told me to get into his car, and asked me what it was that I wanted. I told him what I was about, and gave him JT's letter. He said he was glad that I had spoken to him, as he was on his way to a meeting of council officials and would follow up the possibility of council schools donating their unwanted, surplus to requirements, educational resources to our project. The supportive parent was in the class assisting the children with their plaster of Paris models. He is a great help. I brought him up to date with developments. I received a letter from a resident in the village offering material that could be useful in Grenada. I showed her letter to another teacher, who was doubtful whether it would be of any use and, furthermore, doubtful that the IT equipment on offer from the other school would be of any value and that the knowledge on the gift of compact discs was out of date.

On the way home I stopped off at the other school to see the acting HT who appeared interested in our educational resources for Grenada Relief Project effort. She said that I was welcome to the computers that they intended to junk. I called Supportive Businessman and he told me that The Tea Room would donate what would have been the commission for displaying his pictures to P4/5's Enterprise Fund. Generous of him. I called the kind local resident to thank her for the donation of compact discs and materials, and asked if they could be delivered to me at home. We'll have to wait and see whether or not they will be of any use at all. What is one man's meat is for another poison.

Wednesday 23/03/2005

10:10 a.m. Classroom. Earlier today on the way up the road through the village, and between the view of the bowling green and the Edwardian tenements, I saw Jim of the Island Community Links organisation, who I had got to know years ago when a group of us started, what was later to become Island Waste Watchers. I got off my bicycle and went over to speak with him about my current project. Primary 4/5 are temporarily packaging up their models, which will be sold by them later at the village gala day in May. Their handiwork is sale worthy, and each pupil has taken time and effort to produce a plaster of Paris picture frame that can be sold. The success of this exercise is due to one of our supportive parents, who has given of his time to come into the class and work with the children over many weeks.

11:20 a.m. P4/5 are busily involved in pricing their models, adding the total amount of money they wish them to be sold for, with much discussion among themselves. *'See the toys in the cloakroom Mr H, can I price them?'* asks Leanne. *'Certainly, off you go and take your time. How much are you getting? Wow! Put*

Tuesday 29/03/2005

your name on it.' I said. My enthusiasm, and theirs, will one day go all the way to Grand Roy Government School in Grenada, West Indies.

6:05 p.m. Home. On the way back down the road I stopped off at the Discovery Centre to see John, manager of the local tourist board, to follow up on our meeting several weeks ago. On arrival home I called the British High Commission in St. George's, Grenada to speak with the High Commissioner, who I learned is based in Bridgetown, Barbados, my island of origin. He told me that he had got the 'Supportive Businessman's' email but he was too busy to do anything about it.

7:30 p.m. Home. Well, a short while ago George, the local government officer ex-Royal Navy and indefatigable RNLI representative and fundraiser, telephoned me to say that while he was at the meeting being held at the council headquarters he had sat next to Councillor Dick Walsh and he showed him the principal's letter and he asked him if the council could do something for Grenada. The helpful councillor then showed the letter to the director of community services.

The councillor thought it would be a good idea and commended our school and P4/5 for this project … we'll see what transpires. It is wonderful to get this help from George; sometimes, more often than as not, it is who you know and who you happen to speak to, that brings unexpected results.

Tuesday 29/03/2005

11:50 a.m. Classroom. At the break I read out to the assembled colleagues the letters I had received from the Minister of Education and Labour in Grenada, the letter from the travel company and the Scottish Beekeepers Association. They listened without comment. The head teacher said he had received a letter from Councillor

Walsh, enclosing a copy of a letter he had written to the director of community services. I can wait and see what develops from my wheeling and dealing.

Friday 01/04/2005

3:25 p.m. Classroom. At the lunch break I gave a copy of email from the British resident High Commissioner for Grenada to the head teacher. This afternoon I met the other Mrs Drummond (the bankers from Hampshire) from the keep across the bay who were here to open the school's Easter Eggstravaganza fete. They were interested in P4/5's enterprise project effort to bring a little relief to the school in Grenada, and perhaps one day to other schools on the Isle of Spices. She purchased a couple of the models. And so it goes. Sowing and reaping. I continue to journey hopefully.

Thursday 07/04/2005

Home. I called Macmillan Caribbean. Their Caribbean representative has not replied to my letter. I was told by the person who took my call that some publishers in the United Kingdom had sent some books out to Grenada, but could not tell me whether any had been sent to Grand Roy Government School.

Friday 29/04/2005

6:45 p.m. Home. I called the Ministry of Education and Labour and spoke to Rhonda who gave me the minister's telephone number. We chatted. GRGS now has two roofs covered and the morale in good. Hopefully Juliette Smith will be in touch with them before too long. *'Can you be bothered to keep on bothering? I can.'* I spoke with Francis, a volunteer, to call him on Thursday 1 May at 10:30 a.m. *'What are the objectives of the charity?'* 1. Education. We are engaged in the supply of fit-for-purpose, recycled and new, educational resources to wherever they are needed. The organisation is worldwide in scope and reach. 2. I hope to create an organisation with wholly transparent principles. Open an account at the local bank. *Are you not going over the top with this project?* I ask myself.

Wednesday 11/05/2005

11 a.m. Classroom. I spoke at the break to Barbara Liddell, the schools supplies manager for the council's Department of Community Services, who is very helpful, and who tells me that as a result of a meeting with Councillor Walsh and others she had some more 'action points' to type up and was going to contact the council's transport department to make arrangements for the storage of the educational resources that have already been collected from the council education authority schools. She said they were trying to chase up those schools that have yet to indicate that they have supplies that are surplus to their requirements. She thanked me for getting in contact with her. I should be thanking her, for being so efficient in setting in motion this process of resource collection and salvage from schools in the local authority. She is absolutely brilliant.

Earlier, before the school day began, I walked across to see the owner manager of the boatyard to where he is creating a car park on the shore, with truckloads of stones he hauls every day from the local quarry, to ask him if it were possible to move the 20-foot reefer container for storage into the boatyard. He said that would be okay and it would be less likely to be tampered with.

Where to put the unsold items from our last sale, on Saturday 27 April 2004, for storage? I think the pupils feel a sense of ownership of this project. At the moment we are working on their Caribbean alphabet frieze. I have a meeting with Supportive Businessman and the manager of the bank to discuss this charitable project; to regularise and make it transparent, the financial arrangements and source of funds etc. Notes from that meeting: 20-foot seaworthy ocean freight container to be collected a week before shipment to J&J Denholm Ltd depot in Greenock, which will either be shipped to St George's, Grenada or from another port in the United Kingdom. I must get hold of the precise details of these arrangements. It is happening!

4 p.m. The bank manager's office, meeting with. The 'organisation' will be wholly charitable in its objectives but it is not a 'charity' per se. Making it a charity at this stage would involve bureaucracy, solicitors etc.; I am seeking the bank manager's advice from a financial and banking point of view. I will need to keep a journal account of minutes of these meetings. We are agreed that we don't want to have a lot of administration to involve secretarial work. We decide to open a treasurer's account; start some sort of an organisation and open an account in the name of it. Chairman, secretary, and treasurer, with a working title of 'Educational Resources' with a business self-help, social entrepreneurial ethos; need to raise money by the sale of surplus resources? The immediate cash challenge is to raise money to ship resources to Grand Roy Government School; the bank manager is to find out the best arrangements for a financial basis of this organisation – it is a not-for-profit body. We need to draft a form of words to articulate our intentions and goals. Materials collected and donated can be converted to cash. We need to capture the imagination of the community. All donations and funds raised deposited into the account at this bank. The manager will let us know about another meeting next week. I am now on a learning curve. There will be no turning back from here on.

5:45 p.m. Home. I called the Honourable Claris Charles, the Ministry of Education and Labour, in Grenada. Not in office. She never is when she learns who is calling from Scotland. I told her secretary I would call again at the same time tomorrow. I would

Wednesday 11/05/2005

like from the ministry a list of schools in Grenada and their priority needs in terms of educational resources post Hurricane Ivan. Could Her Honour let me have this information as soon as possible. The transatlantic phone calls are costing me a fortune. I am glad that no one else is about the house or they will have my guts for garters.

9:35 p.m. Home. I called the school supplies manager, Barbara Liddell, whose team are going to deliver surplus school supplies to me at the boatyard. I misunderstood, the 20-foot seaworthy ocean freight container for Grenada does not arrive at Sandbank Community Centre car park until we are ready to load it. Oh! Find out the estimated time of arrival of the container in Grenada. I will call John, who is the freight forwarder at Denholm Bahr Ltd in Liverpool: the company are doing all the necessary paperwork for free.

Call Supportive Businessman to tell him that council vans are bringing resources over to the boatyard. I will have to get my head round the logistics of it all. The name of this game. I sent an email to Mademoiselle Maryse Faure Taylor, the French Consul in Grenada, to whom I was introduced by my cousin Wendy Lloyd-Rees, who accompanied a team of insurance adjusters to Grenada shortly after Hurricane Ivan. They had met at La Source Hotel back in September 2004. I spoke with John Sas to clarify arrangements for delivering the 20-foot ocean freight container to Grenada. He is extremely helpful. He gives me clearly stated instructions to follow: *'We'll get a price worked out for you. You will have two hours to load the container and you may require a forklift. Okay. Don't worry, we will keep in touch when the time comes. Okay,'* he said.

I called the island blacksmiths asking them if they could pick up my 20-foot Gray Adams reefer from the yard of the estate factor, from whom I had purchased it and deliver it to the boatyard today, where it will be used for the temporary storage of donated resources from this island's community to be shipped later to Grenada. I asked the secretary in the blacksmith's office to send me the invoice for the delivery.

8:30 a.m. Classroom. I went over to the boatyard to speak with the manager and owner to let him know when my ocean freight container, ordered by Denholm Bahr Ltd, was to be loaded with donated educational resources from council primary and secondary schools, which will be delivered to the Holy Loch Community Centre (formerly the original Sandbank Primary School where I had taught 1991–1992), a week before delivery by articulated lorry from Freightliner Ltd, Container Base, Coatbridge.

Make an appointment to see the bank manager for Wednesday. Pay the blacksmiths invoice for transporting my wee storage facility. I call the manager of Community Services, responsible for the council's school resources. There was no need, for she called during the lunch hour today. We are all a little clearer now of the whole process of collection, storage and delivery of the 20-foot ocean freight container to Grenada. I must try and obtain as many computers in top condition and working order to bridge the Digital Divide.

12:30 p.m. Lunch hour. P4/5 Classroom. I called the community services manager who had called me earlier. I clarified further the arrangements that I had made with the freight forwarder, John Sas, on behalf of the firm Denholm Bahr Ltd, based at India Buildings in Liverpool. Today The Book People delivered P4/5's Enterprise Project order for books for Grand Roy Government School. On return from school, I called the Prime Minister of Grenada's office and spoke to Barry Collymore who told me that he would let Kirk Seetahal, the public relations officer for the Ministry of Education and Labour, know about what we were trying to do here on this island off the West Coast of Scotland for one of their devastated government schools. I received a reply to the letter I wrote to Gerry who said he would let his clients and absentee landlords know

Wednesday 11/05/2005

about the project. The community services manager in Dunoon told me that along, with others in her department, they are now clearer that they will require somewhere on the mainland where collected educational resources deemed surplus to requirements could be stored temporarily prior to collection for shipment. I suggested that I could help with this uplift of resources if the education department could grant me a short sabbatical, which would do me just fine to sort, select and inventory the resources being shipped to Grenada. She laughed. I must be joking.

3:50 p.m. I am not long back in the classroom. The 20-foot Gray Adams storage container, formerly for the transportation of frozen chicken, was brought up from the estate factor's yard by the local blacksmith and his lorry with a hydraulic crane attached. Martin, the boatyard owner, was present to help offload it. The sun was shining out of a clear blue sky. A big day for us all.

Isle of Bute Schools, with the assistance of Argyll & Bute Council, ship from Holy Loch Community Centre, Sandbank, a 20-foot ocean freight container of fit-for-purpose, surplus-to-requirement educational resources, to Grand Roy Government School, Grenada, West Indies.

6:06 p.m. Home. I have just cycled back from the town where a supporter has dropped me off, having given me a lift in from the boatyard. Her husband had driven me from a local church hall, which had donated a load of good quality wooden-seated tubular-metal-framed stackable chairs, that were a little bit rusty, and some IT equipment. These we unloaded and stored in the storage container. Great excitement: some of the great kindness and helpfulness from many individuals, which was to make this initiative possible. Alastair offered to let me have some enamel paint from his shop to smarten up the chairs a bit, after I have removed the rust. I saw Robin the joiner aboard a yacht in the boat shed: a classic, bespoke, locally built vessel. I asked him if he could put a window in or block off the opening at the rear of the container. He said he was very busy but would do so as soon as he got the chance. Yesterday an order of Grenadian comestibles a la Fortnum and Mason arrived; earlier in the week a box full of Grenada Tourist Board brochures arrived to be distributed to discerning people. And so it goes and I keep going, going on. Stay on track and stay the course, I can do no less.

Saturday 27/05/2005

3:30 p.m. Home. I have returned from working in the storage container at the boatyard, where I was painting up the recent donation of chairs from the church hall.

Wednesday 01/06/2005

6:06 p.m. Home. I called the Grenada Port Authority. Not particularly helpful. I then tried to contact the Member of Parliament for Edmonton, East Alberta, Canada, Peter Goldring – a potential ally. No joy. I then wrote a letter to my Barbados contact Dr Fraser, who was a couple of years ahead of me at the Lodge School, St. John parish, Barbados (my years there were 1955–1961), to see if he and his contacts will assist us. We were in the school cadet corps together. He is Dean of the School of Medicine and Research, UWI, Cave Hill campus.

I then tried to call the principal of Grand Roy Government School.

Thursday 02/06/2005

11:30 p.m. I arrived home earlier to see, in the hallway, boxes of books – secondary school texts which are a donation from Greenock High School. Brilliant! To cap it there was a letter from Grand Roy Government School dated 2 May 05, along with 14 letters from their Grade 4 Class with replies to our Primary 4/5. The pupils in P4/5 were thrilled to get replies to the letters they had written to their fellow pupils at the Grand Roy Government School. And so the tenuous links between the two schools, made months ago, are becoming stronger.

Later I asked P4/5, the social enterprise entrepreneurs, 'Do you think we should use some of this money from the gala day, together with the money raised from the sale of your toys and books at the village hall back on Saturday 27 April 2004, to buy some books for GRGS class libraries?' They answered with a resounding, 'Yes, Mr H!'

Monday 06/06/2005

1:30 p.m. I was called by the acting head teacher at the big primary school earlier today to tell me they had 'stuff' and did I want it. *'Yes please,'* I said. I am to collect a gift of new books from Karen at Print Point, the local book store and stationers. SG from the other small primary school kindly donated a lot of almost-new classroom stationery for my next shipment. She told me that her son builds websites. I am not ready to hype, or publicise, what I am up to just yet. I am to meet A W Transport up at Rothesay Primary School tomorrow at 10:30 a.m. to uplift a donation of classroom furniture and textbooks. Also call AD to get the donation of the reading scheme from the Red Cross depot. Unwanted, surplus-to-requirements, educational resources, which are still, in my opinion, fit for purpose are being junked in huge quantities as the PFI/PPP new school building being built here on the island is rolled out. No way! To salvage whatever I can that can be useful to this hurricane-devastated school, is my mission, as long as the contractors will let me have it. I'll accept whatever resources are being offered prior to disposal into landfill. I wonder whether it would be possible for me to set up a company to purchase these resources and sell on in the impoverished Third World? One of my 'zany ideas'. And why not? for I am unable to sustain my philanthropy, such as it is, for much longer. Issue of sustainability? For how much longer can this profligate and short-sighted waste of resources continue? I am to call AD by 11 a.m. to collect the donations at the Red Cross and RPS, with AW's Transport and friendly and able assistance. AW would not accept payment for the uplift. Bless him, Lord!

Boxtainer tell me that they have storage containers for use in secure premises; I am calling some more outfits: Container Services, Walsall, West Midlands, have second-hand containers which are cargo worthy. CSC plated £1,200 second hand!! No other competitors. I was speaking to Elizabeth, the sales director, who asks me, *'What do you do?'* I replied, *'I started and run single-handedly, with pro bono support, a surplus-to-requirements educational resources foundation with a global vision, with a present focus of supplying schools on the island of Grenada in the West Indies that were demolished by Hurricane Ivan. The hurricane struck the island on 7/8 September 2004.'*

I asked her if her firm could grant a reduction in the price of a container on account of my humanitarian initiative. *'Sorry we get asked that about 10 times a day and we don't go that far,'* she

Monday 06/06/2005

said. And then she said, *'Are you making this up as you go along?'* which caught me off guard. *'No, I am definitely not. I have just put into words, for the first time ever, what it is I am trying to achieve ever since I began my teaching career in Scotland in 1975, when I was appalled, then, by the amount of fit-for-purpose educational resources being thrown away,'* I replied.

Why not? We are living in a world of constant change and development, and from my side I want to leave as light an ecological 'footprint' as I possibly can. I am thinking on my feet and more often as not, flying by the seat of my breeks.

Ad hoc planning for the time being and following my gut instinct. I have not been this way before. No one is holding my hand and showing me what to do next, or giving me any feedback. I am all on my own and enjoying every minute. I call Steven at the building supplies to see if they will donate funds in exchange for putting their advertisement on the side of the storage container, the Caribbean Hurricane Relief Depot, out at the

The Caribbean Hurricane Relief Depot.

boatyard which is parked just inside the main gate, where all can see it. He was not interested. I spoke to Howard at Freight Container Services (Scotland) Ltd about the purchase of a second-hand container. He said he would get back to me. He then went on to tell me, *'The price of steel is shocking, but we do go up that way.'*

Wednesday 08/06/2005

9:10 a.m. Classroom. I gave a cheque for £120 to the Book People for the GRGS books. This money came out of the P4/5 Enterprise Account at the RBS branch in the town.

7:25 p.m. Home. I replied to the emails from Diana about my order for De La Grenade Industries Ltd Caribbean comestibles. I spoke with JT, Principal of GRGS, and was encouraged by what she had to say about our efforts here in Scotland to assist in the recovery of GRGS. I must continue to just get on with it!

Monday 13/06/2005

7:50 a.m. Home. *'I'll get back to you,'* said Cameron, director of Air Ecosse at Glasgow Airport. I had spoken to him about the possibility of his firm airfreighting the five boxes of stationery, new school textbooks, and new class library books to GRGS. No problem.

11:05 p.m. Earlier this evening I attended a Parent-Teachers committee meeting, where I asked them if they would contribute to the cost of airfreighting the pupils' gifts of stationery wallets. They were almost unanimous in assent to this proposal. They gave me a cheque for £200! Motion passed thanks to the Chairperson's unequivocal support.

Wednesday 15/06/2005

5 p.m. Home. I spoke to Cameron Geddes, who gave me a quote for 20 kg to deliver wallets to their office at Glasgow Airport tomorrow afternoon! The office is located in a small industrial estate opposite the easyJet office. All systems go!

5:20 p.m. I finally got through to the Minister of Education and Labour in Grenada, The Honourable Claris Charles. I, *the consignor*, will send the boxes to her, *the consignee*, and she said she would deliver the boxes to Grand Roy Government School. I received an encouraging message earlier from Cameron Geddes to tell me that the arrangements were coming together. Our first shipment of educational resources to the Grand Roy Government School, Grand Roy, St John parish, Grenada, West Indies, from the island of Bute, Scotland, United Kingdom.

Ross of Ecosse World Express. Ecosse World Express air-freighted five boxes of new classroom resources from North Bute Primary School, Isle of Bute, to Grand Roy Government School, Grand Roy, Grenada, West Indies.

How it all Began

Thursday 16/06/2005

10:30 p.m. Home. I am tired. After school I got the four o'clock ferry to Wemyss Bay with the boxes of wallets containing extras of new library books and textbooks, and collected Marion from her school, who was to navigate us to Ecosse World Express, Unit11, Glasgow Airport. The people there were really friendly, efficient and helpful. The young team were Ross, Robert, Paul, Stuart and Rhona. I wish them all the best. We now await news from Grenada that this gift has been appreciated and found to be useful.

We had journeying mercies which were not taken for granted all the way up and back down the motorway. I have begun to make arrangements for our second shipment of educational resources to Grenada.

Friday 17/06/2005

8:10 a.m. I sent an email to John Sas, freight forwarder at Denholm Bahr Ltd, Liverpool, to let him know that the Argyll and Bute Council's schools supplies manager Barbara Liddell had called me yesterday to let me know that the council were now ready, after 24 June, to receive the 20-foot seaworthy ocean freight container at the Holy Loch Community Centre. This was formerly the old Sandbank Primary School outside Dunoon. The council had generously offered to store surplus fit-for-purpose educational resources at this secure site over the past month, however the roof of the building was now leaking and the resources could be damaged. The pace for another much bigger shipment is quickening. I proceed one step a time.

Saturday 18/06/2005

11:57 p.m. Home. I am tired. Marion helped me this morning to get the P4/5 Enterprise Project stall set up at the local secondary school PTA's gala day, which was held in the car park and playground. Here I met some generous and friendly folk. Some kind soul gave me a coffee and a rock cake. I met Mr Bodo from Germany, who works for IBM over in Greenock, and who is over here to participate in a Heart Start cycle-round-the-island fundraiser. He comes from Helmstedt where my mum, sister Diana, her husband Major Jim and Sarah Jane, Michelle and David lived, serving the British Army in an army quarter during the seventies. I stayed with them one Christmas holiday.

Johanna Louise counted the takings, which amounted to £75, and which will be spent on Grenada Organic Chocolate bars and also on defraying the costs of the big shipment. I am yawning my head off. I helped David clean the fish tank and planted out a PTA stalwart's gift of vegetable seedlings. It has been a wonderful day.

Thursday 23/06/2005

5:15 p.m. Home. I spoke with Leanne at Ecosse World Express, who said that the five boxes from the pupils and their parents at the school arrived in Grenada yesterday and were signed for by M. Julien.

Chapter Two

I Make Arrangements to Deliver More Educational Resources to Grand Roy Government School

Saturday 25/06/2005

9:25 p.m. Home. I was out to the storage container Caribbean Hurricane Relief Depot, Boatyard, Port Bannatyne this morning by 8:30 a.m. I was painting the last five chairs, all of which I sanded free of rust with bright blue paint, which was a donation supplied from A&ES paint and decorators supplies shop in the town. Colin the prawn fisherman and Andrew the businessman came by to find out what I was doing, and I stopped work to tell them. Gordon the joiner and son Arron delivered a load of empty cardboard boxes from DCM's paint and decorators emporium, which was a welcome donation, and this interruption encouraged me. I cycled home for lunch and was back out there again this afternoon under a beautiful clear sky. I met a village resident and very keen yachtsman in from sailing. We chatted and he wished our venture well. He told me that he had spent some time in St Lucia's Marigot Bay. Another Caribbean connection.

I tidied and swept out my premises. I put Greenock High School's gift of English curriculum set book texts on the new pine shelves. I am clearing the decks. I am organising and inventorying the clutter: every donated item, stage by stage. Step by step. I despise not the day, nor the moments of small things. Little gifts, both wanted and unwanted, each one of them are tokens of support from this community of good island people.

Tuesday 28/06/2005

4:40 p.m. Home. I am not long in, when I receive a call from John Sas at Denholm Bahr Ltd. 'David, I've got the ship. It's going to sail from the Port of Felixstowe on the 11th of July and arrives in Port of Spain Trinidad, West Indies, on the 23 July and the container will be trans-shipped to St George's, Grenada WI. Exciting news.

Wednesday 29/06/2005

12:10 p.m. Premier island haulier, Alan, has kindly said he would transport all of the resources from the Caribbean Hurricane Relief Depot at the boatyard to the Holy Loch Community Centre, Sandbank, Dunoon. Alan said he would do it just for the price of the ferry crossing from Rhubodach to Colintraive, and he and his team would help me to load his van this afternoon. Brilliant! Bring it on! I call the supportive businessman to let him know that the transport across the Kyles has been sorted. It's all systems go now, for what I dream may be the first of many shipments of seaworthy ocean freight containers, loaded with cargoes of useful and still surplus and fit-for-purpose educational resources, sailing to distant ports, where beleaguered communities eagerly await them. Only time will tell. Onward and upward. I travel on. I am humbled at this moment by these developments which have occurred over such a short period of time, only accomplished with the goodwill and help of many individuals both here and across the watta.

Thursday 30/06/2005

2:50 p.m. Caribbean Hurricane Relief Depot. A Gray Adams 20-foot reefer at the boatyard. I have been sorting and packing a donation of English and science school textbooks, all in good condition and of relatively recent publication from the Greenock High School. DTB, J, N and C drove by and saw me. I waved, they stopped and I am to call DTB first thing tomorrow morning to meet the ferry at Rhubodach at 6:30 a.m. along with willing helpers.

3:50 p.m. AE and team of R, K and F with a stick, arrive with the van as promised. It was a hurried load of IT equipment, monitors, keyboards, towers and boxes of books, which I shall inventory tomorrow. The little van is now partially loaded but I still have boxes of English textbooks to load.

5:30 p.m. Amy, the journalist on the *Oban Times*, took a shorthand version of the story thus far; I stressed that the movers and shakers in the council hierarchy were to get a mention. I am to call her tomorrow when I learn from John Sas, the freight forwarder in Liverpool, the name of the ship and shipping line that is taking the 20-foot ocean freight container with its cargo of 'gifts', from which port in the United Kingdom, and the date of sailing. I also called Georgia, the journalist on the *Dunoon Observer*, regarding a photo shoot and article of the container being loaded. I have just learned the following details of this shipment from John Sas: '*Vessel details are as follows: The East West Central America Shipping Line based in Rotterdam sailing from the Port of Felixstowe on the 11th of July 2005, due to arrive Port of Spain Trinidad, West Indies on 23rd, then unloaded and reloaded on to a Bornuth Line vessel based Miami, Florida for St. George's Grenada 28 July 2005.*' He told me to have the inventory of the of cargo and documents for the Freightliner Ltd haulier ready.

Friday 01/07/2005

7:45 a.m. First Day of The Holidays. I, the Young D, Marion, David Brown and Julie, Alan Ewing, Team and van are all in the

Friday 01/07/2005

playground of the old Sandbank Primary School, now the Holy Loch Community Centre. I am sitting on a beautiful table, which was donated by Mr and Mrs Masterton of the Tartan Shop in the town. There is a flock of crows cawing. Marion has gone with young David to collect the key from the school services supplies manager of community services BL at the council's headquarters. It is quiet this morning in Sandbank Village, the first day of the summer holidays. Traffic is starting to build up on the main road in front of me. As I look up to my left there is a forested, misty glen, beyond which is the Benmore Botanic Garden, which we love to visit. I passed this building, now called the community centre, every school day in 1991–1992. It was a long haul to a wonderful school, where the staff and pupils helped to keep my career afloat.

I met someone who had just came out of the pub across the road and she said, as I walked over to speak to her, *'A lot of people have moved into the area. The building is being vandalised.'* On hearing that the building had been broken into I became unsettled, and sure enough, when we opened up, the contents of school supplies had been turned over. But in the face of the mess, we did not weaken.

8:30 a.m. Freightliner Ltd artic driven by Danny from Coatbridge, Capital 20-foot ocean freight container number CLHU2451793, arrived and drove into the playground. He reversed the trailer so that the container door opened in front of the main entrance to the building. John Sas, who had talked me through the whole process to this stage over the telephone, told me that the driver should have a form that I had to sign, of which he will need a copy. I am on a learning curve right enough. The trailer is on hire from FRS Coatbridge. Barbara Liddell, school supplies manager, was key to this whole process. We all set to and began to load the container. John had told me that the opening to the container sat five feet off the ground and I was worried that it would be too high, but no, we managed fine to load chairs, filing cabinets and lots and lots of great stuff. NG Primary 7 from Strone Primary School, Dunoon arrived to lend hand, which was greatly appreciated. By 12:15 p.m. the container was fully loaded: a feat accomplished by collaborative team effort. Danny sealed the container with seal HJSE623490.

12:50 p.m. I call BL to let her know that the container was now on its way, due in no small measure to her.

1 p.m. I had a brief meeting with Barbara Liddell to return the keys to the community centre and later show our appreciation with a gift of flowers for all that she and her team had done and, not least, many thanks are due to the drivers of Argyll and Bute Council Education Transport, and the Transport Administrator EM, who BL said, *'She was a great help.'*

1:30 p.m. On the way back we stopped off at the Colintraive Hotel for lunch on me, which we enjoyed, and we felt we had earned a little bespoke cuisine. It has been a beautiful light-filled day. I met CW, who is RW's brother, and he was telling about when he had worked aboard a chartered catamaran in the Caribbean, visiting the islands such as St Kitts, St Barts etc.

To do for next week: I make arrangements to visit the Port of Felixstowe and call Tom at the port, who said, *'You sound like a Scotsman.'* He has not heard me speak for long enough to discover that I am definitely not a Scotsman. He then told me *'You can come down to the port and see the vessel. Actually, the vessel sails on the 13th and, oh!, can you call me at a sensible time, I am on holiday.'* *'I am sorry,'* I said. He then told me that if I was coming down to Felixstowe I should call Rod, the managing director of EWL (UK) Ltd.

Call Lilian, Director of Libraries, the Main Library, St George's, Grenada, to find out what the book situation is post Hurricane

Ivan; call Sandra, Morningside Library, Edinburgh, about their offer of the entire children's collection of library books. She had once told me, *'David, Edinburgh is awash with books. Let me know when you are making a shipment.'* Later this week I must speak with the boatyard owner to see if it would be alright to have the signwriter put some sponsorship advertisements on the side of the storage container. Martin is working day and night, fulfilling his dream of creating a marina from scratch: making endless trips to and from the quarry for boulders to fill in an area for a carpark prior to building a causeway, behind which there will be a marina attached to the pier that he is constructing, truck load by truckload. Martin inspires me.

Ring Eddie about hiring transport to collect library book donation from Morningside Library; try and see if I can get a second-hand dealers licence? Speak to someone in the council officialdom. Who?

Monday 04/07/2005

10 a.m. Young David and Dad have a meeting with Andrew of the Mary's Meals charity. They have a 'Back Pack' project which encourages children, students and pupils here in Scotland to RECYCLE their back packs/haversacks, 'bergens', to help their less fortunate chums in the ill-divided world. A great idea. He told that I can call their warehouse to see if they have any materials surplus to their requirements. Medical things/educational stuff ... Scottish Executive Charities Commission? I am going to have to get what I am trying to do on a proper legal footing with a constitution etc. For the time being, I'll run my not-for-profit initiative, an ad hoc, fly by the seat of my breeks, social entrepreneurial and philanthropic project for as far, and for as long, as I can. When we arrived up that long, busy, arterial main road into the city Andrew Parker was reading a book called *The End of Economics*, or something similar. He is a millennial – bright, switched on. I called him later when he was attending the G8 Conference at Gleneagles Hotel where Scottish International Relief had a stall.

12:50 p.m. Home. I have just spoken to John, the journalist on *The Felixstowe Flyer*. I am to call him on Wednesday to let him know when I am coming down to the biggest ocean freight container port in Europe; call Howard, container dealer/broker, down in Newark, Notts; I need to acquire and understand the vocabulary of logistics global transport in the 21st century, not like it was at Hanschell & Co (later Hanschell & Larsen) in Bridgetown, Barbados in the late 19th and early 20th centuries – phrases like 'bill of lading', demurrage, etc. I was baffled by the logistics terminology. Who is Magnus McFarlane-Barrow, Scottish International Relief? Andrew Parker? I called Gerry Copsey. I then spoke to Joyce the gatekeeper at J&J Denholm Ltd, Glasgow, the group commercial director Jane Harris's secretary, who was supportive in what I am trying to do.

For tomorrow morning it is the first ferry across the watta to meet with Andrew who works for Scottish International Relief. I call on Anita to collect educational resources: reading schemes currently being stored at the island's Red Cross depot.

4 p.m. I have just been speaking to Rod at East West Indies Lines in the Port of Felixstowe and he complemented me. *'That's a nice thing to do. I will call you back later in the week,'* he said.

Thursday 07/07/2005

David the Young and I drive over to the farm steading which overlooks Loch Ascog to view a curtain-sider parked in the farmyard, which is in a poor state and not worth it. I am to collect a donation of new books from Print Point, many thanks due to Karen, Martin and Matthew, and there are more resources to be uplifted from the big primary school. I am to call Eddie about his tariff

Friday 08/07/2005

to collect the books from the Morningside Library. Nine boxes of books! It does not make sense to travel all that way to bring them back here. No way! I will need to have them collected by a haulier based in Edinburgh and stored temporarily in the city until I am ready to have them shipped. Start looking for sources of transport. Call Sandra next week 11th/12th and make arrangements with a carrier to collect nine boxes of children's library books from the Morningside Library in Edinburgh, as they are running out of space. Urgent!

Friday 08/07/2005

Home. I call Rod Wise to let him know my estimated time of arrival at the Port of Felixstowe. Get a banner for the storage container or signage – Caribbean Hurricane Relief Depot. Public relations.? I call Steven at the builder's merchants. *'Can I ask you the nature of the call?'* he asks. Yesterday I called the office of the High Commissioner for Grenada in London, The Right Honourable His Excellency Mr Joslyn Whiteman. Later I called the Minister of Education and Labour in Grenada. *'She's in a meetin,'* she said.

10:45 a.m. Home. Earlier I went into the local travel agency to make arrangements for our travel to the Port of Felixstowe. Helpful and efficient, Amy Elisabeth is sorting bed and breakfast accommodation for us in Felixstowe town centre. Monday 11 July, be at Glasgow Central Station to get the 10 a.m. train change at Peterborough. We come back up on Wednesday. I have just spoken with Rod Wise, operations manager East West Indies Lines Ltd, to let him know when we arrive. David Alexander, loyal and brave young man, is accompanying his old dad all the way to the Port of Felixstowe. Good on him. Speak to Donnie the electrician about the purchase of a generator; Bob's birthday party to be held at the Ettrick Bay Tea Room.

11:20 a.m. I am having coffee with Bob McEwen making arrangements for his birthday party tomorrow. Remember to bring my CD player for the Cuban music.

THE LORD'S DAY 10/07/2005

I called Francis, the chief education officer at the government of Grenada's Department of Education and Labour, at home! *'Thanks for tinking of us. What goes round comes round.'*

Prepare a press release. What's that? Something like the following I guess: where it started, why I thought it should be done, my personal background. The back story. I am a Barbadian born and bred, West Indian with hurricane experience of Hurricane Janet 1955, which swept over the island of Barbados, known as the Land of the Flying Fish. What do I hope to achieve. My vision? Both now and in the long term? And how can folks and supporters, private and corporate, help me and 'us' to achieve our goals?

Monday 11/07/2005 – Wednesday 13/07/2005

The trip to the Port of Felixstowe. What's ahead? It goes something like this: we travel down to the Port of Felixstowe overnight, back up to Kilbarchan. Home today. No gains without pains. As, and when, I hear from Principal Thomas that GRGS has received the 20-foot ocean freight container shipment of salvaged educational resources I then must sit down and write thank-you letters to councillor Dick Walsh, Barbara Liddell, Rod Wise EWL Ltd, the CEO of Argyll and Bute Council Mr Hendry, Tom Hatherall, Diana from Clydebank in the Shipping Office, John Sas and Jane Harris.

11:30 a.m. Ipswich Railway Station platform. I visited the Learning Point. Chatting. Write a letter to Rosalind, Director of Children and Young People, Endeavour House, Ipswich. For 14 July: contact Sandra about the collection of books from Morningside Library on Friday 15th and also Steven, the janitor of RPS, about the collection of donated resources; call Donnie the electrical contractor about connections/plugs for a light fixture in the storage container.

Thursday 14/07/2005

6:45 p.m. Home. I was out to the storage container early today. Martin, the owner of the boatyard, has kindly lent me drive one of his Ford transit vans. I donned my blue boiler suit and never, ever having driven this type of vehicle before I had to drive by FAITH up to RPS to collect a donation of classroom furniture before the building is demolished. The janitor was there to meet me and helped load all that nourishing food for young brains. I took a detour to Homebase to collect DAH and on out to the boatyard to unload, and back to collect another load, and back out and home for lunch. We returned to the yard to shift the furniture round to the back of the boat shed, where it will have to be stored under plastic sheeting for the time being. It has been fun driving through the town in the van. It has been a long day. DAH is no slouch, he is a mighty great help. I cycled home in the rain. Earlier I called JT in Grenada – apparently the five boxes of NBPS gifts of classroom stationery and new class library books have not been delivered to the school.

Wednesday 20/07/2005

8 a.m. The Boat Yard, Port Bannatyne, Isle of Bute. The Caribbean Hurricane Relief Depot Storage Container. Cool but there is sunshine coming through the small window at the rear. I am packing library books and taping boxes (donated by DC Murray Ltd). I am looking forward to my homemade flask of tea and fried egg sandwich. I met Campbell walking his dog. He used to keep a boat here 40 years ago.

10:06 a.m. I squared up and tidied up. I borrowed the boatyard broom. I boxed the books from RPS, and St Andrew's Primary School's and the Morningside Library's books. The sun is still shining through Gordon's window, that he fixed gratis for me; I can see Margaret's flowers in the boat tub, on the other side, waving in the breeze. It has become chilly. I am going to put a lick of paint on the flexible door of this Gray Adams reefer. I am waiting for Billy, the St Andrew's Primary School janitor, who shouted on me in Guildford Square yesterday to tell me he had pencils and all sorts being thrown out. I think I'll hang around for a wee bit longer and leave a note. *'Are ye sellin' stuff?'* asks Eddie, and tells me, *'Ah got two houses.'* Good on yuh.

11:40 a.m. I am heading home. I think I have done enough for one morning. Billy Burger hasn't showed, perhaps he did and I wasn't there. I painted the door and my hair as well.

2:50 p.m. He asks me, *'You are a charity worker?'* 'I guess so. I am a self-funded entrepreneurial charity worker,' I reply. *'You've got to be one, haven't yuh?'* Curious man. *'What are you doing?'* I try to tell him. *'What's the point?'* he asks. 'I like to be busy doing good, or think I am doing good, and I just keep on going, going on,' I said.

Later I met the printer and his grand wains.

Thursday 21/07/2005

The curious man returned to ask some more questions. John comes from Preston in Lancashire. He is semi-retired. A joiner to trade. He tells me that he has not long come back from Vancouver, British Columbia, where he was appalled by the decadent standard

Monday 25/07/2005

of living – the amount of waste. Then Liz came by, who told me that they had given away her precious doll to a charity shop.

I put more shelving together and restacked the boxes. I then went round the back of the boat shed and tied down the tarpaulin over the furniture. I chatted to Betty when she came by and helped her to fill the watering cans for her and Elaine's Submariners Memorial Garden up the road. *'He wouldn't give me peace till I did it,'* she said, speaking of her Memorial Garden to the midget submariners who gave their lives in WW2 learning the hazardous skills of operating midget submarines in the fight against National Socialist Nazi German tyranny. Betty supports what I am attempting to accomplish.

2 p.m. I am awaiting a call from Jane Harris. I wrote a letter, no reply. I am just off the phone to Councillor Walsh in Dunoon, who gets things done. He told me to send the invoice to BL, which I shall do right away. *'We'll have to find a line for that,'* he tells me.

Monday 25/07/2005

10:15 p.m. Home. Earlier today the head teacher of St Andrew's called to tell me that they had computers in the basement of the school for me to collect at 1 p.m. It has been a busy day out at the storage container.

I had been working in our garden until the head teacher called to tell me that they were ready to have their surplus-to-requirements educational resources uplifted. All donations are gratefully received here, thank you. I have not long spoken to Dorothy, responsible for Argyll and Bute Library Services, who is sympathetic to our project and has kindly offered to keep withdrawn library books for me. *'I'm with you,'* she said. I spoke to Diana from Clydebank, who works for EWL Agencies Ltd Felixstowe. I had called to confirm the arrival of the container in Port of Spain,

Grand Roy Government School

Trinidad, W. I. Today? Sometime. To give us a call when she comes up to Scotland for her mum's birthday.

11:50 a.m. I spoke to Gerry to let him know when my next container will be ready, as he has just told me that a client of his travel firm, Just Grenada, has recently returned from Grenada with the intention of sending IT equipment and books out there. We'll have room for more cargo. He has given me the name of Anne, who takes the firm's photographs of various hotels who buy his package holidays on the island.

6:45 p.m. I have just returned from the boatyard. I set off at 1 p.m. and stopped at the Tea Pot where I met Mrs CD, janitor and care assistant of the Port School. I gave her the latest news about the delivery of the container. The ship arrived in the Caribbean, Port of Spain Trinidad, today. It left the Port of Felixstowe on 13th July, and will be trans-shipped from Trinidad to Grenada. She kindly offered me a coffee. I thanked her and told her that I was going to borrow a van. I cycled on and opened up the big box, and paused to enjoy the view of Hilton Farm perched way up on the hill, and the green hills beyond. Later, Martin arrived back with the van. I walked across to the portacabin office and Mary, the boatyard office manager, phoned the school for me. She is someone who has wholeheartedly supported my work. A friend and supporter from early on. Martin once more loaned me the van. The janitor gave me boxes of felt tips and stationery from Mrs Gunning, children's toys from the McCarry family and two refurbished bicycles from the school basement. For all of this I am most grateful. I met Joy walking past all the way out to the Ardmaleish Yard to apply for a cleaning job. She is a spirited soul. I told her that I would get one of her bicycles repaired.

Later that afternoon, Jack, Adam's younger brother, and his chum Owen, who said *'You know my big brother,'* helped me to unload the van with some of my own boxes of extracurricular resources from 'the office' upstairs at home; cludgie you mean. I stood for a while and chatted to Iain. He complained, *'Someone has moored their boat on my mooring.'* I think he stays along the road. He had the island bookshop for a while – it is now a café for Goths. Then Patrick and his missus, from Preston, Lancashire. They have connections with relief work in Kenya. I think they are retired engineers and with a team are refurbishing engineering tools, lathes etc. and shipping them out. A great work. I told them that I was looking for an exceptional digital artisan. Then Diarmid, the master mariner from Cork or thereabouts, came by with his son who is a civil engineer. Tomorrow, if I can borrow the van, I shall be back across to St Andrew's PS to meet The Janny to uplift more IT from the school cellar, or the dunny as he calls it.

Tuesday 26/07/2005

The Boat Yard. I came out here with Billy the janitor at St Andrew's Primary School. We have transported IT equipment from the school cellar in his van. He has been very helpful. I met the signwriter who is interested in the project. He said he would speak to the local builders' merchants about a sponsorship advertisement on the side of the container facing the main road. I pay CBS Ltd for seven plastic bags and two wing nuts. An idea. I will write a letter to the chairman of Barr Construction Ltd, Ayrshire-based contractor Anthony asking would they sponsor a container with educational resources salvaged from the two island schools prior to demolition, with which to refurbish or rebuild a school in Grenada? This firm have recently won £100 million of work over the next two years in the school's sector in Argyll and Bute, north Ayrshire and Glasgow.

Wednesday 27/07/2005

10:30 a.m. The Boat Yard. I have just had a Tea Pot pre-fried bacon roll and a milky coffee. I am now ready to pack a donation of books from the Greenock High School English Department: this came thanks to Elisabeth the speech therapist and Alistair the painter and decorator, who delivered them. It is another beautiful day here.

11:15 a.m. I was talking to Diarmid, master mariner from near Cork, South West Eire. Snatches of his conversation. *'I have sailed all over with my class yacht, which was built in a Tighnabruaich yard by Mr Smith. I own the only yacht in its class left. It's a throwaway society. I know a nice wee spot for a house on the Yucatan Peninsula,'* he said.

2:50 p.m. A couple of wheels, head honchos that is, from Barr Construction came by wanting to know where the owner of the yard was. *'He's out there on that digger,'* I told them. Then Adam, the young master and heir to the family fortune, came by, *'What are you selling?'* he asked. Nothing and everything. The day is bright and warm by turns. I am at peace with myself, and the world is rushing by as I pack books and think.

3:55 p.m. I have just been talking to IC who told me he was moving house and he might let me have some 'withdrawn books', *'Madam wants to buy a boat. Is this your collection point?'* he asks. That's good of you.

4:30 p.m. Today's 21st century world young team, of Jack, Robbie and Owen, came by for a chat; the latter tells me that he is going to become a game keeper when he moves up to Aberdeen.

Thursday 28/07/2005

8:36 a.m. The Boat Yard. There is a cold wind blowing in from the north-east, rippling the bay and turning the anchored yachts in to face the wind. Bushy clouds are sitting on top of the hill

Monday 01/08/2005

above Hilton Farm, which in my opinion has the best view on the island of the Kyles and the Firth of Clyde. I was talking to Betty, who was telling me about her weekend at a composting conference in Edinburgh. She is filling her watering cans and bucket to water the plants in the Submariners Memorial Garden to the brave young men who lost their lives to perfect midget submarine warfare. Get to work. I am going to box the rest of the Greenock High School's gift of textbooks.

11:15 a.m. I am shutting up shop for a while.

Monday 01/08/2005

8:15 a.m. It is dry and cool. There are big puffy clouds hanging in the sky. I can hear Martin picking away with the pneumatic drill attached to the front of the machine. He is extending the area of the boatyard by removing several cubic yards from the cliff face at the back. I must find out the name of that kit. My storage container could be a lot bigger, it is already jammed packed with great stuff. I meet Bill, who is refurbishing a custom-built Nova Scotian yawl. *'I was in BP,'* he then looks across at Martin, the owner of the yard, tearing away at the cliff face with the digger, and says, *'He never stops.'* *'We need more like him on this island,'* I said.

A short while later a dog walker came by with three lurchers, holding their leads in one hand and a bag of poo in the other. She was telling me about being cat-called on the way out of the pub with a carry oot. *'Thanks for listening to me.'*

This morning I spoke to Bob of EWL Central America Line in the Port of Felixstowe about 'the ins and outs' of transatlantic shipping – costs etc. He said he would call me back with a rate. *'You can count on at least £975 plus cost of transport to port, plus ferry rate for a 20-foot ocean freight container from the island, plus cost to ship container to destination £2,400,'* he said.

Grand Roy Government School

Tuesday 02/08/2005

8:45 a.m. The Boat Yard. Here I am again. It's dry. I am blanketed by thick, humid cloud and there seems to be an endless flow of traffic on my doorstep. I called SC about sponsorship of the next shipment of surplus-to-requirements educational resources to Grenada. Would this firm be interested be interested in the publicity? I speak with Macmillan in the Caribbean, he asks me, *'Could you let me know how much money you and the pupils have collected so that Principal Thomas can make her own choice of books. Keep up the good work. None of us know what's over the horizon.'*

11:30 a.m. I spoke to Andrew at Scottish International Relief. He told me that they can use IT and educational resources if GRGS does not want them.

11:50 a.m. I spoke to Winifred at Ravenstock in Coatbridge.

Saturday 06/08/2005

1:42 p.m. The Boatyard. Earlier I received more of the Good Stuff from St Andrew's Primary School. Yesterday afternoon David the Young Yun gave me a hand. Martin lent me the van. I am chuffed tae bits that he trusts me with it. It is cool, but dry this afternoon. I am now going to box some books. I was talking to Tam Boag wi' a cup of tea, one for each of us, which I had fetched from the Tea Pot. The first one fell off the dyke. I dropped off my bicycle. He gave me one of his favourite sayings. *'Lang may yer lum reek, Davie, with other people's coal,'* he has seen the stars pitch during his long years in this place.

Monday 08/08/2005

9:09 a.m. The Boat Yard. It is a beautiful morning. Kames Bay is like a pond. All is quiet in the yard except for the rush of traffic on

Monday 08/08/2005

the road. I am going to get packing in good faith. *'Good morning, Sir,'* I say to Martin as he walks out towards the Samsung Crane … sound of a telephone ringing. I speak to myself. *'Stop stalling, Hanschell, and get on with your own WORK.'* The throb of a powerful engine, the treads squeaking and creaking.

11:20 a.m. A truck, Hebrides Haulage Ltd, Stornoway, pulls into the yard and the young driver jumps out. Chrisfrom the seventies, the Boys Club at The Sandyford Henderson Memorial Church, 13 Kelvinhaugh Street, Glasgow, and he recognises me! WOW! He is delivering a package for Ambrisbeg Ltd. He asks me, *'Do you still go to church?'* I was challenged by that direct question, we had only just met. *'It's amazing who you meet in here,'* said Margaret.

11:45 a.m. I am going to break off for lunch

Chapter Three

Back to the Port School

Wednesday 17/08/2005

8:50 a.m. Classroom. This morning before school I showed Ally, who is a digital artisan, and his missus the storage container with stored IT equipment and he said he would test the lot to see if they were working once I had got electricity connected to the Caribbean Hurricane Relief Depot. I told him I was trying to get hold of a generator.

Thursday 18/08/2005

I must establish that, in Grenada, there is an unequivocal willingness and commitment from them to receive, from schools in Scotland, the surplus to requirements fit-for-purpose educational resources that are becoming available in large quantities, as a result of the closure of schools and the new build schemes. The confirmation must come from the government of Grenada Ministry of Education, who so far have shown a reluctance to speak with me, and from the schools in Grenada that I have been able to contact directly. I have put the burden on myself because if I can help to re-equip/refurbish just one Hurricane Ivan-devastated school my effort has been worthwhile.

9:30 p.m. Home. I have been speaking to Mr McIntyre who tells me, *'We are in dire need.'* I received a call from Joy along the road, whose bicycle I had arranged to have repaired some time ago. *'Can you use 10 reams of paper?'* Yes please. Thank you very much. I speak with Mr Philbert, the seller of textbooks in St. George's,

Grenada, who tells me that he is being rushed off his feet. I ask him, *'Are hurricanes good for your business?'* Don't be a smart ass. He represents the commercial competition versus the Caribbean Hurricane Relief department of good works. I called Alan, the Member of Parliament for Argyll and Bute at his Westminster constituency office, Dunoon. I had written to him some time ago but got no reply. *'I'll look through the files,'* he tells me.

Tuesday 06/09/2005

8:35 p.m. Home. Earlier I had a meeting at The Bike Shed with David and Kevin: both of whom are towers of support and encouragement to me. Kevin tells me, *'In 500 words express what you, David, want to achieve, not including any projects to date: what's new, your latest project/venture; another shipment on its way is being prepared; who are you collecting surplus educational resources for? Design a logo. What's new? Does it/IT tell you something? The photographs are to be electronic. Part Two of The Story; the logistics; who is helping you to shift and ship these resources?'* he said. J&J Denholm Ltd etc. EWL. Kevin is very helpful. He has offered to build a website pro bono (www.grenadarelief.org.uk). I call Computer Repairs Straight Forward IT. What is the best approach? Kevin recommends I speak to Len, island business man, who might help me to put this project together and thereby raise my initiative to another level. I am not sure what Kevin means by this. Perhaps this individual who works for Highlands and Islands Enterprise can help, perhaps not. Kevin suggests that I set up a charitable trust/organisation that is small, sustainable and reliant on goodwill and pro bono support, with a minimum of administration necessary to function in a transparent way that will allow full control to me, until such time as it grows beyond my capacity to manage it or it no longer fulfils its function. A form of words is important. What do I mean precisely? I try to come up with the form of words. What I started way back at the beginning of the year is becoming something much bigger, and more complicated. Do I stop while I am ahead, or do I continue?

(The decision I took to continue with the project was to prove my undoing. Well was it? Yes and no. Read on and decide for yourself.)

Wednesday 14/09/2005

4:35 p.m. Home. I call the Grenada High Commission in London and spoke to Laurence, Mr Sandy is out. I then called the office of the Ministry of Finance and Planning. No joy! To follow that I call the Permanent Secretary – no satisfaction.

Monday 19/09/2005

Today I asked the High School of Glasgow rugby team to help me shift Ninian Dunn's gift of a 20-foot polytunnel frame around to the back of the boat shed, which they kindly did.

Thursday 13/10/2005

Midday. Home. I'm back here in the kitchen. This morning I met Ally of Island Computer Services Ltd. I'll meet him next Saturday morning to make arrangements to get as many computers as possible in the storage container in working order. I also made arrangements with Jim the blacksmith to borrow the boatyard diesel generator so we'll have some electricity connected up. I was off to the yard this morning and met the signwriter. *'I've got a Grenadian flag,'* he said. The signage 'Caribbean Hurricane Relief Depot' will emblazon the sides of the storage container. Hanschell Relief Resources Plc, or something, tongue in cheek. I walked down to the Tea Pot for a takeaway cup of tea. I emptied the rainwater that had accumulated on top of the tarpaulins covering the stored furniture at the back of the boat shed. I had a long chat with Jim the blacksmith, who is one of my supporters – someone I count a trusted friend from the early days out here.

I met Martin bringing the yachts in, and I brought him up to date on the first ocean freight container shipment of fit-for-purpose, salvaged, educational resources to Grenada; so far no news from the beneficiary school in Grenada, West Indies, of so much island goodwill from this little West of Scotland community. I contact the other Martin, who said he will loan or rent me a shredder.

To do: contact Freightliner Ltd Coatbridge about their tariff/rate to deliver a 20-foot ocean freight to the Port of Felixstowe, and permission regarding loading the pallets into a container at the container base terminal. Marion has just told me, *'You are not a Team Player.'* True. I must try negotiating for a reduction in the costs of transportation of the next shipment to Grenada. I spoke to Mick of Roadways, Coatbridge Terminal about the size of pallets required when the next cargo is ready to go (each pallet must be shrink-wrapped), and to get in touch with him when I am ready. He is very helpful – another supporter and friend at the other end of the line.

Monday 17/10/2005

I call Edwin, EWL Rotterdam and speak to Leo. He tells me, *'We'll see what we can do for you.'* I love that kind of a reply.

11:06 a.m. Home. On the way back from the wee town carrying a bag of sausage rolls and a wee sliced loaf I stopped off at The Tea Room. I received a warm greeting from Jean, the restaurateur, who immediately asked after Amy. She gave me a coffee. Very busy. Lenny appeared, who I've wanted to speak to about the next shipment and the possibility of obtaining the surplus-to-requirements educational resources from the local secondary before they are scrapped. I would like advice from Lenny about shipping these fit-for-purpose, valuable, educational materials worldwide to inadequately resourced schools that would only be too glad to receive them. He tells me, *'My business contacts don't read dossiers, just send me an email of what you are about and I'll put it in my own words, and when I see the council chief executive next week I'll speak to him.'* The way 'business' is conducted in The Real World is by a nod, a wink and a handshake, and perhaps a backhander as well. I am a slow learner and I will never be a player in that league. I approached Donald the weaver on the way home to ask if he could drop by the house for a chat, to see if his firm could supply or donate pallets and a roll of shrink wrap for the pallets. *'What do you want from me?'* he asks. I do try.

11:50 a.m. I call Freightliner Ltd, Coatbridge and speak with Agnes the traffic controller, who is always helpful and friendly. Possible sponsors of this next shipment? *'We'll see what we can do for you,'* she said. Wonderful words that encourage me to continue.

11:55 a.m. I called Fraser, the account manager at Freightliner Ltd, to ask him whether his firm will consider the possibility of waiving the transportation charges to the Port of Felixstowe. If you don't ask you don't get. He is very positive to my request for assistance. He kindly told me to contact him as and when we are ready on the wee island to ship the cargo, which he emphasised must be palleted, shrink-wrapped and inventoried awaiting transport to their container base at Coatbridge.

2 p.m. I spoke to Ray, freight forwarder at Denholm Bahr Ltd in Liverpool, also helpful, who told me to call him when the cargo is ready to go.

7 p.m. I received a call from Mae in Glasgow to tell me that her church has been collecting for the Glasgow Play Schemes Resource Centre and would I be interested. I thank her and said I would be in touch. I have to watch out in case I am no longer able to handle the resources. All of it good stuff.

To do for 18 October: call Sandra the librarian to make arrangements to collect the donation of books from the Morningside Library in Edinburgh. Call Donnie and Buckeridge electricians to install lighting in the storage container. Ask Jim the blacksmith whether it would be possible to borrow the diesel generator for Saturday morning.

Wednesday 19/10/2005

2 p.m. Home. I called Edwin at EWL in Rotterdam about the possibility of a reduction in their shipping firm's tariff. He was not positive. *'We are a commercial organisation and are unable to assist you in your aid project.'* I know full well that you are a business, I just wondered whether you guys would cut me a little slack. Nae chance.

3:50 p.m. I called Grenada and spoke to Vic Wallace, the resident United Kingdom High Commissioner. No result. Called J&J Denholm Ltd in Glasgow and spoke to Graham and left a message for Jane their group commercial director who, way back on Friday 18 March, offered a helping hand.

Monday 24/10/2005

Home. A meeting in our kitchen with David and Craig, the outstanding editor and journalist of the local newspaper. We discussed an article for the local newspaper at great length, which is a trade-off of my energy and enthusiasm, plus initiative, effort and the collaborative success to date, subsumed into a 'business', Educational Resources Ltd or such like. It is a suggestion with which I am not at all comfortable and nor with the negativity expressed. I suggested that I contact Anthony Rush, the chairman of Barr Construction Ltd, contractors for the new school and college joint campus, to see if they would be willing to sponsor the next shipment with the materials salvaged from the primary and secondary schools before their demolition, which could be used in the construction and refurbishment of a Grenadian school. Hmm, that idea of mine did not go down very well. I said that I did not want to include the storage container out at the boatyard as part of the assets of this business as it is my private property. I am definitely, at this point, reluctant to go in that direction.

To do: pay the signwriter from the Educational Resources account as and when the signage is put on the side of the Grey Adams 20-foot reefer Caribbean Hurricane Relief Depot; prepare draft of talk; write a letter of thanks to councillor Dick Walsh, Mr H, Ms CW and Ms Sandra Wright; obtain a list of all my transatlantic telephone calls to Canada, USA, Barbados, Grenada, Holland, United Kingdom etc. Money spent to be reimbursed from Educational Resources account.

Saturday 29/10/2005

1 p.m. Home. I am not long in from The Boat Yard. I had a long chat with Tommy from Castle Street, who is a ships' carpenter. He was telling me about the cargoes his ship had brought from and to distant places: crayfish tails from New Zealand to Hamilton, Bermuda; grain from Halifax, Nova Scotia, Canada to rot on the docks of Mumbai (Bombay).

1:30 p.m. It is raining heavily on the roof of this Gray Adams reefer box. Cars are swishing by on the main road just a few feet away. There is a cool, damp breeze blowing in off the bay. I have just flat-packed most of the unwanted computer desks that were gifted to North Bute Primary School. They were disassembled by Mrs CD, the caretaker janitor, and she had gone to the trouble of drawing up a plan for reassembly. She is a great help to this project.

Saturday 29/10/2005

I met Jacqui walking her Boxer dog; an Arnold Clark rental van has just driven in to the yard; Murray, Adam and Martin are busy out in the yard; leaves are turning brown. I came earlier to find the table on which I am sitting had been donated. My heart is full of gratitude to all those anonymous donors. Yesterday afternoon, after school, I brought the collapsible tables the school's janitor said I could have that were being thrown into a skip, along with about a dozen infant, tough-plastic-seated, metal-legged chairs, some big chairs, a trolley, and a computer table. I stowed these welcome resources for the time being under the tarpaulin behind the boat sheds.

Well, here I am at this present fleeting moment, sipping the last of my tea having scoffed the sandwiches I made up this morning. I am expecting the signwriter Malcolm, who said he'd show up to put up the Caribbean Hurricane Relief Depot signage. I keep busy and I am going to pack some books from the box of books which were delivered to the school from the other primary school by Billy the janitor, Mr Fixit, two weeks ago.

The Caribbean Hurricane Relief Depot, the Boatyard, Port Bannatyne, Isle of Bute. We went from air freight to ocean freight.

2:10 p.m. *'Ow much is that glowb?' 'Sorry, I am not selling it,'* I said. *'Then I can't buy it?'* he said.

4 p.m. Meeting of Education Resources Project at the boatyard in the storage container: present – me and DTB. Received a further donation of educational resources (school furniture, school textbooks). Priority remains the packaging, boxing, palleting, and shrink-wrapping of the substantial stock stored behind the boat shed. It was noted at this meeting that David was of the view that the newspaper article of 28 October was excellent, but there was no mention in the article that any financial donations should be handed in at the local branch of RBS, and there was no mention made of our call for assistance in building a website, and these items had been stressed at the last meeting on Monday 24 October. David has agreed to take this up with the journalist with a view that they be included in a future edition of the newspaper. He agreed to write to the CEO of TSC Ltd HQ in Falkirk. We discussed other topics and the meeting closed in good order at 4:30 p.m.

Some notes: feeder vessel to Grenada, contact Eric Hassell & Son Ltd, marketing director Erica Luke, operations manager Noel Walcott have been appointed exclusive agents for East West Indies Lines, which is a member of Wethold International B. V. Head office Boompjes, Rotterdam on the banks of the River Maas. Port Agent Bridgetown, Barbados.

Sunday 15/01/2006

David the businessman and I had a brief meeting. It was agreed at that meeting that the £500 in the Educational Resources account be made to me to defray my payment of the bill from Denholm Forwarding Ltd of £1,971, also that he would write a letter or an email to councillor Len regarding the surplus-to-requirements educational resources that will be coming available as a result of the closure of the two schools here on the island. The meeting closed at 4 p.m.

Thursday 26/01/2006

5:35 p.m. As I was on my home from school I met Harry, the chef at The Pier at Craigmore, who came out to speak to me and said he'd given my idea of holding a Caribbean Supper/Dinner some thought and he would mention it to the proprietor.

Thursday 16/02/2006

Home. The movers and shakers at Rococo Chocolates in London, Chantal, James, Fergus and Millie, paid us a visit and brought us bars of Grenada Chocolate and a bound copy of photographs they had taken when they visited Grand Roy Government School in Grenada. I called Robin Swaisland in St George' Grenada, West Indies.

Tuesday 11/04/2006

8:55 a.m. Home. Howard, the container dealer has just called and wants to know if I still intended to purchase the 40-foot ocean freight container in Coatbridge. *'Yes,'* I said, but The Lord will have to provide the means with which I can purchase it since I am unable to sell the BS&T shares at the moment. I will need to have confirmation from the Grenada government that their education system can still put to good use all the of the surplus educational resources that I am able to send to them.

Thursday 13/04/2006

I had a meeting with D. Hunter of Smart Successful Solutions. I dropped in to see Jim the metal foundryman, who is now running the island Community Links office and I gave him a copy of Robin Swaisland's letter to Mr Pierre, the Permanent Secretary to the Minister of Education and Labour.

Tuesday 18/04/2006

Kerry came to the school to ask if I was still collecting donations for Grenada. I told him that we were and that the office manager, MC over at the boatyard, had the key to the Caribbean Hurricane Relief Depot and he could drop them off with her when it suited. Toys!

Friday 21/04/2006

4:30 p.m. Home. I am off the telephone to Fraser the accounts manager of Freightliner in Coatbridge. He told me that he had never heard of Calder Container Services yard, but he said he would consider bringing the container down to the island, which is a wonderful offer. Prior to that I called Howard to finalise my purchase of the 40-foot ocean freight container. I am now awaiting a telephone call from Robin Swaisland in Grenada and queried whether or not he had a reply from the Permanent Secretary. He said he had not, but he said he would walk across the road to his office and speak to him.

Monday 24/04/2006

5 p.m. *'You will never fill that thing!'* said Jim the steam engineer. Later he remarked, *'How have you lasted so long out here in the yard. You must be crazy.'*

I told him that I had to keep going and see my initiative through to the end. On my arrival this morning at school, after preparing for the day ahead, I went over to the boatyard. A beautiful day of sunshine. Martin was in the portacabin with Jim the blacksmith.

Monday 24/04/2006

I waited until it was convenient to speak to the former. He went to a battered notebook and called one of his associates and that's all it took: one telephone call. He told me that, all being well, a 40-foot ocean freight container from Coatbridge would be in the boatyard tomorrow. I must call John and thank him for his generous offer earlier to assist in the transport of the container up to Coatbridge later this year.

Chapter Four

The Shipping Clerk Purchases a 40-foot Ocean Freight Container

Tuesday 25/04/2006

10 p.m. Home. I was greatly excited, and in trepidation, to take delivery today of GSTU8958639 – 40-foot x 8-foot x 8-foot 6 inches, built in San Francisco, California, and manufactured in 1991. I think aloud about this rusty, bumpy, big box, *'I would guess that it has not been inspected for a long time and this will have to be arranged at some time in the future. The container is a bit worse for wear and tear. Ach well, I'll just have to make the most of it.'* Robert, the artic driver, lives on a farm in Airdrie. He is a chum of Martin, who had called him yesterday morning, and he brought the container down from Coatbridge Container Services yard. I had been speaking to Tom. *'Please advise me before collecting the container, to enable me to arrange for the container to be lifted on to a trailer,'* he said. *'What does the inside of the container smell like?'* I had asked him some many weeks ago as I dithered as to whether or not to go ahead and take the plunge into the big time, and start swimming out of my depth. I had purchased the container from Howard Clack Freight Container Services.

A beautiful morning after settling in to the day job, I walked around to the boatyard and across the road to see an artic lorry and trailer with a San Francisco, California, 40-foot ocean freight container and the owner driver, Robert Hyslop, who asked me, *'Are you a born again?' 'Yes, if you mean by that, am I a Christian, yes, I am,'* I replied. *'Well I think you have been had. This container is no longer seaworthy,'* he said.

Tuesday 25/04/2006

When I saw the rust all over the container my heart sank, but not for long: when he opened up the container doors there was a clean smell of a tropical hard wood, teak, possibly more likely bamboo, which resonated from the Caribbean, and no internal rust. Later, Jim the blacksmith told me that I had got a bargain, which made me feel a lot better.

I was back over at lunchtime and took some photographs. I was glad, with a mixed sense of trepidation and gratitude, and the realisation that there was nothing else for it but for me to keep plodding forward and upward. After school, I went back over to see Jim who loaned me a grinder and goggles, and gave me a new padlock, a pair of new gloves, and an extension cable, and told me to get my boiler suit on. He would have the diesel generator in place beside the container. And what was more important – he gave me self-confidence.

When I had got set up and was about to grind some of the rust off, he reappeared with a tin of red lead paint and face masks, followed by his spaniel. I couldn't have asked for more. Jim's

Even then I was dreaming big – going over the top – which was to lead to many pickles.

professional help and kindness that afternoon had encouraged and strengthened my resolve. Then Mary and Mr Carroll came over to see how I was doing. The supporters. I called Howard of Freight Container Services (Scotland) Ltd to let him know the container had arrived and he would be paid in due course by Mr Hyslop.

After the Scouts were dismissed from their hut adjacent to the boatyard, Robbie, Mark, Jack, Adam, and Robert came by to lend a hand in the boatyard where I have been loading the big container with children's toys, and stowing empty boxes courtesy of DC Murray Ltd (thanks to Alistair, Liz S, Liz and Gordon).

Thursday 27/04/2006

5:28 p.m. Home. I received a message this morning at the break from the school secretary that the head teacher at the big primary school had told her, *'We are getting rid of all our textbooks.' 'That's great, you can let me have them. When do you want me to come and collect them?'* I asked.

Friday 28/04/2006

9:40 p.m. I am back home. I have been out at the boatyard filing, grinding and scraping rust bumps off the ocean freight container and helping Martin shift stuff. It was a beautiful evening. Lots of light from a clear golden sky. I was in a state of flow completely absorbed and focused on the task in hand.

Saturday 29/04/2006

10:50 a.m. The Boat Yard. Caribbean Hurricane Relief Depot. John brought along a computer, printer and a keyboard. I was talking to Mr Timmins from Cumbria who ships tractors to America. He remarked, *'Wouldn't you wish that all your teachers at the academy* were like that.' 'Aye, and they would all end up in Lochgilphead one day like me,' I replied.

I was chatting earlier to AP and Jim. It is another glorious day of spring sunshine. Martin was operating the crane, and with helper Michael from England, along with Jim, we shifted my container into position behind Margaret's boat of flowers, '*That's my daughter's boat,*' said the gentleman from Cumbria pointing to a big yacht. I met a couple who were walking their three Pomeranians. Then I met John the butcher, loyal supporter, who sold his business because of arthritic knees and now lives in a bungalow.

Monday 01/05/2006

10:20 a.m. The Boat Yard. John the neighbour across the wall from the school playground has just brought me his wheelbarrow, '*Thank you John,*' I said. '*No bother,*' he replied. I have been here since 7:30 a.m. shifting IT equipment from the Caribbean Hurricane Relief Depot to the ocean freight container in the parking lot across the main road. I met Colin, an Aberdonian telecommunications engineer who is living on board his yacht, which is in the yard. He was telling me about what it was like working in Dubai and Bangladesh, and the problems of Third World countries. This guy has been around the block a few times.

'*I am not religious, but all my family are,*' he said out of nowhere. He went on to tell me that he knew the Reverend Mr William Still of Gilcolmston Church (who had preached at my home kirk in Glasgow and with whom I had corresponded briefly). '*He preached hell fire and damnation, but he was a really nice man,*' he said.

Later I met two yachties from England. Ray, from Oxford, who tells me that he and his missus who is an artist, as in a painter, holiday regularly in Tobago. He is wearing green overalls and has an upper-class accent, as one would expect from that neck of the woods; his friend Walter doesn't say much. It's a wet morning. I kept on task. The sun is beginning to break through, but there are still sodden clouds over the village of the port. I chatted briefly to Her Self and her three dogs. I must make the effort to keep track of the Dear Folk I meet on the voyage. I have just had my roll and tea, and so its back tae wuk. Naething else fur it, Jimmy.

11:05 a.m. I have just met Bob, who tells me, *'I've moved to a small flat at the port from a big house on the Serpentine Road.'* And he tells me that he is related to Inspector Park, who is now based in Dunoon. He kindly offers to assist in the collection of useful stuff to send in the next shipment to Grenada. *'I'll speak to him and see what he can scrounge for you.'* He is also offering me furniture, for which he now no longer has any room. He tells me that Andy of Beach Watch Bute had mentioned to him about our project to deliver reusable fit-for-purpose educational resources.

11:50 a.m. I have just met Dougie. *'I know all the Denholm People. We have a wee hoose at the front,'* he said and offered to let me have a printer they no longer need.

1:15 a.m. I am heading hame for a bite. I have moved all of the IT equipment into the 40-foot ocean freight container. A little earlier Haike and Catherine, who had been out for a jog, came by with warm welcomes and I thanked them again for their photographs of Saturday 26 November 2005, which were taken shortly after I had finished loading the second shipment of Bute Aid onto Mr MacMillan's (Cranslagvourity Farm) cattle truck, while here I acknowledge Stanley of the Ardmaleish Boat Yard, whose helpful word had facilitated this uplift. I returned to sweep out the depot and finish painting the stern of the 40-foot ocean freight container. While there I met Archie, I should be wearing my hearing aids, who tells me that he is 83 years old. He left school at 14 and served his boat builder apprenticeship here in this yard when boats were being built. Later he was a diver in the Royal

Navy during WW2. He is Diarmid, master mariner from outside Cork's, chum and he drives Diarmid about the island when he visits. Archie referred to him as a *'poor communicator.'* And he said to me one day, *'Davie we live in an ill-divided world.'* Eddie whose head shakes badly, the way I remember my Scottish Granny Ashie's used too. Eddie has a sense of humour and he is laughing at the way Martin never stops working and at me always out here in the Caribbean Hurricane Relief Depot. *'You never stop do you?'* he said. It has been a long day right enough.

Saturday 06/05/2006

10:40 a.m. I am in the Caribbean Hurricane Relief Depot having a break. I have just come off the roof of 'The Hanschell Freight Hurricane Relief Ocean Freighter' where I have been chipping rust bumps off. I began work out here at 7 a.m. I am about to have a bacon roll and a cup of tea, which I have not long purchased from the Tea Pot. As I was about to climb on to my bicycle, a piece of rubbery bacon fell out of my roll in front the tavern and I picked it up and put it back into my roll. The seagulls were not going to have it. EEEE! I got a taxi from Mr McNeil who has only one eye, who used to drive MacKirdy's beer barrel lorry into the builder's merchant, to collect five litres of green paint and back out again and got stuck in!

10:45 a.m. Mick the yachtie came by with a gift of a computer and software. I then met Mr Crawford who is a boat builder and aeronautical engineer, who stays on a farm up the back, of whom Jim the blacksmith said, *'To him, nothing is a problem.'* He tells me that he had a boatyard out in British Columbia. He is another individual fae the port with a Caribbean connection. He tells me, *'I could have bought two lots at Marigot Bay, St Lucia.'* We were chatting away. He was telling me about his pontoon invention. Car tyres are filled with styrofoam. He is an interesting and very clever man. He once brought a cargo of Sitka spruce back from British Columbia to the island with which he built aeroplanes! A 20th century polymath. We need thousands of his ilk in these dire times of CLIMATE CATASTROPHE.

10:50 a.m. It is a beautiful day. There are big puffy clouds drifting across the bay. I hope they don't come to anything much, and give me long enough to paint the top deck of the ocean freight. My friend and supporter George said *'Davie ye can weld a bough and stern on the container, and ye can sail the Seven Seas with yer stuff.'*

7:19 p.m. Home. I put a coat of paint on the top and starboard side of the container. I was talking to Peter who has a flat down the road where he tells me the neighbours will not join in to do the necessary repairs. I met him last summer. When I finished work, I went along to speak to Betty and Elaine Jukes at the unveiling ceremony of their Submariners Memorial Garden, where I was in conversation with Jim, blacksmith and Andy of Beach Watch Bute.

Saturday 13/05/2006

2:21 p.m. I am sitting on one of Mount Stuart Estate's office desks, which came thanks to the factor Nick. I am drinking a cup of milkless, sugarless tea, having eaten a packet of salt and vinegar crisps and a tasteless bacon roll from the Tea Pot. It is a beautiful warm and sun-filled day. This morning, after dropping Amy and Johanna off to catch the ferry to go to Greenock to get their haircut and shop, I drove round to the Island Motors and David put air in the tyres. Nothing is too much trouble for him. He is as positive and welcoming to me as ever. He said words to the effect of *'I was doing good work.'* I drove up to Foley Court to collect two small items of furniture, which Mary had told me about on Friday morning. I drove out here to the boatyard stopping off at DC Murray to buy a tin of grey paint to paint the inside of the

Monday 15/05/2006

ocean freight double doors. *'You can call it Hanschell Aid,'* said Alistair, who has given me some more boxes from Liz at the painters and decorators. Back home and then I went back out to the yard on the bike. I am taking a break. Robbie and Jack stopped by to speak to me. *'I'm bored!'* said Jack. I was chatting to Steven, whose boat 'Bonhomie' is parked beside the ocean freight container. Sponges. Oh! I forgot to mention that Norrie and Hilary are yachties. They have connections with the Caribbean and Grenada, in particular the Gibson of Glasgow publishing empire (see their best seller *First Aid in English*). They came across the road after I had hailed them. *'I kind of like the idea of living on a boat,'* said Norrie. He was telling me about a bad experience he had on a yacht in the Sound of Mull when the yacht nearly capsized. *'We had a yawl once but it was a wooden boat and we spent too much time on it,'* he said.

6:30 p.m. Back home. I am awaiting the return of my bicycle, which I loaned to a stranger on the way to the tearoom. I have just received a gift of surplus paper from Mrs MacMillan who looks after the Russell Street Church Hall. I have received a reply from George Lyon MSP to tell me had written to Douglas Hendry, the council's director of community services, recommending that I be offered the surplus furniture from the island schools that are due to close later this year. We'll see! I had cycled out to Ettrick Bay to see George last week and he was as good as his word. Good on him! Another Supporter.

Monday 15/05/2006

9:10 p.m. Home. Martin called a meeting at his home to wind up Bute Waste Watchers, which muggins, among others, helped start up and run many moons ago. It has been 'absorbed' by the local housing association. Are there any patrons out there willing to support my RECYCLING and REUSABLES initiative?

A 40-foot Ocean Freight Container

Thursday 18/05/2006

Home. I have received a donation to the Educational Resources Project of £100 from Colette and Craig and their family, which will be deposited in the account 'Educational Resource' fund at the RBS branch in the town. I then sat down and wrote them a thank-you letter, which I will deliver to their door on my way to school tomorrow.

Friday 19/05/2006

Classroom. Stuart from the Book People brought some empty cardboard boxes over to the Caribbean Hurricane Relief Depot.

6:30 p.m. Home. I am currently engaged in transatlantic telephony thanks to Alexander Graham Bell, Marconi and a host of many unsung others before them and since. I spoke with Robin Swaisland who is the senior projects manager for the Agency of Reconstruction and Development, Grenada. Build Back Better. He told me that Ricky was checking out about schools on the island in need of refurbishment and educational resources. Robin said he had written to Mr Pierre, Permanent Secretary Minister of Education and Labour, about the offer of further shipments of surplus educational supplies from Scotland on 10 April 2006 but had had no reply. I keep pressing. I also called Mr St John, chairman of the Grenada Port Authority. No result for my effort. What's my/our telephone bill going to be? Don't ask. The cost of embarking on something like this, or anything worthwhile, will be huge: but I can't stop just yet.

Monday 22/05/2006

Twenty-two million containers worldwide. Where did you get that fact from? I called Rococo Chocolates in London and ordered some bars of Grenada Chocolate. The Coady-Booth family are off to the Isle of Spices to visit the source of their bespoke chocolate and told me (bless them!) that they will visit Grand Roy Government School in Grand Roy, parish of St John. I called Blue Sky and spoke to Jeff and later to Tracy who suggested I call Conrad at Container Brokerage. I spoke to Joyce the gatekeeper at J&J Denholm Ltd in Glasgow, who is the group commercial director Jane Harris's secretary, about the offer from their firm of a possible discount on the next shipment. I have high hopes. There is no harm in asking. She suggested I call Denholm Bahr Ltd at India Buildings in Liverpool, which I did right away and I spoke with Ray who told me that ocean freight containers have a seaworthy expiry date. *'Oh, no,'* I say to myself, *'does that mean my 40-foot ocean freight container ain't going to go anywhere?'* He told me that it will have to be inspected. Anyway he said, ending on a positive note, that as and when I was ready to ship what I had collected/gathered/been given to let him know, and he closed our conversation with, *'We'll do something for you.'* On hearing these words I was encouraged. Not all my telephone calls have been a waste of time and family funds. Earlier this afternoon I deposited a cheque for £150 into the Educational Resources account.

To do for Tuesday: contact Mandy Meikle about the Community Woodland Scheme; call Gerry who has returned from Europe about Grenada's continuing need to rebuild and reconstruct its school infrastructure and bring him up to date on what we here on the island have managed collectively to achieve on Grenada's behalf.

Wednesday 24/06/2006

I called Conrad who suggested I call Tom at Calder Container Services in Coatbridge, who could let me know whether or not my container can be re-plated. He said the disintegrating rust process would not stop and the sooner I sold the container the better.

I heard what he said with dismay, perhaps I have got myself in a pickle? Tom Deas then put me through to Tom Walker, who is a plater inspector and container surveyor, who said he would get back to me, and he would let me know what his fee was for coming over to the island to inspect the container. What I have got myself involved in, is becoming more complicated than I had bargained for. All of your own making, laddie.

Thursday 25/05/2006

I collected a computer from Donald the taxi and Lorraine and took it out to the ocean freight container. That was generous of them. I looked at the big box and hoped it would pass muster.

Friday 26/05/2006

4:30 p.m. Home. I received a call from Jean offering me the remaining material from their sale-of-work goods left over after the Port Gala Day. Kind. These offers are coming from all directions and temper my resolve to see this next shipment through to delivery, whatever the verdict on the ocean freight turns out to be. If it is not seaworthy, it can be sold on the island for storage of farm equipment etcetera, and I will have to make sure that the next ocean freight I purchase has been inspected fit for transport overseas. I live and learn. Every day is a schoolday in life's open-source academy.

5:30 p.m. Home. While I was outside preparing to repot the Pet Supplies delivery of plants (fuchsias, dahlias, parsley) I gave Sue (engineer, principal teacher of mathematics at the secondary school) a wave and crossed the road to speak while her dog chewed a piece of driftwood. *'I am clearing out books and equipment from the academy's mathematics department stock cupboard, do you want it?'* '*Yes please,*' I said.

Saturday 27/05/2006

10:50 a.m. Home. I am just back home after cycling into the town. I went up to the builder merchants and Ronny gave me duff hardware, plastic bags and a bucket. Bless him. Back down Castle Street and around to Bishop Street Post Office to collect a sample box of Grenada Chocolate bars and then it was around with collections to leave them at the taxi rank. Print Point was closed until 10 a.m. so it was over to Musicker Café for a chat with John and Sue and then back around to Guildford Square to Paula's for a coffee. I later collected a banner from Martin at Print Point. I cycled home, where I am going to make another batch of marmalade. I made nine jars altogether. Marion and David made covers for the lids and Amy Elisabeth designed and made the labels. I received a call from Gerry, of Just Grenada. He tells me he eats Grenada Chocolate, *'It's got a lot of potential,'* he said. What has?

It is now 11:50 p.m. I have just remembered I met Andy in the Cowal Builders Supplies car park. He has offered me Land Rover parts! Yes please. Why not? Someone will need them on the Isle of Spices. Scrap broker.

Sunday 28/05/2006

10:50 a.m. The Port Park. Gala Day. The sun is shining on the page. Pop music is blaring oot across the Port Park. I have set up my stall. There are withdrawn library books from the Morningside Library in Edinburgh, some are new and never been borrowed, pot plants and jars of marmalade. Mrs Janey J had driven me down the road to the Caribbean Hurricane Relief Depot to load up plants and books in her Waste Watchers recycling van. She is a helpful and generous hearted soul for whom nothing is too much trouble. I then went down later to the Tea Pot for a roll and square sausage and a mug of tea. I am now just waiting while thick clouds with patches of blue in between them are gathering over the hills above Hilton Farm. There is now a strong breeze blowing in off Kames Bay.

7:40 p.m. Home. The sun shone through for a while until it clouded over and I was sprinkled, and there was a strong westerly breeze all afternoon. Arran, Jordan and James, former pupils at the school and from the Clan O'Dunn, wheeled my barrow and trolley to and from the Caribbean Hurricane Relief Depot with the resources and materials that had not been sold at my stall, and that of the Port Committee for which I donated £50 in exchange for all of it. I mistakenly had thought it was the Water Aid charity. Amy, good to her word, had baked two pies for me to sell. One apple, the other a Victorian sponge which was purchased by Margaret.

Amy later brought me a flask of tea. Kindness. Mary gave me a salmon sandwich and a Tunnock's wafer. A lot of goodwill and kindness this day. I sold all the plants at a profit of £40 plus. There is no other way but forward. Oh! Janey J kindly offered to take my stuff back to the storage container, but my former P3/4/5 pupils stepped in with assistance.

10:30 p.m. I have just remembered! Another gift of new stationery came from Mr and Mrs Gordon (Katelyn's great-grandparents) this afternoon.

Wednesday 31/05/2006

8:45 a.m. I met Buckeridge Electrical electricians Gus, Ryan and Nicky who arrived at the ocean freight container to install wiring for electrical outlets/switches for the diesel generator. Gordon the joiner put boards on the ceiling to attach light fittings.

7 p.m. Back home from taking some textbooks and unwanted educational resources from RPS out to the ocean freight. David Alexander is a big help. Bless him, Lord! I have made arrangements

Friday 02/06/2006

to meet Tom Walker, registered container surveyor/inspector, on Saturday 10 June, who will call me from Wemyss Bay and I will meet him off the ferry. I received an email from Maggie regarding my query to her about the need in Grenadian schools for more resources. Not encouraging, however I shall try to exhaust/investigate the situation there on that island as thoroughly as I am able to do, before sending any more help. Perhaps I should draw a line under my humanitarian project at this juncture? But I still have got to send this 40-footer somewhere, assuming it will prove seaworthy despite the rust bumps.

Friday 02/06/2006

1:49 p.m. P4/5 Classroom. *'Mr Hanschell there's a man to see yuh,'* he said excitedly. It was Alex, from Bobby Beattie's storeroom beneath the old swimming baths, with a petrol generator. I asked him if he wouldn't mind leaving it at the boatyard office. *'He'll take £40 quid aff,'* he said. *'Great!'* I said. It is a beautiful afternoon. Sunshine has broken up the thick, grey clouds that hung over me this morning. I had better turn my attention to the day job, or else.

4:35 p.m. I am just home. Blackbirds are singing from the tops of trees out the back of the cottage and other whistlers in the branches have joined in the chorus. After class I went over to the yard to where Alex had left the generator in the safe hands of Jim the blacksmith and young Adam, his unofficial apprentice. The latter helped me trolley it over to the ocean freight container and said he would make me a base for it to control the vibration. I stopped off at the garage to purchase a small portable tank for the gasoline and a few litres of unleaded. Home. *'Call me when you have had everything wired up,'* said Ally.

9:10 p.m. Marion has called me in from working in the garden to return a call from the Coady-Booths, who had told me several weeks ago that they were on their way out to Grenada and said that they would visit Grand Roy Government School. Chantal came on the line and said, '*They are using absolutely everything you sent!*' How did that news make me feel? Just magic. It took me from the depths to back up on top the big cliff at the back of the cottage with its panoramic views of the Costa Clyde.

Chantal put me on to Mott who is visiting with them, who comes from the USA and runs the cocoa estate which is one of the suppliers of cocoa to Rococo Chocolates, with whom I spoke briefly. We are on a similar wavelength. '*I hear you are mining the waste stream up there in Scotland,*' he said cheerily. For sure. He tells me he is off to Dundee and Arbroath to purchase chocolate making machinery. I gave him an invitation to visit us.

Saturday 03/06/2006

11:25 a.m. The Boat Yard. The sun is shining brightly. I have just helped Jarvis with his inflatable down to the shore. Low tide. He tells me that he used to sail on Hogganfield Loch, which I frequented once upon a time after school at Sunnyside Primary School, up the other end of the loch in the relatively new scheme of Craigend, built on the fields of Comedie Farm, as a supernumerary to the Glasgow Secondary Schools Sailing Club. And I spent not a few evenings in the dank basement of Smithycroft Secondary School, patching the Kestrel class dinghies with fibreglass paste. I was hoping that I would earn some time for myself and actually get out on the watta to sail, but that was not to be.

Well, here I am again sorting through the Port Improvement Committee's bric-a-brac from their gala day stall. Some men's, some women's, and some children's unwanted gifts and treasure. Useful bits and pieces, crockery, kitchen utensils, all of value to someone, somewhere else. I shan't cowp it, be certain of that. Get the good of it, I said, midgie skip raker in the 21st century wasteland. I will keep on working and stick to the task in front of me. I paused to speak to Colin, with a schnauzer on a leash. He is from Aberdeen. We had chatted some time ago and he tells me again that his family belonged to Gilcolmston C of S. He knew Mr Still. *'He preached fire and brimstone and he was a really nice man,'* he said. Colin is not long back from working in Chittagong, Bangladesh. He was telling me about talking in a Dubai hostelry to absentee Arab landlords who have skyscraper properties all over the United Kingdom. He is a telecommunications engineer on contract. He is an interesting individual.

Soon after, I had a long conversation with Betty who is trying to get her boule's pitch, up at the Port Park, off the drawing board and working again. *'I get visions all the time,'* she said. Bless her! She is one of the Port People along with Elaine who have contributed so much to the well-being of the local community: among their successful projects are The Good Natured Garden and the Midget Submariners Memorial Garden. She is another kindred spirit, who has been around the block not a few times and is still doing good work with an indomitable spirit.

Monday 05/06/2006

5:15 p.m. Home. At the lunch break today at school I went over to see Mrs Carroll, the business manager in the boatyard office, about a delivery of empty cardboard boxes from DC Murray that may have been put at the depot. I met Gordon the joiner and Jim the blacksmith who are always welcoming and helpful to me. The former offered me a computer table. *'Do you want it now?' 'Yes, please,'* I said. He put it into his van and brought it over to the ocean freight container.

Where is all this stuff going to go to if I learn in a week's time that this box ain't goin' anywhere? I'll cross that bridge when I come to it. First thing this morning, a beautiful day. On the way up the road to school I dropped off the payment in cash for the generator at Bobby Beattie's emporium. I then I cycled on to the garage to get another tank of unleaded for the generator. Ally phoned to tell me that he couldn't make it this afternoon. I shifted cardboard boxes from DC Murray Ltd over to the big box.

Wednesday 07/06/2006

8:05 p.m. Home. I have been printing some pictures/photographs/digitals of the ocean freight container. I was over to the Caribbean Hurricane Relief Depot after school to find about seven boxes of a gift that was promised from Mr Love, the proprietor of The Wee Light Shop, which he said I could have when he came to my stall at the gala day last month. Remember to thank him. I changed into a boiler suit and transferred them across the road. I then had a long conversation with Jim the steam, formerly an oil tanker's engineer: he was describing someone he knew as *'All shadows and mirrors, that man.'* He was telling me about his recent visit to New Zealand to visit his sister and the decline in the standard of education in the United Kingdom, and in particular Scotland. He served his time on Clydeside.

It is a beautiful light-filled afternoon. Container Inspector. Consultant with CT Engineering Services. We'll just have to wait and see. *'We are back from Grenada. It's really a great sight. They are using everything you sent,'* said Chantal from of Rococo Chocolates Ltd. That was the message on our answering machine. I was encouraged by those words.

Friday 09/06/2006

I called Tom Walker the container inspector to check that he's coming tomorrow. I then called Ally, the digital artisan formerly of the National Engineering Laboratory in East Kilbride, to see if it would be convenient for him to be at the ocean freight container tomorrow afternoon to check over the IT equipment and I will have the generator up and running.

Saturday 10/06/2006

4 p.m. Home. Well where do I begin? From the present and go back to this morning of this lovely warm, cool wind, bright and sunny day, when I set off on the bike to meet Mr and Mrs Walker off the 8:45 a.m. boat. I had been outside drinking a second cup of coffee, just chillin' out, when Amy Elisabeth shouted, *'Dad, there's a phone call for you.'* I got Alan from the Isle of Barra (via Durban, South Africa) banker, now taxi driver, to meet me. I thought the taxi waiting by the Victorian toilets was his partner in the business, so when I saw the ferry approaching the pier I went and asked him if he would run me and my guests to the port. At that moment Alan appeared. Oh dear! An embarrassment of taxis. I apologised. The former drove us out. On arrival, Mr Walker had a look at the ocean freight container and said it looked alright but he would have to look underneath it. What do I do now? Should I disturb Martin and leave the inspection for another time? I went over to his home and rang the bell. No answer.

Mea Culpa. I had forgotten to tell Martin that I had made arrangements for the container inspector to come this morning. I did not think it necessary to have the crane ready to lift it. I kept my cool and, oh, a final inspection can wait as and when the time for shipment comes. Alan returned at 10 a.m. and dropped us off at The Pier at Craigmore, formerly The Tea Room. Jean kindly let us in as it was not officially open at that time. Staff were still vacuuming the carpets. Harry the chef joined us while the scones were baking. He was telling us about his time in Grenada when he was out there training staff at La Source Hotel, and also what it was like for him growing up in the Lanarkshire coal mining village of Cardowan. He told us that his parents now live across the main road in Stepps, where I boarded with John and Nan at

5 Alexandra Avenue from 1975 to 1982. He said that area had changed greatly. The Walkers live in Chryston, which is further up the Cumbernauld Road.

I got along well with Tom and Betty Walker, they appeared to be in sympathy with what I was trying to achieve. Mr Walker sure knows all about containers. He knew Howard, from whom I had purchased the ocean freight container, and said it was a small world in the scene of trade in containers, where he acts as a consultant based with CT Engineering Services Ltd in Coatbridge. *'How much do I owe you?'* I asked. *'Eighty pounds,'* he replied. I gave him one hundred pounds. I am always paying over the odds and I am perhaps unnecessarily generous. He told me that he would send the receipt and would vet/suss/inspect the suitability for shipment of any future containers from Glasgow.

Later I met Alastair at The Tea Room and thanked him for the cardboard boxes. The Walkers and I walked back along the front into the town, chatting en route. I said goodbye to them and waited for a bus at Guildford Square. While waiting for the bus to the port, I met Robert and Christopher's gran who told me that their grandad has cancer. *'I have turned the sitting room into a bedroom and the nurse comes every day,'* she said. Their gran offered me £5 and I thanked her for her generous donation and asked if she wouldn't mind depositing it into the Educational Resources account at the RBS branch in the town.

I am back out at the boatyard shifting and sorting through the boxes of bric-a-brac and spent some time tidying up the boxes that were in the ocean freight container, from the primary school where I taught from 1990 to 1991, until 1 p.m. when Ally the digital artisan arrived. The generator started with the first pull.

l left Ally to get on and do what he could do. I had to get a taxi from Charlie while I was waiting for a bus, having left my bicycle at the pier when I had gone to meet the Walkers this morning. I cycled home. David the Young is okay, he was watching a soccer match on TV. Later I cycled back into the town, returned some books to the library and here I am back out here, it is shortly after 4:20 p.m. I think I will tidy up some more and head home. It has been a very busy and fun day. The fine weather helps.

7:20 p.m. I called the Coady-Booths. *'We took loads of photographs. We were at the Horse Guards parade. Welsh Guards. Everyone was there. Fergus hoped Grenada would win the World Cup,'* she said.

To do: see Martin about whether it is possible to have the ocean freight container lifted for next week and to arrange another inspection with Tom Walker as he and Mrs Walker will be on the island staying in a local hotel; ask Jim the blacksmith if he would weld brackets inside the container to hold up the light fixtures. *'This wiring has been done by house electricians. You go from one crisis to another,'* said Jim the steam. As I scribble these thoughts/remembrances/reminders, it is time to stop and return to my precious home life, so drop it now! I need to register as a charity and draw up a constitution/statement of my intentions etc; send email/query to Conrad at the Container Brokerage. I have had no word from Colin in Houston, Texas about the possibility of resale of my dry ocean freight container in the Caribbean. Is there a market niche? How do bank/giro credit slips work for account. I am a numpty but I can learn how to operate these business processes.

Monday 12/06/2006

5:10 p.m. Home. Just before I left school this afternoon the school secretary said there was a call from Ivor at the museum, *'I've got some educational material for you. Four Open University courses.'* Thank you very much, Ivor, could you drop them off at the boatyard office.

5:30 p.m. Home. Call from GJ council office at Kilmory in Lochgilphead regarding sources of funding – has kindly offered to do a search for me. I am being attacked right now with a migraine. I managed to thank Mr Love of the Light Shop for letting me have the bits and bobs from the shop before he closed down.

Saturday 17/06/2006

10:03 a.m. The Boat Yard. I am in the ocean freight container, cars swishing by. Rain drops bouncing off the metal roof. I have a massive pile of sorting and sifting to do. Martin came by earlier. *'Is yer man coming back to check the container yet?'* he asks. I told him that Mr Walker had called yesterday, and would call in again next week. Martin said he would be available with the crane to lift it when we ready. There is a good heavy rain coming down. Get tae wuk.

Friday 23/06/2006

8:51 a.m. The P4/5 Classroom. I am just back from the yard. I thought I'd recollect this little record of events from the ocean freight container earlier. As I was walking across the yard Martin hailed me. *'I want to borrow your generator.'* Certainly man. Glad I'm able to lend you something after all your unstinted help and encouragement to me. And then he says. *'Donald wishes to borrow it.' 'Oh, okay.'* I cross the road and there was his nibs and Tim, to whom he introduced me. With the help of the latter, we lifted it out and over to his car. Donald is a prospective fish farmer against whose plans I had registered a written letter of complaint. Love your enemies. I couldn't say no to Martin, he having lent me so much over the past two years. Unconditional goodwill rules the ocean waves and here on terra firma.

9:45 p.m. On the way home from the staff meal at the Waterfront Café, as I was crossing the road, I met someone, a supporter, who asked me if the first two 20-foot containers had got to Grenada last year. I said that they had, and I was flying out next month to see where the educational resources had got to, and then she said, *'Oh, at your own expense?' 'Yes,'* I said. This supporter is always interested to learn how things are going. As I walked up the road, to post the payment for the milk, I met Iain the spark who is also a publican and lives along the road. *'How's your charity going?'* he asks. He was telling me about his work in the Azerbaijan oilfields after the breakup of the Russian state, and, despite the dire poverty of the people, he was impressed by their hospitality and willingness to share what they had in the midst of the wealth of natural resources.

Sunday 25/06/2006

9:50 p.m. I had a visit from Neil the roofer, a supporter with whom I had a long conversation. He told me that he was working on the roof of a house and felt that he had to come round with a donation. *'I want you to have this,'* he said. I invited him for a coffee and gave him a quick résumé of the work done so far. He told me that what I was sending had love in it. *'Love in a box,'* he called it. I told him to hang onto his cash, but not let up on his wonderful goodwill support for what we were doing. This morning I received an email reply from Maggie in Grenada giving me the name of guest house where we might stay.

Wednesday 28/06/2006

5:10 p.m. Home. Before leaving the classroom, the classroom assistant came up the steps to tell me that the big primary school had some more resources for me to collect. On the way home I stopped off at the Discovery Centre and met the former manager, who is now the manager of the Pavilion. I asked him if he would introduce me to the current manager to see if the centre/ Visit Scotland would let me have some freebies to take out to the

A 40-Foot Ocean Freight Container

Tom Walker Chartered Container Surveyor and Martin Stirling of Stirling Yacht Services Ltd, Port Bannatyne, Isle of Bute.

Grenadian pupils. No problem. He generously gave me a large box of plastic rulers with a magnifying lens at one end to take out to the Grand Roy Government School and the Bel Air Children's Home.

I am cycling onward when I got nearly as far as The Tea Room and saw one of the supporters walking their dog. I stopped to say, *'Hi!' 'Norrie has a $20 dollar Eastern Caribbean note, which he found in an old wallet, and he'll bring it along for you,'* she said.

First thing this morning the school PTA treasurer said she had a cheque for the work/project and who was she to make it out to? I said Grand Roy Government School and DV, I will be able to hand it over to them next month. After the end of term school service in the Port Hall a parent came over with some money for me. *'I heard you were going out to Grenada,'* she said. *'Yes,'* I replied. *'Would you take this?' 'That is very generous of you, but would you mind depositing these funds into the Educational Resources account at the bank?'* I said.

I am not long off the phone to confirm our booking at the Roydon's guest house in St George's, Grenada, West Indies, with all the modern conveniences and cooking facilities, and the landlady Mrs DeFreitas sounded friendly.

Thursday 29/06/2006

4:05 p.m. Home. This morning the journalist/editor/photographer, and friend, Craig came to take the photograph of the P4/5 class and were handed a cheque for £263 from the school's PTA to give to Principal Janice Thomas of Grand Roy Government School. As I was about to leave the school this afternoon a teacher from another island school drove up Castle Street, stopped her car, and gave me a large carrier bag of school textbooks. Earlier Jane called to say they had some IT equipment for the depot.

6:30 p.m. I have not long returned from having had a look at a wonderful donation of primary curriculum textbooks (SPMG mathematics, maps etc.) and classroom furniture at the big primary school. All of it in mint condition, from the Primary 7 teacher. Stephen the janitor told me I can collect it any time.

A 40-FOOT OCEAN FREIGHT CONTAINER

Friday 30/06/2006

10:06 a.m. The Boat Yard. The Caribbean Hurricane Relief Depot. About this time a year ago we were journeying over to the Sandbank Community Centre in the village of Sandbank, on the outskirts of Dunoon, to load our first 20-foot ocean freight container shipment of surplus to requirements, fit-for-purpose educational resources, gifted to us over the past year by schools on the island and on the mainland, for Grand Roy Government School on the West Indian island of Grenada. I have just been on the phone to Tom Walker, container inspector/surveyor/plater based in Coatbridge with CT Engineering Services Ltd. I told him that I had spoken to Martin, and that he would have the crane to lift the ocean freight container, the Giant Green Box, off the ground, so he could inspect underneath and determine whether or not the container is still seaworthy and can be 'plated' up to date.

The crows are cawing in the woods above the boatyard. It is a damp, grey, drizzling morning, but there is plenty of work for me to do in here, so if that's the case get cracking!

2:30 p.m. Earlier I had a visit from Nigel, curious to discover what I was up to. He had his grandson with him, who suffers from Crohn's disease, who told me that he likes reading and he said he liked science fiction, so I gave him the trilogy *Hitchhiker's Guide to The Galaxy* from among the many boxes of withdrawn library books, which he appeared to appreciate. He told me he has an interest in marine biology. I told them about what I was trying to achieve, whereupon Nigel got out his cheque book. I said he could deposit his donation in the Educational Resources account if he wished, but I did not handle any funds directly and I was not registered as a charity, and so far, I had self-financed this social entrepreneurial initiative by myself, out of my own funds (through the sale of Barbados Shipping and Trading Ltd shares, which I had inherited from my two Barbadian great aunts, Mrs

Louie Gittens and Miss Phyllis Manning). *'So, you are not a registered charity?'* he said. *'I am not a charity at the moment, perhaps one day I will be,'* I replied.

Also earlier, I had another visitor who told me he worked for Quarriers, and who has a holiday flat along the road. He offered to lend a hand, which I graciously declined. Perhaps one day, if this exercise in entrepreneurial philanthropy/autonomous self-directed NGO aid takes off, then perhaps I'll be looking for helpers. In the meantime, I have an amorphous team of supporters and friends on the island of Bute who give me all the help I need at the moment. As Iain would say, *'You know where you are going.'* Right enough I do, only by FAITH. And I'll fly solo and by the seat of my breeks for the time being.

Monday 03/07/2006

8:15 a.m. Caribbean Hurricane Relief Depot, The Boat Yard, Port Bannatyne. The craws are cawing in the woods above the yard. It is humid and hazy. Sunshine is going to break through sooner or later and it is going to be a cracking beautiful day. I am sitting on one of Jim the blacksmith's gifts of metal chairs at the computer table given to me by Gordon the joiner. I have just met Martin and his right hand, who has given me a copy of the *Business Yellow Pages*.

Yesterday afternoon I took Ronnie from Lenzie, who had come by Delhi Cottage looking for help to have his bicycle puncture fixed and/or looking to get a puncture repair kit, up to The Bike Shed in the Bush. *'Sorry we are closed, it is Laurie's Birthday.'* said the proprietor of the shop. I persisted. *'I just want a bicycle repair kit.'* David the bicycle mechanic extraordinaire, and the toff that he is, not only gave Ronnie the article but loaned him another bicycle.

It continues to be hazy and muggy, but dry and overcast. Stop dawdling. *'Get to work!'* I am going to set aboot taking an inventory, and pack texts and wonderful library books. I stopped to speak to Archie the multi-skilled: a boat builder and wise resident of the port (he served his time in this yard when boats were being built). He says. *'Are they still suffering out there? We live in an ill-divided world.'* *'I am going to find out,'* I replied.

Earlier today, John lent me his van to go up to the big primary school to uplift a generous donation of educational resources. Nothing is that simple. I couldn't get it to start, *'Press the button after switching it on,'* he said helpfully. I went to the janitor's house and Stephen the janitor came to the door with a cheery and helpful smile. He let me have two trolleys and I loaded the van with assorted texts, some dated but still with sound content (a bit like the prime mover perhaps), and stationery etc. Back up the road with journeying mercies. Parked the van and I walked down to the Tea Pot for a bacon roll, a packet of Walker's salt and vinegar crisps and a cuppae tea. There I met Sandy, who is a friend of the Fisher Folk group, who lent me one of their tapes, and Alastair, master painter, decorator and picture framer who came by with a stack of cardboard boxes. We shot the breeze. He is another supporter and helper. Earlier I went round the back, where the 40-foot ocean freight containers have been converted into workshops, to pay Jim the blacksmith for welding the bar below the double doors of my freight container. He tells me, *'Your money is no good to you here, Dave.'* Knock me down please. He wouldn't take any payment. Another supporter and helper from early days. I am humbled, so just get on with what I have to get on with.

It is hot and steamy. I am being acclimatised for our flying and fleeting visit to the Isle of Spices. *'Will you send me a card?'* Amy asked. *'I certainly will.'* I was also chatting to Tony with the speed boat. He has come up from Bristol and told me he had been brought up in Ruchazie, near the banks of the Monklands Canal (now the M8 motorway), and near to Hogganfield Loch, East End, Glasgow, in the late 1950s scheme: I trod through that housing scheme many a day and it was where my GP's surgery was. Another resonating connection.

4:45 p.m. I was talking. *'Do you ever stop?'* I have typed enough of this screed for one night. Sandy has just lent me another tape of the Fisher Folk, who are friends of his.

Tuesday 04/07/2006

7:40 a.m. I am back out to the boatyard and arrived to another beautiful Scottish summer's day. It is warm for the time being and there is a soft breeze blowing in from the north-east over the Cowal Hills. The yachts at anchor in Kames Bay are all pointing their bows in that direction. That is how I know. I opened up the storage reefer, donned my boiler suit and I am now across the road in the ocean freight container.

'Are you going home?' asks Bob, Katelyn's grandad. *'No. We, Marion and I, are making just over a week's chartered flight from Gatwick, just to see how the island of Grenada is recovering after Hurricane Ivan and what the school has done with the two container shipments of aid from the island,'* I replied. *'My wife has got something for you to take out. Are you going to be here all day?'* he asks. *'That is really kind of you. Yes. I'll be here all day,'* I said.

12:15 p.m. Amy, a supporter, tells me a little about her privileged childhood in India. She spent some of her childhood in Calcutta and recalls the extreme poverty of its inhabitants, and has just come by with a flask of tea for me. Bless her. She tells me that she is hoping to sell her flat along the road and return south. I wish her well.

5 p.m. *'It is too hot to be working.'* Gordon the joiner and son have not long arrived with Guala Closure Group cardboard boxes ('The technology to protect and promote your brand worldwide.') from

DC Murray Ltd. Earlier I stopped work to speak with Malcolm, a port resident, who tells me that his sister lives at Auchnacloich, which is near the Pheasant Pub en route to Lenzie, that I used to walk past on a Saturday morning on my way to Kirkintilloch for an outing. I would walk from my lodgings in Stepps to do a bit of shopping, visit the library, go into a café for coffee, and along to visit shut-in couple Gordon from Glasgow and Mavis (who came from Pudsey), who were friends of my landlord and landlady. More connections. Get back to work and stop your blethering.

5:20 p.m. Along comes Derek the sassenach, who asks, 'Ow much you want for that globe ovah theah?' I tell him it is not for sale. 'I will give you £20 for it.' I tell him it is still not for sale. 'C'mon it's only plastic. I got two boats ovah theah! Get it out of display then.'

Wednesday 05/07/2006

10:55 a.m. The Boat Yard. It is a beautiful day. I am going to pack, sort, inventory and box children's books, both fact and fiction, all gifted from the Morningside Library, thanks to Sandra, the librarian, who said to a while back, 'Edinburgh is awash with books.'

Amy has just donated two bags of new bed linen. Get cracking, there's work to be done. It's nice to be nice but …

1:25 p.m. Stuart, with a flat down the road, appears. 'Can I ask what you are doing here?' 'Certainly,' I said. So I pinned his ears back. Why don't you bin it all that stuff! No way!

1:55 p.m. I have just had the pleasure of meeting Nisbet, photographer, and John Senior. 'He who has led, will lead. These are the words I am leaving you with for the present,' the former said. Another encouragement for me to press on.

Chapter Five

The Fact-Finding Trip to the Isle of Spices

Wednesday 05/07/2006

10:05 p.m. Gatwick Airport South Terminal. We are sitting upon a balcony where Marion and I have claimed a wee space to spend the next few hours until our direct flight to the island of Grenada, via Excel Airways, leaves tomorrow morning, above the clouds on a Boeing 737. The mind boggles. I will be glad to be back on the ground.

Amy and David drove us to the pier and waited until the ferry docked. It was a hot summer afternoon. The Firth of Clyde was like a pond. Johanna, who was staying behind to keep her gran and her Aunt Catherine company, said goodbye to us at Delhi Cottage.

There is a Unique Gifts shop with a display case of models of Concorde. Every person I see has a mobile phone. I am still without one, still lost in 21st century technology, and this traveller goes in faith. No expectations, except to trust and that, somehow, I will be led to the people I am meant to meet and learn whether or not further shipments of surplus-to-requirements educational resources are required. The waste stream miner. A miner of the waste stream. The aristocrat of skip rakers. Getting the unwanted and salvaged goods to others, so that they might be able to get the good from them. I am glad that Marion is with me, but sad that, for once, except for the times when we left Scotland to journey south to attend the funerals for Mum and later Di, we left Amy,

David, and Johanna behind with Grandad and Gran at 4 The Grove in Kilbarchan.

Thursday 06/07/2006

Time? at 35,000 feet above the Blue Planet. We met Mr La Guerre from Belleview, St David's, an agriculturalist who gave us two nutmegs.

6 p.m. We are still above the clouds. Traid.org 'Funding international development projects through the sale of quality second-hand goods' is not rocket science. But I am not selling anything. I am at the moment collecting and giving good stuff away, only it's costing me and those closest to me.

3:05 p.m. Grenada time. It is hot and humid. Marion is trying to phone home. We have booked into Roydon's Guest House. There is a panoramic view of Grand Anse Bay. I have met the proprietor Mr DeFreitas, who was welcoming, and I handed over US$500 for our week's stay. We are in a large Miami, Florida, USA-style brand-new shopping mall in downtown St George's, the capital. There is no sign here so far of the devastation to the capital, St George's, infrastructure wrought by Hurricane Ivan in September 2004. We have had a banana milkshake each, and I scoffed a tuna burger. Grenada schools have begun their holidays, so there was no answer when I called the Grand Roy Government School number.

8:10 p.m. This small, modern, two-level apartment building with construction of an extension, which is sited at the edge of a busy main road (and there is a constant flow of traffic in both directions below the small one room apartment where we are staying), is spotlessly clean and well furnished with all the mod cons. We have just had our first Grenadian visitor, Miss Padlett, who is from the Jehovah's Witnesses – a lovely soul. *'People must show appreciation,'* she exclaimed with conviction.

We are serenaded by a chorus of whistling frogs in the unkempt vegetation at the back of the apartment building. I am sitting on the balcony, which overlooks this constant movement of vehicular traffic moving up a steep hill to my right. I miss the company of Amy, David and Johanna, which is part of the cost of coming here on this 'mission'.

Friday 07/07/2006

5:32 a.m. *'Good morning, Grenada,'* I said out loud and clear from the balcony, to all and sundry. The dawn is breaking on the other side of the island. There is a chorus of the little frogs and cicadas? A white egret just flew past. The traffic is starting to build up on the main road below me – I feel like a bird perched on this newly built balcony. I met Donald the builder who lives nearby and whose firm is building another set of identical apartment buildings. A little bird about the size of a wren but more colourful – what once as a boy in Trinidad I might have called a Picoplat – has just perched on the electricity wire in front of me. (See the book on Caribbean birds, *Birds of Trinidad and Tobago,* 2nd ed [Macmillan Caribbean Natural History], by Roger Neckles and Richard P Ffrench [Lodge School schoolmaster who never taught me, who I thought looked like a bird himself]. It's the current definitive work on birds of the Caribbean). There are clouds, coloured golden orange, on the hill up to my right, which have caught the rays of the rising sun. There are the tiny lights of fishing boats out on the bay. The lights from the hotels and apartment blocks at the other end of the bay are still on. I am going to make Marion a cup of tea.

6:30 a.m. The day has long begun.

On both visits to the Isle of Spices, the Hanschell family were made welcome.

8:10 a.m. We are now sitting in the foyer of the Minister of Education and Labour's, spanking new office with a view of St George's Harbour out of the window on my left. I am waiting to see the minister. She's going to Paris next week, she said. Which I overheard from one of the secretaries. We got a little minibus, crowded to the doors, from outside the guest house to here for $2 Eastern Caribbean currency and walked up the steep hill to the new offices of the government of Grenada's compound in the botanical gardens. I recalled the time when Dad, Mum, Diana and I came here off the ship that had docked in St George's Harbour, which was taking us to Trinidad in 1950, and went to visit Dad's cousin Michael Albert Hanschell.

8:50 a.m. We are still waiting. Patience. I got talking to Marva one of the secretaries. She is friendly and tells me that her family came from Barbados to settle in the Isle of Spices. She asked me if I would talk with her son who has just left school with no

Friday 07/07/2006

What lies ahead of us today?

qualifications as she had identified with my own narrative of leaving the Lodge School in Barbados in 1961 likewise, and what I had managed to achieve since. She is a gentle soul and we invited her and her family, the Andrews, who will call on Saturday at 7 p.m. at the guest house. *'We will be on the lookout for you from the verandah,'* I said.

I can hear voices. *'Everyting is a lot bettah now in Grenada. Would you bring tea for me please, Rae,'* she said to her own secretary.

10 a.m. We had a worthwhile meeting with the Minister of Education and Labour. I am to get their specifications for information technology equipment. *'We will get a driver for you and take you out to the school so you can see for yourself all the educational materials you send dem,'* she said, at which point the gentleman we had noticed earlier was introduced to us. Kirk is responsible for public relations in the ministry. It was arranged that he would call

These beautiful flowers grew wild behind the apartment building where we stayed in 2006.

for us on Monday 10 July at 8 a.m. and has arranged a meeting with the staff of Grand Roy Government School to hand over the cheque from our island school's Parent-Teacher Association.

We are now in the office in the Diocesan Centre, at 2 Church Street, of the Roman Catholic Bishop of Grenada, who I had spoken to on the telephone on another of my many transatlantic calls before I left Scotland earlier this week. This contact had been given to me by supportive Nora in the Food For the Poor office in Miami. *'Why are we waiting, why are we waiting?'* There is a soft, cool breeze from the Caribbean Sea blowing in through a window on my right, which has been thoughtfully opened by the Bishop's secretary.

10:45 a.m. Finally, our meeting with the Bishop. *'Whoever you send the container to, remember to make sure they get the invoice as they will have the responsibility of clearing it with customs and the Grenada Port Authority. Donors in a US parish send me a lot of church pews, we saw them up and use the wood to repair our church buildings. I don't run a museum,'* he said. He is attentive and astute.

Friday 07/07/2006

He distributes what the RC Church receives without favour, no matter the denomination of the beneficiary, which is good to hear. I like this man who is after my own heart. He wants us to keep Tuesday open when he hopes to offer us some hospitality.

2:25 p.m. Home. Sharon, the manager of the Bel Air Chidren's home, told us what they required most were toiletries, soap, pampers, nappies etc. as these items were prohibitively expensive. She told us that her dream was to own a little bit of the Isle of Spices. *'We are very transparent,'* she said. She said she would arrange for us to meet Mrs Sherma Fletcher, principal of the nearby Calliste Government School, where many of the children from the home were educated, tomorrow morning at 9 a.m. Her deputy, Miss Lisa Charles showed us around this modern building and introduced us to the wonderful children.

We made our way back from there to the centre of the capital to another shopping mall at Grand Anse for recuperative banana milkshakes, and out later to the beach and a walk back to the guest house. We met Mustapha, a widower from Egypt, an electrical engineering professor at McGill University who also consults worldwide. *'I am semi-retired. I got married in Barbados in 1973,'* he said. He is all alone. We felt for him. Tomorrow we have meetings with the principal of Calliste Government School (the school had the entire roof of the main building removed by Hurricane Ivan and is based in a prefabricated large shed); the French Consul, with whom my cousin in Barbados, Wendy, had arranged the meeting between 12 noon and 1 p.m.; the Springer Andrews family are coming to us for tea at 7:30 p.m. and we are to leave Tuesday free for Bishop Darius. Monday we are to stay put until we hear from Kurt the public relations person at the Ministry of Education and Human Development.

What can I say to this young lad? If your experience of school has broken your spirit, then you need to acquire creative and meaningful experiences that will rebuild confidence in yourself, so that you are then able to realise your innate capacity to be useful to yourself and to others, or words to that effect. The least we can do is make this Grenadian family welcome on our temporary hearth.

To contact: Mr Mott Green and his team of cocoa farmers and producers of Grenada Chocolate, the best chocolate on the Blue Planet; then Janice Thomas, principal of Grand Roy Government School; Mr Felix McIntosh, educator who had once worked while on a British Council scholarship for the Gibson family, the school textbook publishers in Glasgow. I recall their store on Sauchiehall Street (see their best seller *First Aid in English*); Mr Walter, St John Port Authority supremo; Anne Campbell, a scion of the McIntyre family movers and shakers in the commercial and tourist scene.

6:05 p.m. Marion is asleep. I am sitting on the tiny balcony. It has been a busy day. We were moving about the capital, St George's, in little minibuses here and there. We have met the Right Honourable Claris Charles and the meeting appeared to go well. She told us that the government of Grenada appreciated what had been done for GRGS, which happened to be in her constituency, and she would arrange for a formal handing over of the cheque from the Port School and acknowledgement of what the community on the Isle of Bute had done for this Grand Roy Government School. We'll see what Monday morning brings. We met the Bishop Vincent Darius, who is sympathetic, on our wavelength for sure. He is switched on. *'I don't have a museum,'* he said, meaning whatever they/RC/organisation was given was passed on to those who needed it, most irrespective of their religious or political affiliation.

Saturday 08/07/2006

6:30 a.m. Sandflies are chewing my ankles. Roaring traffic down below me on the main road. The day has begun. I have been up here on the balcony from early.

Saturday 08/07/2006

7:46 a.m. I met Michael, builder of the apartments at Roydon's guest house, Grand Anse, St George's, who tells me, *'We want to get this done for the World Cup next year.'*

8:45 a.m. We are sitting on some uncomfortable, standard-issue design, rusty, American classroom chairs: the kind that have a board attached to the seat for note taking, right. The sun is rising hot and bright directly in front of me. I am not sure of my bearings in relation to where I am on this island. We are waiting on the long verandah of the roofless Calliste Government School for the principal, who said she would be here at 9 a.m., to appear. Are those the red tiled roofs of St George's University down the hill on my right? The Bel Air Children's Home is over the hill behind us. Cows are staked out grazing on the dry rough pasture. A black bellied sheep is down in a thicket at the edge of the rubble and stubble playground, which reminds me of the bit of open ground outside our rented bungalow, Ceres, in the Navy Gardens housing scheme just outside the capital Bridgetown in Barbados: here Diana and I were taken by the nurse to play.

Marion and the children of the Bel Air Children's Home, which was to receive, several months later, a large gift of new resources from Inverkip Primary School.

There is a newly constructed prefabricated classroom building with a blindingly bright galvanised tin roof. Marion and I have just shifted out of the sun and we will just have to keep waiting. Patience. Yesterday we were waiting, waiting for an audience with the Minister of Education and Labour. I recall something she said *'All dat stuff from overseas donated by good people overseas, from the heart, is just left to lie, lots of tings, just left at the port.'* I should have taken note of those words from on high, but they were only to haunt me later while we were waiting to see the Bishop of Grenada, and we continue to wait.

9:50 a.m. We are in a meeting with the principal in her wooden, hutted office, which is adjacent to the prefab classroom. I mentioned to her that what the community on the Isle of Bute and Argyll and Bute Council had done for the Grand Roy Government School might be able to for her school and the community of Calliste. (*I had begun to get carried away with my over-reaching*

Calliste Government School temporary accommodation.

Sunday 09/07/2006

ambition to do good, which would in the years to come go way over the top.) I will have to wait and see what happens. She drove us back to the shopping mall.

4:15 p.m. We have had a delicious lunch and wonderful hospitality from the French Consul at her home above the golf course. She told us of her experience during, and after, Hurricane Ivan and the effect it had on the people of Grenada. *'There are givers, and there are takers,'* she said.

Sunday 09/07/2006

12:35 p.m. *'Go and lime for a bit,'* was said by Mott to Leroy, Frequente, St George Parish, who has driven us up here in 'Deliminator' a mechanic par excellence.

And Troy his assistant who also drove us up here into the mountains via the Grand Etang rain forest decimated by Hurricane Ivan.

Deliminator, a 16-year-old Toyota minivan that was rebuilt by our tour guide, Troy.

'We are having a little meeting. We got a few things going on here, and we have a small problem, so if you guys don't mind, just stick around for a while,' he said. Later Mott graciously gave us time out of his non-stop working day, introduced us to his team and we were given a tour of his small cocoa-powder-to-chocolate, factory, which is situated in the basement of a brightly painted tropical bungalow. He told us that his Arbroath-manufactured, McIntyre chocolate powder refiner has to be repaired. Mott took us upstairs and he served us each with mugs of cocoa, a Gros Michel banana and chocolate nibs for dessert. Mott doesn't stop working. Before long he was receiving other visitors to his chocolate factory. He introduced us to Danny, one of his chocolate makers.

We bid goodbye to an amazing individual and his team. As we were about to climb into Deliminator, a 16-year-old Toyota minivan that was rebuilt by our tour guide, Troy and Leroy gave us each a freshly picked nutmeg (*Myristica fragrans*). Our tour guide charged us EC$100 to bring us up here, and the same again down the road to the capital. He drove us up to Grenville and on to Pearls Airport. He gave us an amusing and interesting travelogue en route. We stopped off in the Grand Etang National Park and he gave me a sweet to feed a monkey.

Many of the rain forest canopy trees on the mountains were blown down by Hurricane Ivan. The regeneration of the forest is slow, and many of the desirable species of new growth flora are being choked out by vines. Leroy had young Troy, who collected our fare, with him as his conductor. A lad who he has taken under his wing to help a relative perhaps. The former has come from a family of 18 on his dad's side and eight on his mother's. He has half-brothers and sisters, many of whom live in Trinidad.

2:05 p.m. Back on board Deliminator, heading back to the capital after a wonderful and worthwhile visit to the Grenadian chocolate factory; there and back we have seen a little of this beautiful and varied Caribbean island.

Monday 10/07/2006

Mott Green made us welcome at his chocolate factory.

Monday 10/07/2006

6:40 a.m. It's Monday morning in Grenada, the Isle of Spices, where there are so many things good and bad for the inhabitants. We are on the lookout for the good in everything and in everyone.

There is a light breeze wafting in from the west. Dogs are barking and the birds have stopped singing. I saw Julien pushing his wheelbarrow with a flat tyre, up the steep hill. He has been doing this routine every morning since we arrived. I went downstairs and across the road in my bare feet, glad to touch West Indian ground, and gave him EC$10 to have the tyre fixed – a gratuitous gesture. There was no one about to see me. HE came down to Earth to give HIS LIFE and gave me a NEW LIFE in Scotland, I would not be here otherwise.

The traffic is starting to build up now. I gave a nod to a passing motorist who clocked me, and who scowled at me in return. There is a panoramic view from the balcony of Grand Anse Bay. A cooler breeze is picking up off the seawater. I have got things to do today. The right people to see. Let it flow.

7:48 a.m. That is Julien coming back down the hill with his wheelbarrow no longer with a flat tyre. He has got a car licence plate T0298 tied to the front of the wheelbarrow. He has just given me a discreet wave. A metaphor. That's all some folk need, someone or something to put a little air in their tyres to make pushing on the road of life a little easier. It is clouding over, another metaphor – I can do without any of that right now. Jim and Jacquie from Trinidad have not long arrived from that island and we had invited them up for coffee. *'It's too steep up those steps for me. I hear you have some high-powered meetings today. We would like to take you two both out to dinner. Sorry you couldn't stay longer, and come down to Trinidad.'* She said these words in a Trinidadian accent. *'That is very kind of you, Jacquie. I would love to return to the Land of the Humming Bird, perhaps some other time,'* I replied. She told me that they were going to stay at Jem's down the road. My family lived in Trinidad from 1950 to 1970. Before we leave this island on Thursday I must try and see Michael of Grenada School Supplies Ltd; Robin Swaisland; Sylvan McIntyre; the editor of the *Grenadian Voice*; Anne Campbell; Walter St John; a

Grenadian beekeeper; and last, but not least, Professor Williams of GRENED, the charity, if only to thank her in person on behalf of all those individuals back on the other island in the Firth of Clyde to whom I gave one of the nutmegs she sent me several months ago.

We are waiting for Kirk the public relations person from the Ministry of Education and Human Development. Agenda: hand over cheque to the principal of GRGS with the Grenada press in attendance. I'm not being serious, who do I think I am?

We were kept waiting until we got a telephone call to tell us that our meeting up at the refurbished, re-equipped, Grenada government school in Grand Roy had been cancelled. Not tae wurry. We'll see yah afta. Later I had the pleasure of meeting Leslie, editor of the *Grenadian Voice* newspaper, a Grenadian of wisdom and stature.

Tuesday 11/07/2006

8:50 a.m. We are on the government of Grenada and the Islands red carpet being whisked in air conditioned, four-wheel-drive-suspension comfort by Gregory and Kirk, the Minister of Education and Labour's public relations person, out to the Grand Roy Government School. Snatches of his conversation. I am concentrating on the scenery – it's great tae be back in the Caribbean. *'There are many problems we face ... we have to prioritise, that's the problem. We are being funded by the Caribbean Development Bank and the EEC,'* he said. Like make sure you get to drive about in a smart 4x4. Notes for an off-the-cuff speech, should I have to make one. How did this shipment of five large boxes of airfreight and two 20-foot ocean freight container loads of aid to a hurricane-devastated island start?

My speech. The prime mover was born on the island of Barbados and brought up there and experienced the effects of Hurricane Janet in 1955, and also lived in Trinidad. I consider myself to be a West Indian first and foremost. I am a teacher by profession and continued my teacher education and employment in Scotland. And I am a late entrant to the field of logistics, in this case moving development aid from one place to another. Two years ago I was doing an environmental studies project on the effects of the weather caused by climate change with my Primary 4/5 composite class at North Bute Primary School, Port Bannatyne on the Isle of Bute. During one of the lessons that I had prepared I shared with them my sister Diana's and my exciting experience of Hurricane Janet in 1955, when we were sent from our schools to stay with my Scottish grandmother, Ashie Howatson Mundell, for safety since she had rented a small apartment in a solid-roofed building made of coral limestone blocks. I then I brought it up to date by describing what Hurricane Ivan had done to the island and people of Grenada on 7 September 2004. My class wanted to help their fellow Grenadian students after they had learned about what Hurricane Ivan had done to their country.

My class, and the rest of the classes and their teachers, began this initiative by putting items of new stationery materials into A4 plastic wallets every week: when these were filled I arranged with Ecosse World Express at Glasgow Airport to fly this precious cargo to Grenada and this cargo was, after some delay, delivered to your school. I then arranged for fit-for-purpose, surplus to requirements, educational resources donated by Argyll and Bute Council's education authority schools to be collected from nursery, primary and secondary schools in Argyll and Bute and stored temporarily until loaded into a 20-foot ocean freight container.

And then I had arranged for the container to be collected by Freightliner Ltd, container base in Coatbridge Scotland, delivered to the Port of Felixstowe in England, and its eventual delivery to your school. During my summer vacation last year, I prepared a second 20-foot ocean freight container shipment of educational resources for GRGS and The Bel Air Children's Home in Calliste. The people of Port Bannatyne, where I have taught from 1992

Tuesday 11/07/2006

to the present in a small village school which is still in continuous operation since 1845, have been very supportive and this cheque comes from the Parent-Teacher Association of North Bute Primary School, who have raised these funds from a stall at the village gala day festival in May of this year. Any questions?

2:34 p.m. We are back at No. 4 Apartment, Roydon's Guest House, having been given the VIP Red Carpet trip to GRGS. We received a warm welcome from the principal and her entire staff. I presented the cheque from my school's Parent-Teacher Association, which was most gratefully received. The principal said the money would go towards purchasing woodworking tools and machinery for their new technical department. There was a table of purvey. Juice and sandwiches laid on for the visitors. Marion and I were humbled by the reception we received from Principal Thomas and her staff. We put a very tiny drop in a huge bucket of need. We saw with our own eyes the resources we had loaded into the 20-foot ocean freight container on Friday 1 July 2005 being used in the various refurbished classrooms, in many cases completely rebuilt. We were impressed by the work being done in that school and we were encouraged to know how they had put to good use the large amount of IT equipment that had been shipped. So much of an effect from so little; my only wish at that point was that every item was brand spanking new and up to date, and furthermore I was personally ashamed to know that all of it had been destined for a landfill site back in Scotland. So much for those who had said to me way back when. *'David that stuff is of no further use, so bin it.'* One of the teachers at Grand Roy Government School is a digital artisan and had furnished a computer suite with the computers that were sent in the two shipments. All our effort and yours had proved worthwhile.

2:45 p.m. Pastor Andrews from the Seventh Day Adventist Church had just called to see how we were getting on. He said Avron was working away energised on Sunday morning. Marsha (Donald's partner and co-worker) has lent me her mobile phone and I am now waiting for Robin Swaisland, senior projects manager with the Agency for Reconstruction and Development, to show up. Earlier I had a chat on the building site office telephone with Walter St John who asked me if I had spoken to Anne Campbell, I said that I was about to call her. Leslie Pierre, editor of the *Grenadian Voice* came by on his way to a funeral to drop off my project file, which I had left with him at our meeting in his office in the Frequente Industrial Estate yesterday morning. It was gracious of him and I said I would write to him on our return to Scotland.

4 p.m. Meeting with Robin. Sederunt: Marion and me. *'I have asked my staff to find out whether what you and your team have done at Grand Roy Government School can be repeated elsewhere at schools on the island, and the answer was definitely yes; the logistics of the ocean freight container becomes my problem when I get it,'* he said. He will contact me eventually. *'I've got your information in my system,'* he said.

5:35 p.m. Meeting and chat with Anne who took us to her home for hospitality and later at 8 p.m. she and Claire, her daughter, took us out to dinner at the Little Dipper, Woburn, Clarke's Court Bay. She gave us some of her fundraising ideas to fund the cost of the next shipment: *Write to Martin of Golden Caribbean asking if his firm would donate, tell him how my firm are involved in assisting you and would his firm donate as a prize a trip to Grenada.* A Trip For Two; write to Michael, chairman of the Grenada Airlift Committee; Anne will give us a complimentary Half-Island Tour for Two ticket; also write to Mr DeFreitas to share in this offer of accommodation as a prize; ask Deyna's for a lunch voucher. For Wednesday 10 a.m. Anne has arranged for me to meet Alvin co-executive director of NULO, the New Life Organisation.

Wednesday 12/07/2006

5:25 a.m. The frogs and cicadas are still singing. Little minibuses are starting to roar up and down the road. A waning moon up to my left is shedding its reflected light on Grand Anse Bay. I can barely read this as I write. Occasionally there is a soft, almost cool, breeze. A bat is still fluttering about the street light; traffic lights and house lights are starting to come on. A surviving coconut palm tree stands alone against the steel blue hue of Grand Anse Bay. A heron, in Barbados I would have identified it as a gaulin (or is it a white egret?), has just flown in from somewhere. A kiskedee is chirping away on one of the electricity wires. A cyclist is pushing his way on the pedals up the hill. A lady has just come scavenging at the garbage collection point along the road from the post office. I could like to live in this small country island nation. It's quiet now but only for a few seconds. There is more of the incessant combustion-engine fuelled traffic. Wealth and poverty existing cheek by jowl, next door to each other. The former oblivious to the other. The latter, looking with unfulfilled longing in through an invisible but impenetrable wall.

5:45 a.m. Wispy pink clouds are drifting away up above the hill, to my right the moon is beginning to turn into a silver dollar. It is becoming warmer now.

5:55 a.m. Julien has come by, pushing his rusty wheelbarrow with a flat tyre. Tiny flies are chewing my ankles and arms. The day has already begun. A tiny bird with black feathers, a dusty red chest and feathers under its tail (the one that flies in and out of the apartment) has found a piece of bread on the tiled balcony floor. Some impressions of the Isle of Spices.

There is a lot of building and rebuilding taking place. A lot of it is large comfortable-looking dwellings, some are multi-storeyed, constructed out of breeze blocks, wooden form work for cement and strengthened with steel rods. There are a lot of people about. Many of the citizens just seem to be hanging about; 'liming' is the local expression. This is a small, beautiful island at a first glance, but there are stark contrasts between those who have, and those who have not, and this makes me feel uncomfortable.

Why should this be? Inequality. Unequal shares of the wealth that is being created I suspect largely from tourism. This state of affairs is unsustainable. I found all of the people that I have met sociable, welcoming, friendly, and helpful; free-spirited insouciant individuality, more like the Trinidadians than my white-skinned uptight Bajans. The only place I have felt uncomfortable was in the newly built shopping mall, where mainland metropolitan North American commercial and cultural imperialism had impinged on my feeling like a West Indian.

After a few days this was short lived; I, who had felt up to that point at home. Homogeneity rules or else we'll crush you. Twenty-first century USA colonialism, full bore, had replaced the Great British, United Kingdom, version: new technology, digital telephony, transport, solar-power panels on roof tops had been embraced. I had never used a mobile telephone until this week and felt left behind. I was the backward country bookie in that department; a lot of people seem to be moving off their smallholdings, the basis of the Grenadians true independence. My dad, David Manning Hanschell, a Barbadian, an agriculturalist from his brain to his fingertips, who loved the soil of the Caribbean and had exhausted himself in a career that largely involved the supervision, management and cultivation of a vast monocultural acreage of sugar cane in Trinidad. He never owned a piece of land, and used tell me he wished he lived in Grenada and owned a piece of ground where he did not have to toil at a monoculture, but could grow a variety of crops, albeit it would be on a small scale. People are moving off their smallholdings of mixed fruit, cocoa and nutmeg trees blown away by Hurricane Ivan, which were inherited from many past generations, looking

Wednesday 12/07/2006

for work in the town. Prostituting themselves because it is not cool, beneath their dignity, to work their own bit of real estate and having to climb the steep hill and dig up in the garden. Like everywhere else, possibilities exist here in hurricane ravaged Grenada (the island did not appear as devastated as I thought it would be) for renewal, reconstruction and the redistribution of land owned by absentee landlords, and regeneration that is sustainable for the long term. A more equitable sharing of Grenada's Blue Planet finite commons.

Dream on bro; agriculture, working the land and being primary producer is associated in the islands of the Caribbean with European colonial exploitation (French, Dutch, Danish, Spanish, Scots, Welsh and English). This resonates strongly right up until the present day, when there was nothing else for the majority of the enslaved populace but to sweat under the boiling hot sun or starve, rather than as way of achieving some personal self-respect and financial independence.

I sing the praises here of Mrs Lewis, in her seventies, subsistence gardener on steep slopes of the Concord Valley, whose nutmeg trees were destroyed by the recent hurricane, but is still able to cultivate by hand the vegetable crops that can be sold in the market. Can I take what you, here in Europe, don't want and wish to throw away, that still has fit-for-purpose shelf life and deliver it to those in the Caribbean archipelago and elsewhere who will be glad to get the good out of what remains in the stuff being trucked non-stop to landfill on the other side of the Atlantic Ocean? WASTE IT or USE IT!

The neighbour to my left, in a new bungalow so designed that the flat roof will become the floor to another storey, is leaving for work in a new car and has just stopped on his way down the hill to give a pedestrian a lift. I am a witness to a good deed. I can see a crucifix on the wall of the verandah. He is driving the talk and some are walking it. As are my Grenadian friends: Mott; Bishop Darius; Kelly; Maryse; Leroy; Janice; Sherma; Sharon;

Lisa; Felix ... and many, many more who I have yet to meet one day. I am trying to leave something worthwhile behind, before I leave this island after a brief visit or back over there in Scotland when the time has come for me to depart forever. Fresh and fading memories of good deeds. I am about to hang up my shirt that has been soaking in the sink and wash these trousers.

11:15 a.m. I have a meeting with Alvin l from NULO. SERVOL in Trinidad started in 1984 by Father Gerard Pantin. Alvin has given me a copy of their recent newsletter. *'We can always use chairs ... in the cultural psyche there are aversions to ? ... I am also coordinator. NGO's tend to help each other ... they cooperate with each other. What you should do is send the same inventory to all recipients. They make the arrangements to make sure that when your container arrives they are there at the port to collect whatever they know beforehand has been sent for them, and they know when it has been shipped, by whom and by which vessel, and the ETA,'* said Alvin, who knows the score.

11:50 a.m. We are still engaged in conversation. *'Have I hit that nerve again?'* he asks. Does he think that a white-skinned West Indian, from a privileged middle-class background, has a guilty conscience about trying to redress the balance by shipping belated reparations, this fourth generation, dispossessed, colonial pied noir of mixed European extraction? What are my motives? Examine them carefully and provide a cogent rationale for what I have been preoccupied with over these many months since reading my cousin Wendy's round-robin Christmas 2004 letter: my 'NGO' working relationships based on unconditional pro bono support, and in due course transparent administration and governance; budgetary accountability, for every penny I have spent in shipping resources. For the meantime all of that complexity will have to wait. And I said. *'Well, I will tell you, Alvin, what motivates me is that I am having an ocean freight* *container load of fun, and that's all the motivation, raison d'etre, rationale I need to do the work I am doing.'*

Thursday 13/07/2006

5:55 a.m. Daylight. Another day in Grenada, West Indies, has long since begun. It has been raining. Sunrise over the hill. I have showered and dressed, ready and willing to face head on, whatever comes my/our way today. It has been worthwhile to come here and I hope that I, and we, can build on our little contribution to what has been achieved at Grand Roy Government School. I have made every effort within the last six days to establish a working relationship with the people/citizens, my fellow human beings, of this small island nation state ... all those who we have met, from government officials to those in engaged in private enterprise, and just guid folk. There is a soft breeze blowing in from the northeast. Those buildings at the far end of the bay were not part of the USA 'private university' of St George's campus, which is further up the much-indented coastline. It is hard to get my bearings.

8:45 a.m. We have just come from saying goodbye to Mr and Mrs DeFreitas, Louie and Carol Anne. We are back on the balcony. The breeze has become warm and the traffic is heavy. Michael, Donald, Richard, and Marsha, who are Mr DeFreitas's team of construction workers on the site, and the cement mixer are all busy doing what they have to do and applying their know-how on this building site of what will be another block of apartments. Just as many other enterprising Grenadians with a self-help up-by-my-bootstraps attitude are doing all over their island today. Breeze blocks going down through upright steel rods locked in cement and form work for the walls in between. As I scribble these notes, the builders outside are pouring over A3-paper size blueprints, each of them confidently competent. The twenty-first century builders of Grenada's today. I have finished off the Oil Down

Rundown, Grenada's national dish that I heated up in the microwave, for breakfast that Kelly, Sherma and the former's lovely daughter, with a seraphic smile, brought us yesterday at lunchtime. It is made from pig snout, tail and other uncertain bits, and finished off with breadfruit.

Write letters with a wee minder to: the staff of Grand Roy Government School who took the trouble from their vacation to come along on 11th July to meet Marion and me to thank us at hand over of the PTA cheque; Anne and Claire for their hospitality; Maryse for her hospitality; Kirk for his arrangements and driver Gregory; Leslie, editor of the *Grenadian Voice* (the statement on the masthead of the newspaper: *'The right alone is right. The wrong is always wrong.'*) to thank him for his interest and encouragement, and to let him know where I go from here, and what I hope to accomplish next; Mott for his hospitality and being so keen to share with two strangers his current problems and hopes for the future; the DeFreitas's for their support and the possibility of their contributing some accommodation at a future date as a prize; Robin Swaisland to confirm with him my plans and intentions and advice on their feasibility or otherwise. Total integrity, sustainable. As light an eco-footprint as possible. Economy of scale. Appropriate aid.

8:55 a.m. We are waiting for Leroy and Deliminator: the minivan has come to take us to the airport as he promised he would on 9 July. *'There he is!'* I return to old clothes and porridge and will continue to salvage ocean freight container loads of fit-for-purpose educational resources from schools all over Scotland.

Chapter Six

My Attempt to Solve the Wasteful Disposal of Educational Resources

Thursday 10/08/2006

10:45 a.m. Home. I call Sandra, the principal librarian at the Morningside Library, Edinburgh. She is on holiday. I spoke to Sam. *'We do withdraw stock from our shelves from time to time,'* he said. I then called Midlothian Council and spoke to Paula the senior public relations officer, who suggested I write to Adam to whom I wrote a letter. *'Our council leader will raise the issue in cabinet,'* she said.

It is now almost 11 a.m. and here I am pecking away at the keyboard with the sun shining out of doors. That was Paula on the phone, wishing to speak to Amy who has returned to work at Chandlers Hotel with David. Bless them both. Wrote to CEO of Barr Construction. I got through to his personal assistant, well almost. Instead, I spoke to Rajinder who told me to speak to Marie, PA to Anthony Rush. I gave Rajinder the group commercial director of J&J Denholm Ltd's name as a reference. I don't know why I did that because she remains incommunicado, inaccessible, never replies to my queries. I could expect no more favour. Wrote to Andrew, librarian, Library Headquarters, Stirling. I was speaking to Marian at the Scottish Executive who suggested I write to COSLA and speak to Anna, Team Leader, Children and Young People, who I spoke to later and who was extremely helpful and is now on secondment I believe. Write to David Kennedy, Press Office, COSLA. Write to Leslie Pierre, editor of the *Grenadian Voice*.

Solving the Wasteful Disposal of Educational Resources

Friday 11/08/2006

Today I received a letter from Robin Swaisland from the Agency of Reconstruction and Development with the Grenadian government's Ministry of Education and Labour and Justice. The Honourable Claris Charles has added another portfolio, listing the requirements/IT specifications and the roof specifications for Calliste Government School. I have decided after visiting that school and meeting the principal I will try and send them a shipment of educational resources.

Saturday 12/08/2006

9:30 a.m. It is a beautiful, clear blue sky day. The sun is shining. I shall go outside in a minute. Jim the baker has just given me the keys to the front door of his former premises, the Old Bakery. I have stopped to scribble this note. I am in here to dismantle the shelving (which would be ideal for a library), cabinets, fridges etc., which he has donated to my initiative, so get to work.

4:55 p.m. Young Steven and David have given me a helping hand with the uplift to the boatyard.

Wednesday 16/08/2006

I called them today to help me shift the Electric Bakery's display cabinets. Call head teacher regarding the uplift of educational resources from her school.

Thursday 17/08/2006

11:55 a.m. School. I am back in the classroom trying to get everything ready. A class to be taught, organised seating, etc. and the rushing off to meet the joiner and his team from Hanson Ltd

Thursday 17/08/2006

outside the Electric Bakery to remove the large plate-glass front window. I worry about where to put the two large display counter units and how they were going to be collected, let alone lifted. I rushed back out to the yard in the car and Martin lent me the van. I was back on busy Montague Street, trying to find a parking space in front of the Electric Bakery, only to discover, as we struggled to lift the first unit, that it wouldn't fit. I had to take the van back to the yard and return in the car to find both units on the street in front of the tradesman's entrance to the drugstore, and there they would have to stay for the time being. I phoned JM and assured him that they would be moved early on Friday morning. I have just had a call from The Super Cargo aka, George, who has received a letter from Eileen the Argyll and Bute Arts Coordinator about a new project idea, *'It's just a floating shoe box … The Puffing Container. My wife died a short while ago and I'm a bit lost without her … Who is your doctor? Geoffrey Orr? He's a nice man. Paint the bottom red, paint the top black, fabricate a funnel, wheel house, bow mast assemble the Para Handy,'* he said laughing. George is brilliant. Mr George. I am to call him this evening to discuss plans for the container. Try and get in touch with John MacMillan; Robert McIntyre; Mr Close; Jim the baker. I need to move the display cabinets, they are still on Montague Street. It serves muggins right! I had to go cap in hand to Jim the local island supremo builder and ask him if he could supply me with a truck with some of his workers. You got some nerve. *'What are ye after noo?'* he asks me.

7:30 p.m. Home. This morning I met Barry, coach of the High School of Glasgow rugby team, as I was going across the road to the Co-op, I told him to see the article in the local newspaper for coverage of our efforts to send educational resources and much else to hurricane ravaged Grenada, and the mention of the help their rugby team gave in shifting stuff at the boatyard. I told him his team could have an ice cream on me from The Tea Room.

9:30 p.m. George in Gourock has called me back and told me to give him a buzz if they let me out of the hospital before lunchtime. We will see. I have been phoning around all evening trying to get transport and lifting gear to shift the two display counters from in front of the Electric Bakery former premises.

John, port resident, and to whom I had promised a jar of marmalade some days ago, has kindly left a cabbage and a swede from his kitchen garden at the door of the Caribbean Hurricane Relief Depot. He is very supportive and helpful. I phoned Mr Close who said he would meet me outside the Old Bake shop at 7:30 a.m. tomorrow. I have tae see Jim the builder later.

Friday 18/08/2006

1:40 p.m. Inverclyde Royal Infirmary. Branchton, Greenock. My ordeal at the urology clinic is over for the time being. I faced it with fellow sufferers: Robert who is a painter and decorator. *'I keep busy. I am always on the go. I just let them get on with what they are trained to do,'* he said. He has an indomitable spirit. He is 84 years old, has steel rods in his legs and has had two hip replacements; James was once an engineer, since he was 15 until he was 48, with J. G. Kincaid ships' engine makers, and now works three nights per week in reception at the Travel Inn. I also meet Laurence, who has lived in Spain for 17 years and is a publican. They were very supportive and have had to undergo this unpleasant procedure of trans-rectal biopsy of their prostate more than once.

George, artist, sculptor, Glaswegian and my friend, came by and picked me up from Inverclyde Royal Infirmary and brought me to his home on the ridge overlooking Gourock and the Clyde. Wow! What a view! Then he took me up to the top of the road for a panoramic vista of the river and the tributary lochs. He made me a cup of tea in his kitchen and heard me out, rabbiting on about my all-consuming passion. I am encouraged and glad to be in the company of this amazing multi-talented and, for all his gifts, modest human being. *'I was going to show you The Puffer that I made for the Kelvingrove Museum. Have you ever heard of the Granny Kempock Stone? Why is it there?'* George asks. Bless him. After a restorative cup of tea, he drove me all the way down to Wemyss Bay and bought me lunch at the Sea View Café. I received this soothing oil of grace on my balding pate with gratitude.

I returned on the 3 p.m. ferry. I was back to the bakery at 4 p.m. The counters and units were still on the street. I went around to the builders on the High Street. I was not too happy having to beg, but there was nothing else for it. *'Look, I have given you a number of estimates and you've never taken any of them,'* said Jim. In exasperation, however, he took mercy on me and my plight and said he would get a truck and some of his staff, their names were not forthcoming, to help me get the units out to the yard.

Sunday 20/08/2006

4:13 p.m. I am out at the boatyard chatting to Bill. *'I'm fae the Gorbals, South Wellington Street? Then Cumbernauld Road, then we moved up to the Bully Wee ... then I got into the navy ... then we had a single end on Caledonia Road ... then we moved to ... '* he said. Bill told me that he saw the film 'Mrs Miniver' in Port of Spain, Trinidad. The island where I lived from 1950 to 1955 with Dad, Mum, and sister Diana. I returned to the island during the summer months of 1964, 1966, 1969 and briefly into Port of Spain as crew aboard *The Sun Ray* bulk cargo behemoth en route for Port Alfred in 1972.

While Bill is talking to me, I'm anxiously awaiting Jim's gift of more refrigeration equipment. I have been here since 2:30 p.m. I have just found the freezer, it was out the back behind Martin's boatshed, damaged hinge but still holding ice. Sight unseen, this beggar can't be too choosy. I am trying to cheer up Bill, who has been recently widowed. He is always emphasising the negative and I am at the other end of that spectrum. I made him welcome to the depot along with Roddy, who came earlier. I spoke briefly to Richard QC and the young lad from Essex who used to tear around the town on his bicycle doing wheelies, and who now has a speedboat and is married. It is a beautiful afternoon.

5:04 p.m. I have missed the evening service and am worrying about being late to collect Johanna. I can't please everyone. Bob and Mrs Gordon said, *'I could have cried when I read the letter.'* The letter to them, which came from an orphan at the Bel Air Children's Home, thanked them for their gift of stationery, which I had handed over to Sharon the home manager in Calliste, Grenada, on 7 July. They had stopped by to deliver yet another gift of stationery. I didn't have time to look at everything in the bag.

I rushed home here to call Jim, spoke to Ruth who said that the freezer refrigeration equipment had been delivered, but where? So it was back into the car and out to the boatyard to find that Isabelle from England had delivered audio telephone, printer and stationery as she had promised a while back. Bless her and her husband. They have moved back up here. Remember to thank Jim with the arthritic knees, Ardencraig gardens, or was it Alison who had dropped off the IT equipment? Martin told me it was in the boat shed. I shifted all the gifts into the depot. I have been very busy, what with dismantling shop-fitted display units from the Electric Bakery. Anyway, I finally shifted them after a think and looking at them, and regretting that I had agreed to accept them in the first place. I gave my helpers £10 each. Treat others in a manner with which you would wish to be treated, with the measure you meet etc.

6:25 p.m. This afternoon I shifted the refrigerators into the little container, and yesterday afternoon I covered over the counter units with one of the tarpaulins and tied them down. They are now situated on the far side of the big container. Whew! I am knackered.

Wednesday 21/08/2006

6:14 p.m. Home. After school I went across to the boatyard to meet George who said he would be there, as I passed him boarding a bus in front of his home on the Ardbeg Road as I cycled up the road this morning. I met Harry and we chatted. Eventually George arrived as I was on the roof of the Caribbean Hurricane Relief Depot, unravelling the string attached to the multi-coloured wind sock. George has brought a boot load of books on navigation, a small wood turning lathe, a spinning machine, and a globe. A treasure trove of useful stuff came from the boot of his car. A beautiful light-filled afternoon.

I cycled into the town and stopped off at Michael the horologist who put a new buckle on my watch strap, on around to Print Point off Guildford Square where I met Captain Charlie, master mariner, the principal of Bantry Bay Fisheries College, Wexford, Eire. He has retired to the island. He expressed an interest in the Grenada project He said, *'My view is I came in with nothing, and I'll take nothing out.'* Same here. He arrived here on the island not long after we did in 1990 and he had been making hazardous journeys driving truckloads of relief supplies to Bosnia. He has also set up a charity to minister relief and holiday time to the children of Chernobyl. Good on him!

Wednesday 30/08/2006

5:30 p.m. Home. It has been a busy day. I received a call from Nick from the estate office, who brought monitors to the depot in the back of his 4 by 4 pickup at 3:45 p.m., followed by a truck load of office furniture, assorted heaters, and to top it all he gave me a pair of new gloves. All of which was much appreciated. Then

I set off to the Red Cross Centre, Barone Road in the Bute Fabrics Ltd compound to meet Anita, who was not there as arranged, and drove to her home on the Mount Stuart Road. She had a large gift of books and videos I took her out to the boatyard to show her the ocean freight container. While awaiting the delivery from the estate I met David (I was not wearing my hearing aid!). He has bought a house in the port. He said he had a lot of stuff and had recently been to Cuba and saw the dire need there ... moved. He said his missus is keen to help and would come back to meet me. Yesterday afternoon Tony phoned to say he had some computers. I can't say no thanks and start being choosy about what I am being given. I'll just have to sort it later. He said he would drop them off tomorrow 4 p.m. here. *'Yes please! Thank you very much.'* I have got to keep moving forward, preparing for the next shipment.

Tuesday 05/09/2006

7:10 p.m. Home. This afternoon 5:15 p.m., there abouts, I was down to the pier to meet Marion off the boat and saw John Junior of John MacKirdy Transport Ltd waiting in his car. I walked over to speak to him. *'Hi,'* I said. He rolled down the window. I mentioned the 40-foot ocean freight container in the boatyard at the Port and he said he had seen it. I asked him if I can count on his firm transporting it up to the container terminal in Coatbridge? He said, *'Yes.'* And we shook hands on it. And then I said, *'I have to see that it is fully loaded first.'*

I met Alastair at the security gate to Clydeport Ocean Terminal and later Peter in the office of Denholm Barwil Ltd, and gave him a copy of *The Buteman* article.

Now **1:40 p.m.** in the office of Iain, associate director, who has just given me Niall, the managing director's, card. And said I was to mention that I had met him and he suggested I write to the managing director of Denholm Barwil Ltd.

Wednesday 20/09/2006

5:35 p.m. Home. I called David at COSLA, who put me onto Anna, who I think is responsible for COSLA policy, who said she would attend to my letter eventually. I then called Niall and received a hearing. *'I have been travelling. I don't like unfinished business,'* he said, and he would give my query and spiel some consideration and said he would mention my request for pro bono assistance to his cousin, John Denholm. (*Who generously, months later, was to make a donation of £250 to The Surplus Educational Supplies Foundation SCO 39331.*) I then called Principal Sherma Fletcher of Calliste Government School, who said they would be glad if I went ahead and sent them an ocean freight container shipment of educational resources.

Monday 25/09/2006

I called the Barr Construction Ltd project manager up at the site of the new joint nursery, primary and secondary school and college campus, hoping to see if this firm will allow me to salvage any materials (kitchen, gym equipment, etc.) before the buildings were demolished. My request was turned down. No reason given.

Saturday 30/09/2006

11 a.m. A little after 11 a.m. I am now sitting in Euan the dentist's surgery. I have just cycled in from the boatyard. It is a beautiful light-filled morning after a wet and windy, blustery, grey week in which I was out every day in weakness and FAITH, trusting only HIM for strength and WISDOM. Earlier, I was round the back of the big shed, where I got a friendly greeting from Jim the blacksmith and his brother- in law. I was tidying the 'junk.' Stripping off the polythene and will have to tarpaulin it all down. Today. Now! I met William. *'I am staying in David Baxter's flat, just in* *case you don't know who I am. Is this an ongoing thing?'* he asks. *'Yes. There is an ever-increasing mountain of need in many parts of our world and I am going to put my little drop in that bucket,'* I reply. As I write this I do not know who he is. David the businessman showed him my operation. 'The Business.' My Initiative. The Wee Project.

I arrived out here about 8 a.m. Opened up the depot and the ocean freight container. I was shifting Jim the baker's shop stuff. I am awaiting the gift of a computer. While I was round the back it was left in the container. On the way back into the town I saw Roddy walking his dog along Castle Street. *'Thanks a lot for the computer, Roddy, I was working round the back of the boat shed when you came by,'* I shouted over my shoulder as I cycled past. And I got a wave from Mrs Dunn, Ailsa and Arran's mum, who was at her back door hanging out the washin'. I took a short break and cycled along to the Tea Pot. Alison's last day. They have sold up. I got a bacon roll covered wi' cling film and a cup of coffee served by Alicia. I went back up the road and saw Betty coming down the road with her lurcher. We stopped to chat. Bless her. She's off to Cape Town, South Africa, in 15 days and is going to climb Table Mountain. She is a bonnie fechter and a friend tae boot. I met Margaret going to the Tea Pot for papers, *'I am away to do a wee stint at the ABC café,'* she said. I met the little ginger-haired lad, *'He's my nephew,'* said Owen, who tells me he is leaving school at Christmas and going up to Aberdeen to find work as a gamekeeper. His older brother ran the disco at the Port Hall.

Saturday 07/10/2006

7:39 a.m. The Depot. Bob and Mrs Gordon, Katelyn's gran and grandad have just stopped by, *'Margaret's bothered wi' her back. It's her age,'* he said. They were here to drop off another parcel of new stationery. They are good people, the best. I have been here since 7:35 a.m. I have been chatting to Amy who passed by earlier with her three dogs and has come back with photographs of her parents and of her childhood in Calcutta. Jim the blacksmith showed me how to tap the rain water out of the lock, which I couldn't get to open. The sun is shining on the rain clouds. Amy EH has just arrived with a delivery of school reading books and assorted textbooks from Inverkip Primary School. Bless her and Marion.

Monday 09/10/2006

7:39 p.m. Home. I have just written to Andrew of Eden Transport Ltd, High Hesleden, Hartlepool. I had flagged the firm's driver down this morning as the transporter rumbled past me while I was standing in front of the ocean freight container. The friendly driver stopped and leaned out of his cab and told me to get in touch with the firm's office. I can but try as I will need to get my container off the island some time.

I arrived at the yard late this morning after I had made David the Young a bacon sandwich. I am whacked as I scribble this. It has been non-stop. Inventorying and boxing books, textbooks, electrical equipment. Frank the musician came by with two large boxes of jigsaw puzzles. We had a long chat and he encouraged me to keep going. Get EWL copies of me and David 12th July 2005. I went down to the New Tea Pot at 3 p.m. for a late lunch. Soup, cheese toastie, a wee side salad and a mug of tea. I left the boatyard at 5 p.m.

Tuesday 10/10/2006

8:25 p.m. Home. I am tired. I have just done the dishes and swept the kitchen floor. It has been a good day. A lot was accomplished. I started at 8:45 a.m. I began tidying the container and then Robert and Calum, former pupils, came by asking if they could help me. I set them to assembling the slotted metal posts which I had dismantled from the Electric Bakery shop. They took apart the shelving and this gave them something to do. They borrowed 'Scoomba' Jim the blacksmith's power drill and he gave them expandable metal screws. This activity kept them gainfully occupied for a while. Calum used the overhead power drill in the boatyard machine shop to drill in the holes on the shelving for the screws. The result is a bit ramshackle, but is an improvement way beyond what I would have been able to do. I can now get stuff off the floor of the container. Visitors: Amy came by to tell me that her rescued sheep dog has a new home; George was showing me how to set up his gift of a pedal-powered band saw; Jim and Gladys from the gardens came by to drop off a computer and a microwave; Murray and his little friend Darren, Stephen's brother. I had a cooked breakfast in the New Tea Pot; a bit too expensive. A one-off treat.

The sun shone brightly and then it cooled right down. Keep plodding on.

Wednesday 11/10/2006

9 a.m. I called Fyne Homes and left a message on Peter's voicemail about the possibility of the collection of a donation of redundant library stock from Stirling Council Community Services. I also left a message on Marie's voicemail, PA to the chairman of Barr Holdings Ltd, as to why they had not replied to my letters.

1 p.m. It is raining heavily, but dry in here, and I am grateful for small mercies. I am slowly getting squared away. This morning, after my arrival, I met Leo, who I met last year shortly after he had arrived on the island from Wales. He was looking for Martin and sought permission to park his loader and truck, which he used to transport his Manitou cherry picker, which he had just used to put a lanyard on Betty and Elaine's Submariners Memorial Garden flag pole. I showed him round the depot and the ocean freight container.

Murray and Darren are sheltering in the depot from the rain until George shows up, as he said he would, to assemble the pedal-driven fret saw. Then David the engineer came by with his dog under a big golf umbrella. We, or they, chewed the fat – the state of the United Kingdom government – and I got back to work until Amy appeared. *'Do you want that telly?'* she asked. *'No, thank you,'* I said. And then she reappeared sometime later. *'Gordon hasn't been blabbing to you has he? I don't want you to get the wrong end of the stick ... I could be in MENSA you know ... I've owned three homes,'* she said. She took offence when I called her a bit scatty and went off, rightly, in a huff before I could apologise. Part of the port's varied and rich human tapestry. I am getting a bit peckish. I'll have to wait until the rain stops, so just get back to work.

Thursday 12/10/2006

8 p.m. Home. It has been a beautiful, sunlight-filled, brilliant day. I tidied the ocean freight container and shifted what Gordon refers to as crap. It's definitely not crap to me and that is what matters. I had been chatting to not a few folk: Jim the steam engineer who has told me more than once I'll never fill the container. (He knows it all. Clever.) And regular visitors from Perthshire, who remember the island during the WW2 era and sitting in a midget submarine. And then I cycled home for lunch with David and Johanna and back up the road.

I met Laurence and showed him around. I had a chat with Jim the blacksmith. Off the phone to Peter of the local housing association, possible offer of furniture from a care home in Inellan. We'll see.

Friday 13/10/2006

8:15 a.m. Home. I am just off the phone to Allan, unit manager of Barr Construction Ltd on the joint campus site, top of the

High Street. He said I could come and have a look at the building before 22 December, decanting as it is being demolished. Now will the Argyll and Bute Council let me take what I want? He heard me out. *'It's admirable what you are doing,'* he said. I am to meet Jean at midday tomorrow to help her shift bric-a-brac from the Port Hall.

2:45 p.m. Barbara's off on holiday. Contractors owner Kerry, admin office. David Logan, Argyll and Bute Council special projects mannie up the wee manse brae. He says there is a possibility of RECYCLING materials, in what was the former big primary school, that are still fit for purpose before demolition … offers of recyclable building materials. We will have to wait and see what happens. I could reroof Calliste Government School with what exists in that school building.

Ha, if only I knew then what I know now, as the saying goes, *'Experience keeps a dear school and a fool will learn in no other.'* And I am some fool, but what else can I do that will keep me from breaking down completely?

3 p.m. I spoke to Lorna, the primary school administrator, Hopeman Primary School, Morayshire. I acknowledged her email.

3:45 p.m. I spoke to Ian, depute head of Speyside High School.

Wednesday 18/10/2006

6:57 p.m. Home. I have had a shower. I went out first thing and arrive at the boatyard shortly after 9 a.m. The sun came through today. I shifted and then demolished the bakery cabinets, which are unsuitable: mis-judgement on my part because I am too eager to get my hands on whatever is offered to me without stopping to think *'how is this piece of kit, whatever my immediate perception of its usefulness, going to be used by the beneficiary?'*

Thursday 19/10/2006

Martin asked Dougie the port scaffie, to come with Argyll and Bute Council Cleansing Department's truck and thanks to him took the units off my hands. I am still hoping that the refrigeration units can be put to good use. I cycled back home for lunch. On the way back I stopped off at the local haulier's yard to see both John Senior and John Junior. There I met Margaret who works in their office. I went there to ask them if they would collect the large donation of withdrawn library books from the Stirling District Council Library Service. *'You are a good salesman,'* said John MacKirdy Senior. *'I went ashore to that tiny island of Meyreau in the Grenadines on four oil barrels,'* he went on to tell me, on learning that I had come from the Caribbean. He told me that while he was serving on a merchant navy ship, in WW2, he was torpedoed off the island of Meyreau in the Grenadines. His firm have generously agreed to collect the donation of library books from Stirling gratis. Bless them both and all associated with them in their long-established haulage firm.

I went back out to the boatyard after lunch and met once more Fiona and Ray off their yacht, *Ceres of Bute*. He had told me last summer that they had holidayed in Tobago WI and the former yachtie was impressed by the smartly turned-out school children in their uniforms. Some of my former pupils at the school came by to see what Mr Hanschell was up to and, as always, I was glad to see them and gave them the time of day. Robert, Jordan, Jack, Nicky, Arran, former pupils and Robbie a contemporary and friend of David the Young who was not at the Port School. *'I admire your patience,'* said Jim the blacksmith who had stopped by.

Thursday 19/10/2006

11:15 p.m. Home. All quiet here. I set off this morning after 8 a.m., later than I had wished. I cycled past John of musicker, hoofing to work. The water, gulls floating immobile in the wind, the hills across the water: there is so much visually for me, and for anyone, to lift one's spirit. I do enjoy riding the Raleigh bicycle (which I purchased from Mr McCansh in August 1990 with my one and only tax rebate). Martin said it was identical to the one he rode to school. I met David, ex traffic policeman, walking home from the old Baptist Church building and walked with him until he turned up Ardmory Road. We talked about living in Edinburgh and where he had lived. He told me why he had done a dissertation on Eternal Life for his degree in theology, as he had to take a large number of funerals since moving to the island. He said he was still a probationer and had more academic study to do.

I changed into my blue overalls: getting a bit worn, but they will see me out. I just remembered, Gordon McFarland, ex-army retired, appeared. *'Jump in!'* Gordon said and took me out to the Ettrick Bay Tea Room for a bacon and fried egg sandwich. The chef showed us later where she had seen a white ferret. Gordon is another connection to the Caribbean. He was telling me about his wealthy expat Cornishman chum Richard, who lives in Antigua, West Indies. Gordon had gone out to the island to recuperate from major heart surgery, to stay with his friend, and while there he saw the eruption of the Soufriere volcano on the island of Montserrat, which has virtually destroyed most of its human habitation. He is a great conversationalist, Greenock lad o'pairts, hospitable, witty and gossipy. And seen not a few stars pitch in his time. I respect him and he is kind to me and knows I am in difficulty.

It was raining heavily. I met Ray off the *Ceres* and he returned my July trip to Grenada photographs. I tied down the tarpaulins on the stuff round the back of the boat shed and then, from out of nowhere, I was besieged by Jack, Robert, Robbie, and Arran, and I got them to help me to wash down and scrub the moss off the sides and top of the Gray Adams Caribbean Hurricane Relief Depot, for which they were each paid for their work, to Marion's annoyance. They were at a loose end for goodness sake. I was trying to bring them up a little. Someone has to give them a little adult attention. As the saying goes in Africa, *'It takes a village to raise a child.'* They were riding about the yard on my bicycle, which to them must seem a really antiquated piece of machinery.

Friday 27/10/2006

Classroom. Lunchtime. David, the *'Special Projects Person'* with Argyll and Bute Council based in Lochgilphead called to let me know that he was returning the information I had sent him and was passing onto various organisations the information about The Aid to Grenada Project.

Saturday 28/10/2006

12:05 p.m. It is wet and grey and damp in here in the ocean freight container. I have not long had Robert and Jack come by and I was showing them the Grand Roy Government School, visit to Grenada, photographs, which Colin had stopped by to return with my project folder: a supporter who said he would contribute to the cost of shipping the next consignment of educational resources to Grenada, to which community has not been decided. We chatted about the inequity and injustice in the process of distribution of aid. The haves and the have-nots. He knows the score. *'And the gap gets wider. Yes, we do indeed live in an ill-divided world,'* he said. Before that chat, Amy and Larry, one of her dogs, came by to tell me that she and her upstairs neighbours are at peace once more with each other, and the man of that household has offered to repair her kitchen ceiling. Great news! She had told me she was born in Kolkata (Calcutta) and was telling me about the privileged upbringing in that city. She is brave soul. I head home. I did not accomplish much today except be a listening ear and have a welcoming mien.

Saturday 04/11/2006

5:10 p.m. Home. A beautiful day here on Costa Clyde. I have been busy taking empty paint tins up to the cowp Shanks & Mcewan Waste Solutions, formerly the council dump. I had a chat with Robert the rich, honcho up there for many years. And it was back out the boatyard. Robert and Jordan were visiting, hanging around, unfortunately I did not have anything that they could do, but I made them welcome all the same; had I deeper pockets I would have had them, and others of their circle, with me crewing one of the many big yachts up the West Coast now, which are in the yard going nowhere. And out of the blue Chris from down south, a recent resident of the island, appears with half a dozen monitors. He had stopped by months ago and asked me if I would like them; then his missus appears with some furniture. More visitors promising stuff they do not want. All donations are gratefully received. Beggars can't be choosers.

I shall call my company shipping line the Caribbean Hurricane Relief Transport Company Ltd. We sail in all weathers. I ride my bicycle in all weathers. I have purchased a 'recycled' 40-foot container, which I hope on inspection will prove to be a seaworthy container to transport resource relief to the islands of the Caribbean and littoral of the South and Central American coast? And to the Africa and Indian continents. Why not? Rangers FC was bought for a £1. There are, at this moment, container ships tied up in ports all over the Blue Planet that are likely to be broken up in the yards of Bangladesh. And there are about three container ships tied up in Striven loch across the watta from here. Dream on shipping clerk.

Saturday 11/11/2006

3:42 p.m. I am inside the Hanschell Freight, Ocean Freight Container GSTU8958639. It has been raining heavily and I have proved that

Saturday 11/11/2006

this big, beautiful box has no leaks and there is a wholesome smell off the teak flooring (or is it bamboo?). There is occasional sunshine through the clouds and the sky is beginning to clear over the tenement roofs of the port. Noise of vehicular traffic swishing by. This day I have forced-willed my being to keep on plugging away.

I came out here this morning at 10:30 a.m. and climbed on top of the depot to unravel the windsock. As I did so, a curious couple walking back towards the village from the Port Park paused to read the banner hanging from the side of the ocean freight container, which reads *'Caribbean Hurricane Relief Transport.'* I hailed them in my 'hail fellow, well met', amiable mode and big friend to all the world. *Would the two of you like to learn what this is all about?'* I ask. *'Who is paying for this? Who wants your rubbish?'* she asks dismissively. *'Lots of people on the hurricane-devastated island in the West Indies are getting it for free,'* I replied. They tell me that they have recently visited Grenada on a cruise ship and that they felt threatened in the St George's Market. I wished them well and changed into my boiler suit.

Shortly after Chris and his wife from Chelmsford, Essex, the recent Isle of Bute settlers, arrived with a folding round table and escritoire. Encouragers and definitely supporters. Welcome aboard. No sooner had I got started boxing more children books than it was time to head back doon the road to join the firm for lunch. I stopped off at the Co-op for bacon rolls and two bags of jam sugar for my next batch of marmalade. On the way I got off my bicycle to speak to Tam Boag. *'How are you Tam?'* I ask. He replied, *'If I had legs I'd run like hell.'* Bless him. He is one of my original island heroes.

Well here I am again and see if I can box some more books, but first I will treat myself to a cup of takeaway hot chocolate from the New Tea Pot, which is under new management, just like yours truly PTL! Then I saw Jenna's mum, the port postie *'We've got two bags for you,'* she said. *'That is really kind of you. Many thanks,'* I said.

Solving the Wasteful Disposal of Educational Resources

Tuesday 14/11/2006

I spoke to Avril, who said, *'The resources must be uplifted at least five days in advance. Desks, chairs, storage units. It is imperative that you are able to organise this collection within the next three weeks.'* The towns of Kirkcaldy and Inverkeithing. Kirkcaldy North Primary School, Capshard Primary School, and Inverkeithing Primary School. I have a big PROBLEM to solve. Collect and store the fit-for-purpose, surplus to requirements, educational resources from three Fife Council primary schools. How on earth am I going to be able to uplift all of these wonderful fit-for-purpose educational resources and classroom furniture, let alone, once collected, how and where am I going to store it all?

The logistics of it? I am now in big trouble and I have brought it all on myself. I can hear the voices at my back. *'You are just too big for your boots. You should have realised long ago that the scale of what you had envisaged, of collecting, storing and sending more container shipments of educational resources from the mainland, is just way beyond your capacity. You have become an embarrassment to all those on the island who assisted you in delivering the two 20-foot containers last year, and not least your lovely family,'* I said aloud to myself. I will just have to climb my way out from under it, step by step.

First I call Tony – he is not in. No joy. I call Fyne Homes – can I get some help with transport? You must be joking. John MacKirdy the haulier, I spoke to John Junior – they have collected the library books from Stirling and will deliver them to the boatyard on Friday afternoon. Good on yuh. *'Sorry our reach does not go as far as the East Coast. May I suggest that you try and locate a registered haulier over there. Good luck,'* he said. I am grateful for all their assistance.

Names come to mind – does Forbes, publican, have any clientele in the haulage business? Where can I rent a van? I need a truck and an HGV licence. Arnold Clark. I called Leo and left a message. I called Gordon with his contacts in the army.

For Wednesday 15 November: call Leo; call Iain at Clydeport Ocean Terminal Greenock to see whether Peel Ports could offer me some pro bono storage or even transport; call Robert about haulage firms on the East Coast. Who to contact? *'Problems, problems, Boy,'* said to me by my Lodge School Physics master Mr Clark, whose nickname was 'Goggles'. I could never get my head round to solving them physics problems. How am I going to collect and store resources from these three Fife Council schools within the timetable constraints? What are the storage facilities available to me in the vicinity of these three schools? Find out what and where there are storage facilities available in Inverclyde? Contact Rainbow Friends, The Lighthouse Trust, upper Port Glasgow near the Playtex factory? Open a Paypal account? No way! I am not going to start begging for money. Transport and storage pro bono? Yes!

5:15 p.m. Home. I am off the telephone to Andrew Wishart and Company Ltd, Kirkcaldy. I got a friendly and supportive reception from the office. I left my details for Mr Wishart. I will call again tomorrow. I need temporary storage facilities in Kirkcaldy and transport to and from the two primary schools. I contact the Scottish Road Haulage Association members … pro bono, gratis, goodwill, a one-off favour … well I can only ask.

Thursday 16/11/2006

7:15 a.m. Home. I am speaking to Scott, in the office at Andrew Wishart and Company Ltd. I eventually manage to speak to Brian, the operations director at Fife Group, Kirkcaldy. The game changer. Salvation Army, Grenadian Consulate. The new education minister was Deputy Justice Minister Hugh Henry.

SOLVING THE WASTEFUL DISPOSAL OF EDUCATIONAL RESOURCES

Friday 17/11/2006

10:51 p.m. Home. This afternoon Colin and Kenny from John MacKirdy Transport Ltd arrived in the classroom to tell me that they had dropped off four pallet loads of books, the redundant library stock from Stirling District Council Library Services, beside the ocean freight container. Later, after school, I went and covered them over with a spare tarpaulin. It is raining wet and miserable, so it's batten down the hatches sailor and don't ever call me a yachtie. John The Sails let me have some rope, as much as I needed, to tie it down. *'Is that you got too much stuff to handle?'* he said. And it is all my own fault and a big problem to be solved.

When I opened up the depot I found bags of uncollected and unwanted jackets, umbrellas, lunch boxes, gloves, scarves etc., all of it good stuff, which had been saved from disposal and brought from the Western Bus Company Depot along the road.

Tuesday 21/11/2006

Home. Mr Munro is to call me after having spoken to their managing director. We'll have to wait and see what happens in that quarter, meanwhile I shall have to get on with what is in front of me.

Wednesday 22/11/2006

3:40 p.m. I called Fife Council. Avril not in her office. I then called Mr Munro, operations director of the Fife Group.

Thursday 23/11/2006

The Fife Council want school furniture and educational resources shifted from the three schools in a hurry. They have arranged to have it all crushed on contract to a demolition firm. Logistics? The prospect for me is not promising. I have to keep calm. The pressure is on me. I have taken on far more than I can handle and ought to have stopped after the second 20-foot ocean freight container was delivered to Grenada in 2005. I could not resist the temptation to accept the offer of more surplus-to-requirement educational resources by simply saying, *'no more, thank you,'* to the offers of good stuff that was flooding downstream into landfill sites all over the beautiful country of Scotland. We'll see. So here I go, and with another throw of the dice I will call on the *Fife Free Press* and see if I am able to enlist their support in preventing the resources in these three Kirkcaldy schools from being destroyed.

Thanks for this RESCUE must go to this journalist extraordinaire Tanya Scoon, who immediately said she would write an article highlighting my predicament and a request for storage and transport in Kirkcaldy. With this response from her I could see that there was some light at the end of the tunnel.

Saturday 25/11/2006

Home. First things first. A little puff by Tanya in the *Fife Free Press* that was to take me a long way into many more shipments. I wrote a letter to the editor of the *Fife Free Press*, and then hopped on my bicycle and into the town, and sent it recorded delivery first-class post. Before leaving I listened to Chris's message once more.

7:23 p.m. This afternoon I supervised the P3/4/5 composite class at their Winter Warmer Bring-and-Buy Sale in the Port Hall. They raised £45. Good on them! I will bank it in the Educational Resource account. I was in two minds whether to head over to the ocean freight container and start on the boxes that I had unloaded last Saturday morning off the four pallets of redundant library stock from Mr Muirhead, operations librarian, donated by Stirling Council Library Services and brought across the watta by John MacKirdy Transport Ltd on 17 November. Thanking you again. Duty called and I got stuck in. There is a lot to do.

Solving the Wasteful Disposal of Educational Resources

The Big Green Box 40-footer ocean freight container is full to the gunnels, but is in no way properly loaded: there are cardboard boxes, donated gifts, and offloaded-on-me computer monitors and school furniture are taking up a lot of space. Marion and David came by with bin bags of reading schemes from the big primary school's Support for Learning Centre. Little by little, I tackle the task of sorting this jumble of treasure and the only way is to keep going on. I haven't been feeling too strong these past few weeks. I am to collect a donation from Chris at 2 p.m. on Sunday.

This encouraging note was left on the front door sometime today: Russell, Eurocentral Freight Village, Motherwell, sales contact. *'David Hanschell. A starting place if nothing else.'* Thank you, Tish and Peter. In the days to come the Scottish road haulage industry will play an essential part in The Surplus Educational Supplies Foundation project to salvage fit-for-purpose educational resources from schools the length and breadth of Scotland.

John MacKirdy Transport Ltd were crucial in making many deliveries to and from the island a success.

Monday 27/11/2006

I called John Russell, he was not in. I sent an email to his secretary. I called Anna at Midlothian Council and left a message after receiving her email earlier. I will take everything. All donations of unwanted fit-for-purpose, surplus to requirements, educational resources will be gratefully received. Midlothian Council's Private Partnership Scheme, involving 35 schools and 8 new build schools, has brought far more educational resources into the waste stream than I can handle, but I kept on digging myself deeper and deeper into a hole.

(Pride was to be my downfall. I became a taker of risks and self-inflicted problems.)

'There is absolutely no way, chum, you are going to be able to meet your verbal agreement to take some of those resources off their hands,' I said to myself. *'That's what you think. You just watch me,'* I said to myself in reply. There is no one, apart from me, to validate what I am single-handedly attempting to accomplish. I have achieved two 20-foot ocean freight container shipment loads of educational resources, and am loading another. I am not starting from nowhere. I shall not buckle at this point. Will there be a reprieve somehow for 'surplus educational resources' or is this initiative going to end badly?

4:35 p.m. *'I am sorry, Mr Hanschell, but we will now have to send all of these resources to the crusher. We are no longer of the view that you have the capacity to collect or store these resources. We respect your commitment and effort,'* said Avril, and my heart sank when I heard these words. There was no way, if I could help it, to allow that to happen. What is my next move?

'Please, Avril, can you and your team give me another 48 hours to have all the necessary logistics arrangements in place?' I pleaded.

'*All right then,*' she said, relenting. Good news? I am to call Invertiel House. I can't do this initiative by remote control, by conscripting others or contracting out my big idea: it's all in my wee hauns and, with my sleeves rolled up, I'll take the consequences of success or failure. It will probably be a mixture of both, only time will tell. I will need a place to stay in Kirkcaldy, a van to rent.

I look forward to help from the fourth estate, the press, which is my last resort to extract me from this pickle of my own making.

Wednesday 29/11/2006

10:35 a.m. Classroom. Avril, of Fife Council, has called me at school and left a message. I rushed down the back steps and around to the office, and the school secretary put me through. It is going to be all systems go! I have been offered transport and storage. The *Fife Free Press* are running a story on the front page of the newspaper and an appeal for volunteers. I have been snatched by a whisker from the jaws of failure. I call the editor to thank them. I'll need a place to stay on Friday night. Avril recommends Invertiel House B&B, Kirkcaldy. Linda let her know my ETA.

Thursday 30/11/2006

8:15 a.m. I call Scott at Andrew Wishart and Sons Ltd about the possibility of transport. *'I'll see what I can dae for you. Nae problem. Whit's yur number?'* I had to give him the school telephone number. *'Could you call me during the break between 10:30 and 10:45 a.m.?'* I said.

3:40 p.m. I call the editor of the *Fife Free Press*. *'Let us know how you get on,'* she said. With those few words my spirits were lifted. 'Rescue of Surplus Educational Resources from The Jaws of The

Friday 01/12/2006

Crusher.' For Kirkcaldy: Stage Coach, Buchanan Street Station, stand 26 at 10:32 p.m. The last bus on Friday 1 December 2006 8:15 p.m.

I received a call from Mrs Brown, the head teacher of Blackburn Primary School, with an offer of educational resources, which I accept.

Friday 01/12/2006

3:38 p.m. The Pier. I am, at this moment, sitting in the waiting room on the island pier waiting for the 4 o'clock boat. I have left the car at the Co-op car park. I have been wheeling and dealing right enough. I am moving with every step into the unknown. First across to Wemyss Bay on the train up to Central Station, from there I walk up to Buchanan Street Bus Station to get a Stage Coach Express bus to Kirkcaldy. I have booked a room at the Invertiel B&B, which is up from the bus station, past the museum and over the bridge.

This morning I called Andrew Wishart & Sons International plc. The answer is *'No.'* They could not provide transport for me tomorrow morning. So I got on the telephone again and called Arnold Clark plc, Peugeot showroom, spoke to Stuart and arranged to collect a van at 8 a.m.. Then I shall drive over to Capshard Primary School, Kirkcaldy, where that is I haven't a clue at the moment, to meet the janitors and hopefully some volunteers that have been moved to assist me by reading an article in this week's local newspaper: an article which has given me some vital puff. Never, never, ever give up. A lesson I have had to learn the hard way.

Last Saturday morning I decided to write a letter of appeal for support, to help me to collect, remove and transport resources from two primary schools in Kirkcaldy to the Fife Group's yard. I sent it registered post before I put in some more time loading my next ocean freight container.

Solving the Wasteful Disposal of Educational Resources

It looks as if I have been able to get a reprieve on the fate of these resources that were awaiting disposal in a landfill site in the Kingdom of Fife. I drove home at lunchtime and called the head teacher of a West Lothian Primary School who had emailed me with an offer of educational resources, which I hope to be able to collect during the Christmas holidays. Everything is tentative, provisional, I have nothing sewn up and that is certain. I then called Balwearie Community High School to speak to Dr Munro, who had left a message for me earlier with the school secretary to say that I had not given them sufficient notice, which is fair enough. This quixotic wild goose 'rescue of educational resources from destruction' crusade continues to be tenuous. Is that the word I am looking for? If it isn't, you choose a more apt one. '*Yur coat is hingin' on a shoogly peg.*'

I make one faltering step forward and then stand still. Some often said my project was dead in the water.

4:50 p.m. I am now on the train. A few minutes earlier, while walking up through the Wemyss Bay pier on a forest of North American pine timber, I met Marion and Amy, who gave me some bananas. Bless them. I said I would call when I got to Kirkcaldy. It's dark outside. Five pound single fare to Central Station. I am journeying onward and upward.

9:52 p.m. Invertiel B&B. I arrived at the bus depot in Kirkcaldy and got a taxi up the road to here as I was not too sure of my bearings. John, taxi driver, wouldn't accept my fare. I insisted. He had stopped off at a petrol station for me so I could purchase a copy of *The Fife Press*, and sure enough there was some puff about what I hope to achieve tomorrow. He was interested. I have received a warm welcome from Harry, the landlord of this fine establishment. He brought me up a mobile, so I could call Marion, a plate of meat paste and tomato sandwiches, a bowl of fruit and a pot of tea. As he read Tanya's article, he said, '*There's a child out in*

Grenada sitting at a desk wi' someone's initials from Scotland.' So far so good. I met another good soul who came on the train up from Wemyss Bay and who got off at Paisley Gilmour Street, who said. *'I'm no from Paisley, ah come from Mosspark.'* She wished me well.

Saturday 02/12/2006

11:30 a.m. I, along with a team of volunteers, have just loaded two full loads of school classroom furniture, in mint condition, into two 20-foot ocean freight containers at the Hayfield Industrial Estate. The following individuals made this collection and storage possible – Brian, Jamie, and Roddy, all of The Fife Warehousing Company Ltd; Alec, janitor Capshard Primary School, and Mick, floating janitor; and Peter of INDIPA, Kirkcaldy, Fife. I had made arrangements with Arnold Clark on the Mitchelson Industrial Estate to rent a large van today, which I did not need thanks to the generosity of the Fife Warehousing Co. Ltd. Roll it back.

Around 8 a.m., well after breakfast at the Invertiel B&B, the landlord, Harry, kindly drove me up the road and around to Capshard Primary School, situated in a version of a Bishopbriggs housing estate 1970s development. A neatly kept warren of semi-detached houses. I could never have found the school on my own.

On arrival I found Brian, the operations director of the Fife Group (whose USP is 'The Whole Package. Storage, Removal and Transport'), at one of the school's prefab portacabin classrooms with two of his workers and two janitors who were in the process of loading a large furniture removal van. He told me that I did not need to rent a van. I was speechless with gratitude. I got stuck in alongside them shifting classroom furniture, all of it in good condition. Then, when it had been loaded, I went with Roddy and Jamie to the Fife Group's warehouses on the Hayfield Industrial Estate and helped to unload the school furniture into two 20-foot ocean freight containers. There had indeed been an article published in *the Fife Free Press*, written by the journalist Tanya Scoon, bless her, who I had spoken to over the telephone earlier in the week 'puffing' my initiative in which volunteers were asked to help with the removal of school furniture. For a little while we stopped to catch our breath; Alec the Janny said that a lot of the books being discarded at the school were not politically correct, and right away Peter contradicted him and said. *'No way! Those children out there just want to learn to READ and WRITE. The European Union has got nothing to do with them.'* Right enough. Thanks for that.

I then accompanied the two janitors to Kirkcaldy North Primary School, built of red granite or sandstone in 1906, where there were classrooms full of classroom furniture in excellent condition. I was daunted for there were two flights of stairs to bring it down, but a few willing and experienced hands made light work of it all. Later, Brian told the foreman that the truck could be unloaded on Monday morning and I was free to go. Words could not express my thanks for what he and his team had organised.

5:40 p.m. MV *Bute* is rolling about a little as we head across the watta. I am glad to be heading homeward. It has been a long and amazing day. I left Kirkcaldy at 12:45 p.m. through to Glasgow on the bus. I walked down a teeming Buchanan Street and got the Gourock train at 3:05 p.m. rather than wait, and then spent a while cooling my heels waiting for a Largs bus. I scoffed a poke of chips at the bus stop and regretted it.

6 p.m. The ferry is heading into the harbour. *'Never, never, ever give up!'*

Sunday 03/12/2006

I wrote a thank-you letter to the editor of the *Fife Free Press* and to Fair Isle Primary School – a gift of furniture came from this school; acknowledge a possible link with the recipient school in Grenada. The issue: these vast quantities of fit-for-purpose surplus educational resources haemorrhaging from school closures all over Scotland – is it the CRUSHER, GRINDER and LANDFILL or REUSE?

Monday 04/12/2006

I receive a call from Avril. *'Do you realise there are 10 classrooms in Inverkeithing Primary School? How are you going to move all that?'* she asks. Well, gone from what I had thought impossible a short time ago and managed, just, with the help of others to salvage a large quantity of educational resources from landfill, I am certainly not going to give up on trying to salvage educational resources from this next school.

I get to work and start calling around. I speak to Marielle Tweedie, journalist at the *Dunfermline Free Press and West Coast Advertiser,* who had called me at school about the volunteers that I needed to remove the resources from Inverkeithing PS; I call the Fife Group, who tell me that they have no more space. I NEED TRANSPORT FAST. I call John G Russell Transport Ltd and spoke to Peter, who is to call me back; call Scott at Andrew Wishart & Sons Ltd; I then call Avril. *'Sorry Mr Hanschell. There are deadlines that have to be met. We cannot offer you any assistance,'* she tells me. I have been on the telephone constantly for almost two hours.

Over the years a B. Mundell truck, Tarbert, has passed me as I cycled to and from the Port School and I have often wondered if their ancestors were related to my grandmother Ashie Howatson Mundell, who was a Mundell from the Inverlael Estate, Loch Broom, Wester Ross – so I thought, why not give them a call? I spoke to James in the office, who took my call. I did not mention my possible link to that Mundell branch of my family, but somehow I felt I was entitled to identify myself as a

Solving the Wasteful Disposal of Educational Resources

distant relation *'fae Kana Dah'*. I told him that I was trying to get pro bono assistance from the Scottish road haulage industry with the collection and storage of surplus educational resources before they were destroyed. *'Do you realise that would mean having to take one of our trucks across to the East Coast empty?'* he said. And then I told him that I did not expect his firm to do that for my project but, if it were possible, could he give me some contacts on the East Coast of Scotland that I might call. *'I just wonder if you can give me the names of transport firms on the East Coast that could/might assist me?'* He then said, *'Okay, I can give you two people to speak to and you can tell them that you were speaking to me. They are: John Mitchell and Duncan Adams.'* And then he said words which are similar to other words that have given me hope on this journey and then he said, *'If all else fails, call me back.'* At which point I pick up the telephone and for some reason I call the second telephone number. *'Could I speak with Mr Duncan Adams please?'* I ask. *'Mr Adams is not in the office. Would you like to speak with Eric?'* he asks. Who is Eric, I wonder? *'Yes, please,'* I reply. *'What dae yuh want?'* he asks brusquely.

I tell him that I need transport to collect surplus educational resources from Inverkeithing Primary School, in the town of Inverkeithing in Fife, to a facility where they can be stored, sorted, inventoried and loaded into a seaworthy ocean freight container, before shipment to a hurricane-devastated school in Grenada, West Indies. *'We'll dae it for yeh. It is not the best way. But my advice is yeh onlie want tae move it once. Call me when you are ready.'* When I heard him say that my heart sang. I have cracked it, only up to the next crisis. I was on a roll from then on. *'Thank you very much, sir. I will be in touch with you as soon as the Fife Council Education Department are ready for me to uplift these resources.'* It looks as though I am now going to have to purchase my second ocean freight container sight unseen, and not inspected.

I am at the mercy of the dealer but I have no other choice if

Monday 04/12/2006

I am going to rescue these resources. I call Howard about parking the container in the yard of Calder Container Services Ltd, Coatbridge. For Wednesday 6 December 2006: call Fife Council, who are cutting me no slack, giving me no quarter and they have awarded contracts to have resources crushed. JUST GIVE ME ANOTHER 48 HOURS PLEASE.

(I should have realised then that Fife Council's (and the other Councils in COSLA) policy towards the reuse of fit-for-purpose, surplus to requirements, educational resources from school closures was completely at odds/counter to what I was attempting to do, and without their support I eventually would end up in trouble, which was to happen some years later. I KEPT ON being of a dogged and persevering nature and being energised for once in my life by the kindness, support and good will I received in pursuing an initiative, a project of my own, which has been acknowledged so far in this account and from the increased support from the Road Haulage Industry.)

I call John managing director of John G Russell Transport Ltd. Let Mr Hume know a day in advance when I was turning up with my container. It is a GREAT FEELING for me to receive these offers of assistance from the Scottish road haulage industry: my first taste of what it is to experience unconditional word-of-mouth support in the big world of business/the corporate sector, in contrast to my three decades of experience in the world of education and with colleagues. Completely different. *(Only my enthusiasm, sense of wonder and gung-ho willingness to collaborate with the youth of Scotland, with no hidden agendas had kept me in that career for as long as it did.)*

I now have a firm commitment from Eric, Duncan Adams Transport Ltd. Time and date to be arranged of the uplift is uncertain. Friends Gordon McFarland and Alan Cowie come with some good news! The latter tells me, *'That's you, a project manager.'* Thanks for that Alan. *'Tell me how do I set up in business?'* I ask him in jest, such is my appalling and miserable lack of self-belief. I call Anna, Team Leader Children and Young People at the

Scottish Office. Project status? WHAT am I? We'll answer that question later. I now have a number of possible sources of surplus-to-requirements educational resources coming, or about to come, on stream from the following: New Fife primary schools: Fair Isle; Masterton; Strathallan; Inverkeithen; Kennoway; St Columba's RC; Holy Name RC; Duloch Community Campus etc. etc. WHAT A WASTE. It is a scandal which the Scottish government, society at large, politicians, and those who wield power in the education system, have deliberately chosen to ignore.

Thursday 07/12/2006

4:55 p.m. Home. Just off the phone. I called Avril of Fife Council to confirm uplift for Saturday. Not in. I received an email from Eric at Duncan Adams Transport Ltd giving me a contact at Maersk in Glasgow. I called immediately and spoke to Lisa, who I am to call when ready to ship this container. And here I am with one ocean freight container in a yard on the island, which has no recipient.

(What on earth did I think I was doing?)

4:20 p.m. I call Inverkeithing Primary School and Inverkeithing High School. I spoke to Katy who heard me out. A positive reception/response. I am seeking volunteers with the uplift on Saturday 9 December. You got high hopes chum. *'Who wants to collect old school furniture from a now derelict building?'* Answer. No one. You would have thought I had done enough calling around at this time of day. I called Westfield Primary School to speak again to Caroline at lunchtime on 8 December to arrange for the collection; I speak to Mrs Rarity the janitor of Westfield P. S, Bathgate, Armadale, to notify on arrival. I make arrangements to collect school furniture on 28 December. DEO VOLENTE.

I am now well and truly out on a limb and it will not be the first time that I fell out of a tree to suffer the consequences. Later I spoke to the head teacher of Murrayfield Primary School, to collect resources on Thursday 28 December. Contact Billy the janitor. There is a large collection. I will need a big van and the educational resources will be stored in the school hall ready for collection.

(I faced the problems of logistics, which I created for myself with this self-directed, self-centred venture with a 'can do' attitude, which presumed on the good will of 'strangers.' I had no other choice but to see the project through to completion. I had set in motion a largely self-financed aid project that did not come to an end until almost 13 years later.)

Friday 08/12/2006

3:40 p.m. Well, here I am once more preparing to leave for the unknown. I am sitting in the Caledonian MacBrayne pier waiting room having just purchased a return ticket. Shortly after the noon break bell, when the P4/5 had left the classroom, I told Mrs ES (the visiting speech therapist who comes once a week for an hour with two of the pupils) where I was going once more this weekend and what for. She seemed pleased that I had managed last weekend, with pro bono support and good will, to collect some several 20-foot ocean freight containers of surplus to requirements educational resources, collected from two Fife Council primary schools.

(But then she said something which I should have taken heed of. 'Well I hope you still have a marriage,' she said. I hoped so too. The consequences of my commitment to a venture on this scale, in personal and family terms, were going to be unforeseen.)

That's the ferry being tied up so I am to cease scribbling.

4:45 p.m. There goes the whistle and throb of engines. Bump and shudder. I met Bill, computer technician and master of a few other trades as well. We shared a cheese sandwich and cups of coffee. He was telling me about a memorial stone to a Covenanter, Iain Ferguson, who had been murdered by Graham of Claverhouse, that he had found in the garden of his Ettrick Dale home across from Kames Bay, which he had passed on to the Clan Ferguson. Prior to this meeting I met Mick the diver who asked me rather abruptly, *'Where are you going?'* I decided to answer since many years ago he loaned me a wet suit so I could be dumped in a tank. This was at a Rothesay Primary School fundraising fete way back in 1990. I attempt to answer as succinctly as possible, and often ignore their intrusive curiosity. I prefer to mind my own business and grant others the same respect.

9:15 p.m. I am now in Room 26 of the Boreland Lodge Hotel. I arrived in Dunfermline at the bus rank shortly after 8 p.m. and I asked the inspector for the bus to Inverkeithen. He told me to get the Edinburgh bus at 8:30 p.m. Bert the taxi driver brought me here from the town centre. I met Yvonne, the landlady, who was welcoming and lent me her mobile to call Marion. All home on deck. David the Young had finished his kitchen portering shift at Chandlers at 8 p.m. and Nevil the chef had given him a chef's meal in the function suite, and got Bill to bring him up something from the bar to drink. Bless them, and all who treat their kitchen porters with kindness.

Prior to getting a taxi, the bus dropped me off in front of The Chippie in Inverkeithing town centre. I was sore tempted to get me a poke of chips, but resisted. I am now going to brew myself a cup of tea. Reminisce. I recall from my bank of recollections. I was last in this town in the summer of 1974, would be middle of July. I arrived on the outskirts early, with the dawn breaking, that Saturday morning, having walked across the Firth of

Forth bridge. I went into a field and had a kip, and saw the sun rising over Arthur's Seat and the distant Pentland Hills. And so began my new life in Caledonia. I had slept uncomfortably under a hawthorn hedge before crossing the Firth of Forth bridge having walked my way out of Edinburgh.

Saturday 09/12/2006

8:20 a.m. A big curtain-sider arrives as I stand in front of the Volunteer Arms pub. The driver in the cab winds down the window and says to me. *'Jump in! I love doing charity work,'* he then opens the door and I climb up beside him. George of Duncan Adams Transport, along with The Young Kenneth, apprentice mechanic, who is sitting beside him. We drive slowly through the sleeping town and up to the vacated school with boarded-up windows. Frank, the janitor, meets us in the playground. He tells me knows Dag Crawford BBC journalist and landlord of the Russian Tavern at the port. It's nae a chance of anonymity for me, just as well I walk the straight and narrow highway. Should I stumble, the whole nosey island will know within seconds. And what's more Frank has a caravan up at the Roseland Caravan Park and thinks McQueen's the butchers are the best.

There is not much time to hang around. Somehow I find the strength to keep up with my companions, fetching school furniture and loading it up onto the deck of the curtain-sider until there is room for no more.

2:16 p.m. Time moves on. *'This train is for Glasgow Queen Street.'* *'That's all I can do,'* says George, who comes from County Donegal, West of Ireland. He kindly waited around at Duncan Adams headquarters until Willie the timekeeper in the office had contacted Eric, who had just gone home, and then Neil the office manager to see whether or not there would be another lorry available for tomorrow. *'Drivers don't work on a Sunday. What you need are some* *containers,'* said the office manager. George kindly drove me up to Falkirk Grahamston Station.

Roll it back: I rose early this morning, having slept fitfully in room 26, shaved and showered. I handed in my key and chatted to the cook who was preparing breakfast and though I could have done justice to a full Scottish I resisted the temptation to hang around. *'There's nae many like yuh,'* said the cook and I decided to push off. I walked on to the Boreland Road over the railway bridge and back up the steep brae past the Town Clock tower. It is going to be a beautiful day. Early morning: best part of my days past, present and future. Rays of bright sunshine glow over Arthur's Seat and the panoramic view of the Firth of Forth side of Edinburgh Town, the Pentland Hills beyond and the scattered bumpy drumlins like pies. I then walked up and down the empty Hope Street and around to the school to see where a 40-foot curtain-sider or a transporter/artic with a 40-foot container could be parked. I met a neighbour of the school (older building, 1875). She told me she was a former pupil of Inverkeithing Class of 1913: all of it going to be demolished. She had gone on to tell me that she had gone to Moray House College of Education (my PGCE class 1974–1975), where she had trained as a teacher and was now retired. It was a pleasure to speak with a fellow alumnus.

I walked back down on to the main street and met James, the Inverkeithen town scaffie and asked him where I could find a payphone. *'Here, use my mobile,'* he said. *'That's kind of you, but I don't know how to use one. I'll need to put my glasses on,'* I said and he tapped the number for me to Duncan Adams Transport Ltd transport office. Willie put me through to George the driver who was well away on the road to Inverkeithing, to whom I gave directions. *'We are now approaching Cumbernauld,'* he said. And I told him I would meet him at the corner of the Volunteer Arms pub. I then went in to Greggs the Bakers, which had not long opened up for the day, and got me a welcome coffee and a corned beef pasty and along to the newsagents and bought a copy of the *Fife*

Saturday 09/12/2006

Free Press to see if the editor had published my thank-you letter for the help I had received on Saturday 2 December. I haven't had a chance to look yet. Frank the janitor, who was at the school gate to meet us, said, '*I hate to see all of this perfectly good school furniture being crushed. I am glad to see someone like yourself going to a lot of trouble to ensure its reuse.*' Thanks to George's skill, who had to shovel a bag full of salt on the sloping driveway, the curtain-sider managed to manoeuvre round the school buildings and within three hours, by 12 noon, the four of us had loaded up as much as we had been able to load on to the 40-foot trailer. We went back to Grange Dock, to the Duncan Adams Transport depot on and over the Firth of Forth bridge (me seeing things, the changes in my life as I crossed it coming the other way 32 years later), then back up the Firth of Forth coastal route to Grangemouth. It has been a beautiful light-filled day in which I could not have asked for more.

3:10 p.m. '*This train will call at Stepps and Springburn. Please take a few minutes to read over these notices,*' she said.

More recollections as the train, at blink speed, moves past where I had once begun to get a grip on making something out of the new life that had been given to me in Scotland, when I lodged in the home of John and Nan Tennent in Stepps. I walked to school along the busy Cumbernauld Road. Remember on Monday to call Avril and suggest if the 40-foot by 8-foot container in the school yard, if possible, could be filled up with the remaining surplus resources. Is the container for sale? Would Fife Council donate it? I can only ask. I am always pushing the envelope. I call CT Engineering Services Ltd, speak to Jean and ask to speak to Freddie. I then called Howard and learn to my amazement that he works with Eric, and they are business partners in Freight Container Services (Scotland) Ltd. '*Eric's my partner,*' he said. '*That is AMAZING!*' I said. Is this just coincidence, part of destiny, or what?

SOLVING THE WASTEFUL DISPOSAL OF EDUCATIONAL RESOURCES

Monday 11/12/2006

5 p.m. I am home and on the phone. I called Tom Walker, container surveyor, who had given me the CT Engineering Services and Ravenstock telephone numbers, and who had spoken to them and they will call me back with prices. I got home from school, to my great joy, to discover that Linda had posted my little book of Common Prayer, which she had found in my room at the Invertiel B&B, which I thought I would never see again. Grateful. Bless them both.

Get in touch with Nick to see if the estate have any spare dry storage, an empty, wind and watertight shed or barn would be perfect; call Denis, Frank and Jimmy, Edinburgh City Social Work Department, to see if they might provide me with any 'volunteers' for possible help with the next uplift.

Tuesday 12/12/2006

Call Howard. John MacKirdy called to say they will transport the container in the boatyard to Russell in Hillington. Call Caroline at Westfield Primary School, Bathgate.

Thursday 14/12/2006

4:40 p.m. Home. I invited Robert, master mariner, round for a cup of tea. He is back from the South Atlantic, Punta Arenas? I called Avril, who had called me at school during the lunch break to tell me that she had spoken to Eric to learn from him that the collection of another container load of educational resources from Inverkeithing PS was possible for this Saturday, 16 December. I called the Grenada High Commission about delivery of resources to schools recovering from the damage caused by Hurricane Ivan. I am getting nowhere with these officials. I have learned that

Saturday 16/12/2006

Principal Thomas's brother settled in London many years ago and is a tireless worker for Grenada. Grenada.

I left a message for Eric Adams. I booked a room at the Boreland Lodge Hotel B&B with Peter and Yvonne, proprietors.

Saturday 16/12/2006

1:47 p.m. Eric has not long dropped me within walking distance of Falkirk Railway Station. A short while ago I had arrived back at Grange Dock with another container load of educational resources and waited in the queue of drivers handing in their tachograph slips to Willie the transport manager. When I finally got to the head of the queue this casually but smartly attired youngish gentleman of average height, from the other side of the counter, looked me directly in the eye and asked me, *'What's next?'* I replied, *'Mr Adams, the Scottish Local Education Authorities are disposing good quality surplus-to-requirements educational resources into landfill. I hope to be able to salvage much of that for my aid to Grenadian schools post Hurricane Ivan,'* thinking to myself *he's going to think this guy has gone over the top.*

(Many months later he told me that, on being asked by a business associate who I was, he told her, 'He's a nutter fae the West Coast.'*)*

He then asked me, *'How are you getting back to Glasgow?'* I replied, *'I'll walk out of the dock and over to Grangemouth town centre, and get the bus up to the train station and the train to Queen Street,' 'I'll see you out in the yard in a few minutes,'* he said. There was a Porsche Carrera parked beside the office steps. I was about to put my bag in what I thought was the boot. *'Get in! The boots at the front!'* he said. And he roared up the road past the Grangemouth oil refinery. He parked the car outside the railway station and looked over at me and said, *'You find the shipping lines, and we will take your containers to any port in the United Kingdom.'* Eric Adams has offered to keep 'The Boxes', waiving all handling and storage charges and fees, until such time as I have sourced a shipping company. And he has advised me to stay within the Central Belt of Private Finance Initiative schools. As we passed the Denholm Barwil Ltd portacabin offices on the way out of the dock, he gave me the name of John, the manager, and suggested I call him and let him know that I had been speaking to him. He parted with these words: *'You only want to move it once.'*

Briefly. Boreland Lodge Hotel B&B last night. Off the bus from Dunfermline. I walked it this time. I was up this time at 5:30 a.m. Recollection: Caldora Café, July 1974, en route to Blairgowrie on foot, stopped off at Gairneybridge, Kinrosshire. Keep your mind on what is in front of you someone said. *'If you want to keep flying, don't look down.'* I met Peter the landlord and his grandson Bradley.

'The next stop is Glasgow Queen Street.' I am going to stop scribbling and drink my coffee and eat my sandwiches as this train moves back west. There is a lot more to write about and recall, not least the long walk I had from the old boarded-up building, formerly Inverkeithing Primary School, to find trolleys from Fleming Removals to shift school furniture to the container.

Monday 18/12/2006

10:20 a.m. Inverkeithing Primary School, helpers and volunteers. Write and thank them: Alan, former pupil of the school (he works for Mr Azaf, the Max's Newsagent, The High Street); the volunteers who helped shift a lot of stuff.

2:45 p.m. Home. To call: Alison, the advertising director of the *Fife Free Press* for some publicity to acknowledge the assistance

Monday 18/12/2006

my/the project/initiative has received from the commercial/ road haulage/transportation/shipping sectors of the Scottish road haulage industry. And at the same time raise the profile/ marketing of what I am trying to do: Highlight the scandal of unsustainable and unnecessary waste of fit-for-purpose surplus educational resources being crushed, ground and trucked to landfill sites by council education departments all across Scotland. The Surplus Educational Supplies Foundation (SCO 39331) has unlimited scope to take advantage of the opportunity that this waste presents. It has, albeit on a modest scale and operating from a shoestring budget, persuaded four authorities, Argyll and Bute, Fife, West Lothian and Midlothian Councils, to release to my NGO educational resources in schools due for closure, which have been contracted out for disposal. Why are these quality educational resources being disposed of in such a wasteful manner? I can do little to change council/COSLA policy in this regard. All I can do, as I have shown already, is to continue to acquire a tiny fraction from this stockpile of educational resources due for disposal into landfill. See Craig, journalist with *The Buteman*, to let him know that a 40-foot container shipment of educational resources, recently salvaged from two primary schools in Kirkcaldy, is awaiting delivery to Calliste Government School. I wish to raise the profile of the Caribbean Hurricane Relief and Transport organisation/project/initiative. Craig suggested I write a letter to his newspaper expressing my appreciation/gratitude/thanks for the practical/indispensable/ vital assistance that this island-based project has received and achieved.

Contacts: John, Denholm Barwil Ltd. Thank you to all who have helped continue to help me to make my VISION a reality. Goodwill in action, turn my IDEA to deliver fit-for-purpose, reusable, educational resources to wherever needed. Constructive ACTION. I now have three 40-foot ocean freight containers loaded with fit-for-purpose educational resources: one at the boatyard at Port Bannatyne and the other two at Grange Dock, none of them so far have been inspected. Are they seaworthy?

(I am now well and truly way out on a limb, and the branch is shaking, but I did not realise it at the time.)

Wednesday 20/12/2006

5:16 p.m. Home. I spoke to Steven of CBPS Ltd this afternoon on the way home and he told me he would put in a word for me with McKerrell Transport Ltd that this firm might be willing to offer me some pro bono transport, but said their focus was their local community.

Friday 22/12/2006

Home. Nick, supporter, factor of the Bute Estate, has given me the keys to the stable underneath the estate office in the town for storage. GOOD on him.

Tuesday 26/12/2006

9:50 a.m. The pressure is on me again to locate suitable transport and storage.

Wednesday 27/12/2006

I am about to call Denis, Lothian Regional Council Department of Social Work, who were once my employers at the Northumberland Street Mental Health Hostel, New Town, Edinburgh from September 1974 to July 1975, where I was assistant to the warden Pipe Major Calum McPhee while I attended Moray House College of Education. I need a Luton van. I call Murrayfield Primary School, Catherine Terrace, Blackburn (off the M8 at junction 4).

Thursday 28/12/2006

I haven't a clue as to how I am going to find this school, let alone rent a van from Arnold Clark in Armadale and then pick up stuff from Blackburn, and then from there to Grangemouth.

What are the logistics of this self-imposed and totally over the top self-inflicted problem? First I have to get the train from Glasgow and then a bus to Livingstone and then another bus to Bathgate. IMPOSSIBLE certainly! I am tae fone Billie the jannie. Stramash, is that the word? I am in a pickle that's the word. I am to call the Big Nissan garage. I haven't got a clue at this point. I am muddling through and stuck with a commitment that I can't meet. I receive a call from Eric Adams, who talks me through the connections for this uplift of educational resources. *As long as we know you are coming,* he said. I will have to call this collection off, which is something I do not want to do. It will be the first one so far and my pride won't let me admit defeat.

Thursday 28/12/2006

10:52 p.m. Home. I am sitting on the edge of our bed recalling the highlights, before they slip away, of the eventful day. David the Young and I were driven at 6:15 a.m. to the pier to catch the ferry for Wemyss Bay and purchased tickets to Glasgow Central.

8:05 a.m. We rushed out and got a purple taxi for Queen Street Station, quickly purchased tickets for Edinburgh Waverly. And while on the train, David set up a call on his mobile phone and called the head teacher of Murrayfield Primary School in Blackburn, West Lothian to let her know we were on our way. David was operating Marion's mobile phone, which I still marvel at and am unable to use properly. Margaret met us at Linlithgow Railway Station car park, where her husband, Gavin from Biggar, drove us back down the motorway to Muirhouse. The sun was rising behind Shotts kirk.

She told me he was the son of a shepherd and a farm manager's son, and had gone to collect a truck from WH Malcolm Transport Ltd's (of Brookfield, Renfrewshire) huge depot. We were then driven back up the motorway to Murrayfield Primary School. The head teacher showed us around the school and introduced us to the janitor and various members of her staff, who had all given up their Christmas holiday time to prepare for an impending Her Majesty's Inspectorate inspection. Eventually her husband, Gavin, arrived with the truck that we loaded with a large gift of surplus school resources, which had all been moved to the school gym. After loading the truck Gavin drove us around to Westfield Primary School in Armadale to collect a donation of 31 pupil chairs: a small village primary school with a lovely atmosphere on entering. Artwork and project work on the walls. We were met by Mrs Rarity the janitor. After loading it was back up the motorway and across to Grangemouth and into Grange Dock into Duncan Adams Transport Ltd.'s depot, where we were met by Niall, the office manager, who was helpful and friendly. Later Eric appeared, who invited us into reception as we had been waiting outside in the yard, and served us coffee and sweets. He had arranged for 'my container' (which I hadn't yet paid for, and which Howard Clack had had delivered yesterday) to be moved to near where we could offload the donation of educational resources from Murrayfield and Westfield primary schools. Eric then got welders, mechanics from the machine shop and Young Kenneth the Apprentice to help us, and within no time at all the job was done.

Eric asked Young David if he would like to drive a transporter – all computerised and drives itself, almost. Brilliant! Magic! Gavin and Margaret then drove us back to Airdrie Railway Station, from where we got the train back to lower Queen Street Station. I walk through my city to Central Station and wait for the Wemyss Bay train, then ferry and safely home. Much, if not all, of this amazing uplift/collection I could not have envisaged. I am humbled by the help I have received today, which had taken me from despair to a successful collection thanks to many folk; unmerited and favourable contingencies, all unforeseen and unplanned by me 24 hours ago, yet all had been arranged and in good order.

Next steps? After all that experience I can do no other but continue this work of salvaging good quality, fit-for-purpose educational resources from being trucked to landfill.

Friday 29/12/2006

7 p.m. Home. I set into the town on the bicycle, sunshine through a mixed clear and cloudy morning, and along up the road to the boatyard where I managed to box and shift the computers, trusting that this out-of-date, obsolescent, unwanted, dumped IT equipment will be reconditioned, refurbished, re-engineered and put to further good use. I met Her Good Self and her three dogs. *'Watch out they nip!'* she said. I stopped for a break. Fry-up brunch at the New Tea Pot: not the same. I must take it or leave it. Then back up to the Big Green Box with the sun shining at the doorway and I managed to bring some order to the jumble of boxes.

This afternoon I was chatting to Malcolm, naval diver, boat builder and once the publican at The Anchor Tavern, and later Samuel Bain. Later the loyal supporters and encouragers (and neighbours of Mr Barraclough QC), appeared and put £20 in my overall pocket. I had met my friend with his friend from Colintraive, Mr McIlwraith the retired dentist, last year while I was loading the second shipment to Grand Roy Government School. Bless them both. *'I am 83,'* he said.

Marion and Johanna have gone up to Kilbarchan. David and Amy are off working away at Chandlers Hotel at Ascog. I am whacked but I am not knackered yet, by a long shot. The terminology and complexity of the whole logistics process, dealing with the customs people, port authorities, consignee, consignor what is the difference, which is which? I am learning slowly. Every day is a school day. What is amazing is the help I have received from so many individuals, that has enabled me to keep going thus far on this journey, albeit, somewhat late, for a man of pensionable age.

Tuesday 09/01/2007

Called Geest Line and spoke to Sandy? I am to quote customs reference of 28 December 2006, if, and when, I get them to ship my container. I then called Alastair of Jonas Brown Hubbard, St George's, Grenada, about the possibility of the Port Authority reducing their handling charges and customs dues. He suggested I contact Calliste Government School and get them to make representations with that regard to the Grenadian government's Ministry of Education and Labour and the 'Port People'. I called the principal of Calliste Government School. I received a positive response and she said she would contact the ministry. She said she had received my letter, which had gone via the island of St Vincent.

Saturday 13/01/2007

10:30 p.m. I spoke to Kevin in the Denholm Barwil Ltd, Falkirk office, who told me that they had moved up the road from Grange Dock. John was not in the office. I called Mr Fleming of Fleming Removals. *'We can do removals. We do a lot of wee things, like work for the Children's Hospice in Kinross,'* he said. I thanked him for his firm's loan of the trolleys on 16 December, without which we would never have fully loaded the container, as the trailer had to be parked outside the school gates of what had once been the Inverkeithing PS playground and we had a long way from the building in order to shift the educational resources from the classrooms.

Set up a collection and distribution network. How? Have ocean freight containers on standby where and when required. I am getting carried away with my big ideas.

Wednesday 17/01/2007

4:30 p.m. I spoke to the young Mr Hopkins at ZIM Integrated Shipping Services Ltd (Liverpool) India Buildings. I sent him an email with my intentions. I spoke to Brian, Fife Group to let him know.

I managed to source sea transport thanks to Anne, Caribbean Horizon Tours and Services, McIntyre Bros. Ltd, St George's, Grenada. I called Duncan Adams Transport Office Ltd. Eric is on the road. I left a message to tell him that I had sourced a shipping line. Frank, technician, of Fife Fire Extinguishers, was in the P4/5 classroom this afternoon and I told him that I had been over his way in the Kingdom of Fife, and why. He said, '*It's taken over your whole life!*' Well not quite.

(He was right, but I did not know then, to what extent it would, indeed, take over my life, and be a burden to those nearest and dearest to me.)

He then went on to say, '*You have an expensive hobby,*' I replied, '*Expensive, yes, it is; at many levels it is costly, but it is definitely not a hobby. I believe it to be a ministry based on faith,*' he smiled at my foolishness.

Contact: Peter, volunteer, who helped with the loading of resources on Saturday 2 December from Capshard PS and Kirkcaldy North PS, unloading them into two 20-foot containers at the Hayfield Industrial Estate later that morning. I thanked him and told him about the planned uplift of resources later in the month; Frank, HT Fair Isle Primary School; contact Tanya *Fife Free Press*, and Brian. I am and will be ever in their debt.

Friday 19/01/2007

4:45 p.m. Home. I called Tom at ZIM and spoke to Cara, who told me that the container will be delivered to the Hayfield Industrial

Estate, Kirkcaldy on Monday 22 January 2007. SeaFreight Agencies, Caribbean Shipping Line. A strategic supporter: contact Roland, President, David, Yamila, Grenada Ports Authority, Carenage, St George's Grenada. Contact Ambrose, Grenada Ports. I called Brian, operations director of the Fife Warehousing Company, Kirkcaldy, who has told me that they will load the ZIM container on 22 January and will take an inventory and enclose it with a bill of lading and fax me a copy. Wonderful!

I called the *Fife Free Press* to speak to Tanya (she was not in), to call her on Monday to let her know of the arrangements for the shipment of these resources to Calliste Government School in Calliste, Grenada. Also call Fair Isle Primary School to let them know where their recent donation of school furniture is going. Pupils might be interested. Call John, MD of Russell's, Hillington depot. Contact Anna, COSLA. Wrote letter. I received a word from John Watt of Denholm Barwil Ltd in the Falkirk office. *'We came up with a rate and sourced direct shipment from Portsmouth ... the final costs of that ... from you, we want inventories and pretty concise information,'* he said.

Saturday 20/01/2007

Kevin, the digital artisan, has generously offered to build my website www.grenadarelief.co.uk pro bono *(Now evolved into www.haitirelief.org.uk)*. I ask him if he will. *'I need you to put the sponsors links and logos on to the site of every company that has helped me thus far,'* he replied. *'No problem.'* I was talking to David, friend and supporter at The Bike Shed. *'It's just different ways of walking ... you can't get on with everybody.'* Wise words.

Monday 22/01/2007

I received a call on from Brian to tell me, *'That's all the stuff in the container. That's everything on. There were only four items fit for the bucket.'* I told him that I was unable to thank him and his team at the Fife Group enough for all their help.

Tuesday 23/01/2007

I spoke to Tanya Scoon, reporter, *the Fife Free Press*, who said she was writing another article. I told her that her help recently from the fourth estate had been crucial in making this next shipment of educational resources to Grenada possible.

Wednesday 24/01/2007

9:50 p.m. Home. This afternoon, as I was walking along Castle Street, I met Jim (known to his friends as Scoomba) and we stopped to chat. He said, *'Davie, if you fell in the water you'd come up with a fish in your mouth.'*

I had been telling him about the recent 'developments' that came out of the blue almost, offers to assist me that occurred just when I thought my collection of surplus-to-requirements educational resources project days were over. He told me that some people had left a donation in the boat shed. Mr and Mrs Pollock and Sandra the taxi driver. I went over after school and put it in the Caribbean Hurricane Relief Depot. The kindness received from so many continues to keep this initiative afloat.

On the way home I stopped off at *The Buteman* to speak to Craig, the editor, to give him Tanya Scoon's name at *The Free Press*. He is always positive and helpful. I thanked him for redrafting my letter of gratitude to all those on the island who had contributed to the success of the two shipments of educational resources to Grenada in 2005, and he continues to support the project. I tried to contact ZIM but the lines were busy. I contacted Neil, public relations and journalist, Aberdeenshire Council.

Solving the Wasteful Disposal of Educational Resources

Thursday 25/01/2007

6:43 p.m. Home. Earlier I spoke to Penny of the COSLA office in Edinburgh, who is now in Anna's job, who is on secondment. I have been on the phone trying to contact Robin Swaisland and left a message for him. He called me back. *'Keep in touch,'* he said.

I then called Anne Campbell-McIntyre and ended up speaking to her brother, Michael, to thank them for giving me Roland's email. And as a result of contacting him, the offer came from his firm, SeaFreight Agencies Lines, to transport the container once ZIM had delivered it to Kingston Jamaica. They will collect and deliver from that Jamaican Port to St George's, Grenada. *'Once he hears yo name, he opened de door for you. Keep up your good work,'* he said and with these few words encouraged me. I had called Roland in Florida to thank him and let him know that Stephen of Tom Kenny's Transatlantic freight forwarding team, at ZIM Integrated Shipping Services (Liverpool) Ltd, had collected the 40-foot ocean freight container ZCSU8083681, loaded and inventoried it with a piece list of educational resources from two Kirkcaldy primary schools in December 2006, from The Fife Group Hayfield Industrial Estate, and would send me their bill of lading. And it is to be delivered to the consignee, Principal Fletcher, Calliste Government School, Grenada. I stopped off at RBS: my funds to pay for this shipment have come through sale of BS&T shares. I cycled up the High Street to see John MacKirdy Senior. I met Junior and his missus: I asked them if they could move the ocean freight container out at the boatyard across to the John G Russell Transport Ltd depot in Hillington Industrial Estate. I gave them John Hume's name as this firm has offered to store it until shipping arrangements have been arranged.

Saturday 27/01/2007

8:42 p.m. Home. A few lines to help recall what I did this day.

Saturday 27/01/2007

I returned from where I had the frames of my spectacles repaired and a rigout for young David, who cooked us a bacon roll and tea. I then cycled up to The Bike Shed, which is behind David's home in the Bush; as always he is welcoming, encouraging and efficient in what he does of keeping my old bicycle roadworthy. I cycled back around and down onto the High Street into Woolworth's and purchased a new washing-up tub for the kitchen and cycled out to the port. It was grey, wet and chilly out there. I opened up the depot to find that someone had put a new bicycle in there.

I went across the main road and opened up the ocean freight container and shifted the large bakery boards, which I had got when I dismantled the Electric Bakery shop 'donation' on Montague Street. Gordon, the joiner, is kindly going to saw each of them into three for shelving, to be assembled in the estate stable on the High Street as and when I receive more donations of books. On arrival I got a welcome from Jim the blacksmith, who is always glad to see me. I had a brief chat with Peter who lives at the port.

I met Martin and mentioned to him that I had spoken to John on Thursday afternoon about moving the container, and he asked me if it was full. I said it wasn't as both the big primary school and the secondary school had not moved into their new PPP/PFI scheme joint campus and the surplus-to-requirements educational resources had not become available. He said, *'Never mind. You can continue to keep the container and the depot here until such time as it fully loaded.' 'That is very good of you, Martin, and please accept my heartfelt gratitude. I could never have embarked on this venture had you not given me the space,'* I said.

This afternoon I met once more Colin, electronics engineer and yachtsman, who tells me, *'We are taking the yacht down to Spain this year.'* He described his trips to the Arabian and Persian Gulf, Qatar, and also he goes to Bangladesh (Dacca and Chittagong). He comes from Aberdeen. It has been a good day.

Solving the Wasteful Disposal of Educational Resources

Monday 29/01/2007

4:41 p.m. Home. I called Avril, Fife Council. *'I have more furniture for you at Kennoway Primary School. It needs to be uplifted on 7 February,'* she tells me.

Johnston Press: speak to Graham, contact given to me by Tanya Scoon. I had stopped off at John MacKirdy Transport Ltd, where I told John Junior that there was no hurry to move the ocean freight container at the boatyard when it was eventually fully loaded as I had still to source a school in Grenada to whom I could ship it.

(A warning that was not heeded for I would soon have more fit-for-purpose surplus from local education authority schools than I could ever possibly store and deliver successfully, but I continued to dig a hole deeper and deeper. But, no, I did not heed advice from Marion, Eric and my own insight, since I kept on contacting education authorities and schools that had surplus school furniture to offer.)

I have no storage facility for my salvaged educational resources in Fife, or anywhere, on a large enough and suitable scale. I had put the cart before the horse. I am now out of my depth. I called Mae Winterton, *Schools For Gambia*. Do they want my stuff?

Friday 21/01/2022

1:50 p.m. This morning I was talking to Ross a businessman in Helmi's Café who has a business in the Gambia.

Tuesday 30/01/2007

4:58 p.m. Home. Spoke to Marie, responsible for surplus educational resources at Newburgh Primary School Fife; and Kennoway Primary School and Community School, Mrs C.

Friday 02/02/2007

Stewart is the head teacher and Mrs D. Cook is the business manager.

Some notes: Liberian refugees? Davina O'Regan (www.allafrica.com). Ellen Johnston Sirleaf is the country's leader; Christian Aid (Scotland); Friends of the Earth (Scotland).

Goal: I need to acquire the skills of logistics and transport ... well I am after these many months (how many now?) not entirely a newbie novice. I am self-directed, a prime mover, (*not quite you are dependent on pro bono support and goodwill in order to collect, transport, store and deliver educational resources*) and I am attempting to be engaged in meaningful work that is within my reach, but has way exceeded my budget to sustain it, and at the same time I have a contractual commitment to my local council's education authority.

Wednesday 01/02/2007

'I doubt very much that you are going to be able to do it this time,' said Paul, the jannie. We'll see. Just you watch me.

Friday 02/02/2007

3:30 p.m. To collect? Be at the depot? From Helen? A printer to be 'recycled.'

10:30 p.m. Home. My friend Robert, solicitor in the town, came by earlier to return Chantal's (of Rococo Chocolates in London) book of photographs that she took when her family visited Grand Roy Government School, in May/June 2006, to see for themselves what the school had done with our first two shipments of educational resources to the island in 2005. The book is on our bookshelf. Robert and I chatted for a while. He was sympathetic to the aims of my project/initiative and kindly offered to come by and lend a hand to shift school furniture if required. *'It will keep* *me fit,'* he said. He mentioned the name of a Brian Stirling, who he would inform of what I hoped to achieve with my venture.

Later Alison dropped by to hand in an article from *The Sunday Times* about Grenada from her dad, Alan, who was the best man at our wedding on 30 December 1986.

Wednesday 07/02/2007

4:45 p.m. Home. I called Brian of the Fife Group and I asked him if his firm could help with the removal and storage of educational resources from more of the Fife schools. He said he would call Avril. *'It's not up to Avril,'* he said. I then called Gillian, who said she was getting in touch with her colleagues in economic development and would call me tomorrow.

Security firms? Offers of pro bono help willing to look after Kennoway PS. No! I am hoping that the Fife Group will come up trumps again. I called Stephen at ZIM. He, bless him, has contacted their transport department and tells me that their haulage costs from Kirkcaldy to Liverpool have been waived. Wonderful! Every little bit of assistance matters greatly.

(I was now buzzing from the thrill of making these connections, and oblivious to the predicament I had created for myself, and the toll of worry that it was taking on those nearest and dearest to me.)

Monday 12/02/2007

4:12 p.m. Home. I called Fife Estates. Gillian to call tomorrow about payment of rates etc. should an industrial unit/warehouse in Glenrothes become available. She is very helpful and supportive.

I can now inform Avril, Brian and the Fife Council schools that it is likely that I shall have somewhere soon, where educational resources can be transported, stored and inventoried before being shipped. *(Great news, or so I thought.)*

Wednesday 14/02/2007

4:12 p.m. Home. I am going to lease an industrial unit in the Glenrothes Business Park. I was speaking to Renwick, Fife Estates surveyor. *'I will cut to the chase, Client Development will let you have the unit rent and rates free for two months. The unit is situated in Fife Food Centre,'* he said. Warehouse 100% reduction rates abatement because the premises will be used for charitable purposes only. *'That is really good news to me and I am so grateful to Gillian, yourself and the team in Fife Council for this opportunity to store fit-for-purpose educational resources prior to shipment,'* I said.

I now have to make travelling and accommodation arrangements. Wunderbar! I am going to stay in the Golden Acorn Hotel, Glenrothes town centre. Now I have to rent a van. I call Mr Fleming of Fleming Removals in Inverkeithing. The collection? It's on. Just when I thought the time had come to lick and lock up. Jack it in. Call it a day. No more shipments. Admit defeat. The cavalry comes over the hill to my rescue, because of my do-gooder, persevering, cussed never, ever give up and can do spirit. A dilemma. To quit or not to quit.

(I knew that my teaching days were numbered. I had been advised to retire, but I had wanted to make 65.)

Thursday 15/02/2007

5:30 p.m. Home. Eric Adams will provide a top liner with driver. I am speechless with gratitude. I am to email him with the address where the team from Duncan Adams Transport Ltd are to meet me. For Friday 16 February: I am to call Renwick. 'Where is the *Fife Food* Centre?' I call Avril; Susan Mitchell, Newburgh PS; Graham Scott the reporter.

The branch I am clinging on to is shaking. I am travelling solo and paddling against the current without a life jacket.

Friday 16/02/2007

9:39 p.m. The Golden Acorn Hotel, Glenrothes, Fife. Christina, the receptionist, is welcoming, friendly and helpful. I signed in at reception. I have just eaten a pizza, with all the messy toppings, from the Spice of Life Tandoori Kebab across from the car park. I don't feel too proud of myself for scoffing that lot. I could, and should, have passed it by. There were youngsters hanging around outside, too young to be puffing on cigarettes. Degradation in the midst of plenty. Glenrothes, New Town no mair, but new to me.

I set off from the house, our home, with Marion to the 7 a.m. ferry. I came back home and had some breakfast and got ready for school. I called Fife Council and spoke to Renwick who is helpful and efficient. He told me that the lease documents will be left at the hotel reception desk for me.

10:15 p.m. I have just had to re-open the self-addressed envelope for the Fife Estates council office, Glenrothes.

I had enclosed the signed plan, which I had used earlier when I hired a taxi to go looking for the Southfield Industrial Estate Food Resource Base Units 1 and 2, when all along I had not noticed that there was a map enclosed. I am now going to post it in the out-of-hours letter box. I am quite tired and there are nipping pains behind my right eye; I have plenty of pain killers, back out the door again.

Saturday 17/02/2007

7:55 a.m. I am talking to Isobel at the reception desk, who is a big encouragement to me. Helpful. She has let me use the phone to call Duncan Adams Transport Ltd, who tell me that they were not sure whether they were going to send a transporter and container.

I am worried. Anxious. Is this it, where all my time, effort and

Saturday 17/02/2007

expense over these many months comes apart? I am in the soup, in the deep end and sinking. Isobel tells she is a fundraiser for Action Aid and works with Sally Magnusson. I finally get through to someone in the office. They are on their way! I am speaking to Stevie, who is on his way from the depot at Grange Dock. *'I've got three passengers,'* he said. He is bringing a curtain-sider TLH8 which will be offloaded on Monday.

2:25 p.m. We finally arrived back at Duncan Adams Transport Ltd, Grange Dock depot.

3:40 p.m. I am on the train, running smoothly on iron rails past the hills of Stirlingshire. I have just left Falkirk Grahamston Station. I took a bus from Falkirk Central where Stevie and his son Daniel had dropped me off, having given me a lift up the road from Grange Dock. It has been a day of full-on spring sunshine, hawthorn bushes in bloom, and the freshly ploughed fields of Fife.

I got up early. I had slept fitfully until 7 a.m. showered and went down to reception and chatted to Isobel, who has done a lot of fundraising work for Action Aid. She is a big-time fundraiser involving the Scottish business world but you wouldn't know that, she is a quiet, modest individual with a calming presence. She was very helpful to me. I was on tenterhooks imagining worst-case scenarios. Could I still expect (taking nothing for granted) was it fair, reasonable, more to the point, presumptuous of me to expect that once, yet again, Eric Adams and his company would provide (as he said he would) the transport to collect the 'surplus' resources, unwanted classroom resources no longer fit for some purposes, from Kennoway and Newburgh primary schools? Well the answer was 'Yes!' He and many others so far on this journey have kept their word to me. Stevie said he a had three passengers with him, Kenneth, and Kenneth Junior (who had been with the drivers on the previous collections, 9 December and 16 December 2006), and were on their way. What a relief. I felt as though a bag of cement had been lifted from my back.

I went into the lounge-cum-bar and ordered tea and toast, signed myself out, thanking Isobel for her precious support, and went outside in the sunshine to wait until 9 a.m. What a thrill it was for me to see the 40-foot curtain-sider coming round the roundabout on the way to Kennoway Primary School, a large 1950s building, which we had difficulty in finding, where we met Robert the visiting janitor, there to open up. I apologised to him for being late. *'I'm not worried. I'm on time and a half,'* he said.

Another school another collection. I have given up another weekend away from my nearest and dearest but I shall be back over here tomorrow morning.

Monday 19/02/2007

I am here this morning, at Duncan Adams Transport Ltd, Grange Dock, Grangemouth. We loaded 40-foot ocean freight container MAEU7412692 *(Which Tom Walker was to tell me later had failed its inspection as being no longer seaworthy, with no ISO certificate. I must now follow that up with Howard)*, which I had paid for with the resources on the curtain-sider TLH8. We also removed the resources from curtain-sider TLH 43 (which we had loaded on 9 December 2006) assisted by Stevie the mechanic and biker, Craig, and Kevin from the machine shop and garage. I met young Kenneth on his lunch break; and Duncan Adams, a gentleman. Eric offered me a coffee.

Tuesday 20/02/2007

I called Gillian at Fife Estates to cancel the lease. I then called the *Fife Herald* editor who was trying to give me a hard time. *'What's the local angle on this?'* he asks. I called Avril and had to turn down the offer from St Andrew's Primary School. For the time being. Distance. I cancelled the lease on the unit in Glenrothes for the time being and will post the key back to Renwick and Gillian, who were very helpful, with some ginger biscuits and a letter as to why I did not need their industrial unit at this time since Duncan Adams Transport Ltd had not only provided transport to collect educational resources donated to my project from two of the Fife primary schools, but also had allowed me to park two of my 40-foot ocean freight containers, when loaded, in their yard at Grange Dock free of charge. But if it were possible, I would at a future date, perhaps, require an industrial unit. My plans for storage and their willingness to provide it had not come to fruition. Move on! I called Falkirk Council Education Department and spoke to the director's personal assistant, who is to call me back. I am still waiting!

Thursday 22/02/2007

I called Peter in Grenada, begging him to cut me a little slack, and left a message for him to call me collect, as if that was necessary. When will I learn? That's flaming that. My container, actually it is ZIM's (ocean freight ZCSU8083681 Seal 093636/HC40CY/CY) loaded with second-hand school furniture was shipped on 8 February 2007 to Calliste Government School, Calliste.

8 p.m. Sandra, librarian at the Morningside Library, has just called to let me know that they had a donation of 16 boxes of books. I said I would contact DHL, as before, to arrange an uplift. This firm had collected a donation of books from the library on 9 January.

(I was to receive another donation of books from this library later on 13th March 2007, which was collected and delivered to the Caribbean Hurricane Relief Depot by John MacKirdy Transport Ltd.)

Solving the Wasteful Disposal of Educational Resources

Wednesday 28/02/2007

4:45 p.m. Home. Earlier Gordon the joiner came up to the classroom to tell me that the shelves he had made out of the Electric Bakery's display unit were ready. After class I went over to the boatyard and we unloaded two of them from his van and set them up in the depot. He has another one in his workshop. I am extremely grateful for Gordon's kindness. Another small but not insignificant encouragement to just keep on getting on with what I know is meaningful work, that in no way detracts from my commitment to my teaching vocation, which I feel has become an extension of it. I left a message on Roland Malins-Smith's voicemail. I called Principal Sherma Fletcher to let her know that a container of educational resources was on its way to her school.

Thursday 01/03/2007

5 p.m. Home. I called Peter, who told me to call him at 12 o'clock tomorrow. He keeps fobbing me off and it serves me right for having a fixation on those who I perceive as being of some material and or emotional benefit to me. I just don't know when to give up altogether on such folk. I called SeaFreight Agencies in Miami, who are tracking ZCSU8083881 (Seal093635/HC40). It left the Port of Liverpool on 8 February, actually Grange Dock, Port of Grangemouth. I was speaking to Yamila in the SeaFreight Lines office. *'Come to Miami and we will teach you some more Spanish,'* she said.

Send a message to Kimani Peterkin. MVA *Hansa*, Griefswald. ETA Grenada 6 March 2007.

Friday 02/03/2007

I came home at lunchtime to call Peter. *'It's 8 a.m. my time. I can't hear you. I am very busy!'* he said. I told him I might be able to meet him in July. He makes me feel very silly. All for what? Because I think, somehow or other, he can facilitate my shipments of educational resources to deserving schools. I have always been too trusting and expecting preferment from the wrong people.

Monday 12/03/2007

4:30 p.m. I left a message for Mungo of Argyll Wind Farms Ltd. He called me back. He lives in Symington, Ayrshire. He suggested I write to Peter Blacker. Before that, Stephen at ZIM called to let me know that he had got my letter, for which he thanked me, and to inquire as to when I wanted to ship 'my next container.' I told him that I was now awaiting word from the principal of Calliste Government School. Stephen, whom I like, said that for the next shipment I could use my own container.

(I was to wait months before I received a belated thank-you letter, but I was able to speak with her over the phone and all she wanted to know was could they keep the ocean freight container! To the effect that they were pleased with what they had received and would be glad to perhaps receive another shipment. I just do not know when to draw the line and say, 'Enough is enough, okay.' But it was to take me not a few years into the future to learn the lesson that nice guys finish last, or as Murray Higgins, sixties journalist of Halifax Nova Scotia said, quoting maybe someone else, 'The meek shall inherit the earth, for their faces are already in it.')

7:05 p.m. Now I am going to write a letter to Peter Blacker, of Argyll Wind Farms Ltd, with an initial inquiry as to whether his firm would sponsor a small wind turbine that could be attached to the roof of the depot at the boatyard and supply enough voltage for light and heat. It's been damp and chilly working in there these many months.

Solving the Wasteful Disposal of Educational Resources

Wednesday 14/03/2007

4:55 p.m. Home. I was not long in the classroom when there was a knock on the door and Cheryl, the Electric Baker's missus, and son arrived to tell me that she had kindly brought a donation of children's toys, books etc. in her car. I let the classroom assistant know I would be briefly off the school premises and left the donation in the depot till time to sort and inventory. The HT took the class for the Easter children's concert song practice after the midday break.

6:10 p.m. Home. It has been non-stop whizzing about. I had been not long in when Tom called offering me whatever he had. *'Do you take clothes?'* he asked. *'Yes I do, thank you very much ... I'll take anything. All donations will be gratefully received here,'* I said. We chatted. He said he'd left a television some time ago and I told him he could let Mary know and she would put the donation in the depot. I had been over at lunchtime to touch bases and bring her up to date on all that had been achieved since we last met. On my return home from school I got a call from Martin at the boatyard to tell me that there would be a pallet load of books delivered in 20 minutes. David called me a taxi.

Andy and Sandra, who had enquired about how to go about shipping resources to a school in Mombasa, Kenya, were telling me about the stationery materials that they have collected. I showed them inside the Big Green Box and asked them if they would send a taxi back to collect me in half an hour. Meanwhile, the local island firm's truck arrived in the yard with a pallet of books, 'Books For Charity', addressed to Surplus Educational Supplies. Many thanks to John Paul and James, the drivers of John MacKirdy Haulage, who had collected them from the Morningside Library in Edinburgh. And many thanks to Sandra and staff who had gone to the trouble of boxing and labelling. Frank the taxi driver came to collect me. *'Will you take stuff?'* he asks. He has always been sympathetic to my project. He asked me if I would collect stamps for him, which he sends to Guide Dogs for the Blind and I would. And so it goes.

I am tired. I was in the midst of cooking supper when I got the first telephone call. Thankfully Johanna took over in the kitchen. I'm hungry and knackered. I can smell the mince. I am trying to keep track of events as this story unfolds. Logistics. Cooperation. Collaboration. Transatlantic telephone calls. Weekend trips across Scotland to collect educational resources. Join the dots. Stay in Grangemouth for a couple of days. The cost of total commitment. What's this all about? *Two 20-foot ocean freight containers have already been shipped to Grenada and you want to send more?*

No wonder when Eric was asked who I was he said, *'he's a nutter from the West Coast.'*

Friday 16/03/2007

7:45 p.m. Home. I have just received a call from SeaFreight Agencies, Miami. I am speaking to senora Yamila, who is letting me know that today they loaded the 40-foot ocean freight container ZCSU8083881 aboard one of their ships in the Port of Kingston, Jamaica, for St George's, Grenada. *'We'll do all we can for you,'* she said. I thank her for these kind words and my spirit soars.

Contact: Mr Peterkin who is the Trans-Shipment Control Supervisor, Caribstar Shipping; Anne and Michael and families; Anne Campbell, Director Caribbean Horizon Tours and Services; McIntyre Brothers Auto Rentals, True Blue, St George's Grenada; Alvin Hamilton; Bishop Vincent Darius; Glasgow City Council Furniture desks. *'I understand that you have some surplus furniture?'* I said. Remind Brian Munro if he could take a piece list.

Solving the Wasteful Disposal of Educational Resources

Monday 02/04/2007

7:20 a.m. I am on the train for Glasgow Central. I have just met Clark, who I met way back on the morning of 19 February 2007 when I journeyed across to Grange Dock to unload the curtain-sider of resources into my second 40-foot ocean freight container. Clark tells me that he used to be the purchasing manager for Rolls Royce at Hillington and now works for Glasgow City Council. He was telling me about the city's efforts to win the bid for the Commonwealth Games, and also that an official in his department has a lot of desks that they wish to dispose of, and he suggested I contact him.

I am being propelled along to Glasgow Central en route for Duncan Adams Transport Ltd.'s depot at Grange Dock. I am travelling hopefully. I was up before 6 a.m. and had slept fully, not helped that my waterworks are totally out sync. A beautiful morning. Onto the old bicycle. I couldn't find the bicycle chain key and remembered as I pedalled towards the Cowal Hills that I had left my pensioner ferry-travel concession card behind. No time to turn back. Not tae wurry. Press on, pedal forward. I bought a day-return ticket to Central on board the MV *Saturn* across the watta. Now rolling forward on iron rails. The sun is like a big lightbulb up ahead, above Port Glasgow town. Get on with it! The train is squealing to a halt at Drumfrochar.

8:31 a.m. Riding the rails. I walked past Clark, telling him that I was on course for Grange Dock, on through the teeming humanity of Central Station; I won't be deflected. I had thought of going along to 20 Trongate, but decided against it. All being well I have a couple of containers to paint. I walked up Buchanan Street and across to Queen Street Station. *'Single or return?'* he asks. *'A return ticket, please,'* I reply.

I asked a helpful rail inspector the directions for the train to Falkirk. I get the train for Falkirk Grahamston platform1, and here

Monday 02/04/2007

I am with sunshine en route. *'We are now approaching Stepps.'* I lived in lodgings there, finding my way through the Glasgow/Scottish experience of remaking new life. *'The next stop is Gartcosh,'* she said.

9:30 p.m. The hotel. I am ensconced on a rickety chair having returned from La Gondola chippie-cum-sweetie shop with a bottle of water.

I had stopped before that to make another call home. Amy, bless her! David had walked back into town to collect my bicycle, which I had left standing against the metal fence down at the ferry pier terminal. Yes, it has been a long day right enough, where I received many tokens of GRACE, unmerited favour.

The taxi I got on arrival at Falkirk Grahamston was driven by Bruce of GBS Taxis. *'I can't even go to the chippie and they know where I am,'* he said despairingly. He took me to Duncan Adams Transport Ltd depot in Grange Dock. Into reception. From the office on my left someone says, *'We were just talking about you.'* Mrs Adams, matriarch, sitting at a large desk, giving me the 'once-over look' from the top of her spectacles, is the boss, I think. Eric appeared from the big open-plan office at the end of the corridor in front of me, took me right into the office area and gave me fluorescent jacket. *'This will save you from being knocked down,'* he said.

(I was always made welcome, and it made me feel absolutely great. And that was to be my experience in many subsequent visits.)

He then took me out into the busy yard, and along, to show me where the container was that I had said I wished to paint; it's another 40 feet! Have I now gone completely over the top? Why paint it? I painted the 40-footer at the port boatyard last year, which I thought would increase its value when I sold it in Grenada, and I would do the same for this one. I was enjoying the ride for all that it was worth. First, he introduced me to the driver of the 'Box Lift' (a large forklift Triton container lifter truck), who would make a space for me. I was made welcome at Duncan Adams Transport Ltd, Grange Dock headquarters. Next, Eric took me along to the machine shop and truck garage to meet Stevie. *'I am going to do another thing for you today. I am going to send Stevie with you to B&Q to buy some paint,'* said Eric.

It is a beautiful day. The sun shone out of a bright blue sky. Stevie took me to a huge B&Q with lots of paint but not what he knew was required. *'Okay, I'll tak ye tae waur ye'll get whit ye want, and cheaper,'* said Stevie. So it was back up the road in the Duncan Adams jitney, across the busy main road and into Economy Autopaints, Falkirk, for me to purchase two 5-litre URK Rapid Coat 170, specially mixed. Chose the colour – lederhosen dark green, a bit too dark but it will have to do, similar to my first big box. I chatted to Stevie while I waited for the paint to be mixed. He is easy to talk to. Straight as a die, open and friendly. *'I'm okay, you're okay,'* he said. He is a biker and is looking through a catalogue on the shop counter. He is looking to sell his motorbike and wishes to buy another. And he is telling me about a ride over to Glasgow with 10,000, surely more like 1,000, bikes to raise funds for Yorkhill Children's Hospital, and of meeting a young patient. *'He knows he's gonnae die,'* he said about a youngster, James, who's got cancer.

I was chatting to a lady behind the counter, suffering in pain, with a schnauzer at her feet. I gave her two of my painkillers. When I told her I was from Barbados she told me that her favourite island in the Caribbean was St Lucia, which she had visited on several occasions. It was back up the road and into the dock. I was anxious about whether I would be able to manage the task in front of me, but with all the help I had received over the last couple of hours I knew I would give it my best shot.

On arrival back at the yard Stevie advised me to purchase two litres of solvent thinners from Bespoke Paints, and he would order a 4-inch-wide roller kit and foam rollers from Dingbro Ltd for me. Bless him, Lord, every single one of them.

Monday 02/04/2007

I waited and waited at the depot gate for their van to arrive. Meanwhile I had changed into my old boiler suit, which Marion had washed for me, and munched an apple that I had hastily grabbed on my way out this morning. Eventually the van came with the order. I didn't have any change, so I gave the Dingbro salesman a £20 note. Later, a young mechanic drove down to where I was rolling awa' on the box to give me the change. I am experiencing evidence of GRACE, unmerited favours in ocean freight container loads.

Stevie then appeared with thin rubber gloves and three new brushes. *'Are you just going to tickle it up a bit?'* he asked good humouredly. I am going to bram it up. Of course, I am daunted, feart at the enormity of this task that I have undertaken. The audacity of this whole project – I am amazed at myself, at my nerve, and barefaced cheek at times like this. It is more than just an initiative project now. I will just have to keep the bit between my remaining teeth and stay with it (whatever 'it' has now become) until there is a satisfactory conclusion to this adventurous misadventure. I ignore my fears and unpleasant imaginary scenarios and keep rolling away on this glorious spring day. I was enabled to persevere in spite of aches and pains. I kept going as transporters/artics and trailers with their ocean freight containers rumbled past in this very busy yard. Stevie the mechanic and illustrious biker, who joins his biker chums for long-distance charity rides, drove down to where I was in a transporter to see how I was doing. By nearly 7 p.m. I was beginning to start on the top of the container, having made a step-up from discarded truck tyres and pallets that were lying about in the yard. The sun was going down in the west, the skyline of old Grangemouth town to my left. I dropped by the office to let them know I was leaving the premises and would be back tomorrow morning to finish the job. I thought it was fine to quit, enough for one day. Eric, who is often out in the yard and in the thick of it, was still at his desk and he said, *'Dae whit ah tell ye. Get a charity, go on the internet and ye'll get lots of lottery money. We don't want to see you put YOUR FAMILY on poverty street.'* I thanked him for his advice, and for all the support he and his team had given me today. I walked up the road and out of the dock. No help from The Seafarers institute-cum-pub when I went in and asked if I could use the telephone … all cards, no more dial ups. It was a long walk out to the roundabout and into the town mall. I stopped at La Gondola Fish and Pizza Bar in the Laporte Precinct for some supper. I chatted with Mrs Cappuccino.

10 p.m. Oh no, not again. I have a sharp twinge of pain in my little finger and I've got a cramp in the tendon from my groin down my inside right thigh as I scribble this note.

Tuesday 03/04/2007

2:45 p.m. I am heading back along the rails to Glasgow Queen Street. The sun is shining brightly out of a cloudless blue sky *'Ding, dong. Please mind the gap. The next stop is Cumbernauld.'* It has been a long day. I finally got the 'roof' topside of the container painted. Perseverance and determination rules. Are they not the same thing? I said goodbye to young Kenneth in the garage and went into reception to wait to speak to Eric before I left. He said I could keep the fluorescent jacket that he gave me yesterday and reiterated his advice to me about the importance of becoming a charity and acquiring funding *(which I did not heed until it was too late, and by that time I was on the verge of financial embarrassment, not entirely due to my own fault, but I will come to that predicament later in this narrative).*

I walked out of the yard and stopped at the Forth Ports security gatehouse and shook hands with the security guard, and left him in a better mood than I found him yesterday morning. Make peace, let not the sun go down on my wrath, if you can help it. I walked up the road and into Grangemouth town centre and got a taxi up to Falkirk Grahamston and I am now rolling back to where I left. I must remember to bring my passport next time if I wish to get into Grange Dock.

Saturday 07/04/2007

I wrote thank-you letters to: Yamila, SeaFreight Agencies; Brian, Fife Warehousing Ltd; Avril, Fife Council; Ben Mundell Transport Ltd; Eric Adams; Joseph Charter, HC Grenada High Commission in London; Stephen, ZIM Integrated Services Ltd. Still to write to: Andrew, Stirling Council Library Services; Sandra, Morningside Library, Edinburgh District Council Libraries.

Tuesday 10/04/2007

6:10 p.m. Home. I have just come off the phone. There was a message from Brian, operations director for the Fife Warehousing Co. Ltd to tell me that 262 chairs and 184 tables were loaded into 40-foot ocean freight container CRXU4103197, which was transported to Duncan Adams Transport Ltd depot at Grange Dock. These resources were a donation to my NGO from Fife Council and were loaded on 16 March or thereabouts. This morning I posted thank-you letters with tokens of my appreciation.

(I became the victim of my own success, because I was no longer able to cope effectively with the large quantities of educational resources that I had salvaged, and was about to make arrangements to uplift the fit-for-purpose educational supplies that were being offered to The Surplus Educational Supplies Foundation from schools all over Scotland, to whom I had given my word to have their surplus educational resources collected and stored. I had entangled myself in a process I had started in 2005 and was not willing to bring to a stop. I had created an impossible task for me to complete successfully.)

Solving the Wasteful Disposal of Educational Resources

Friday 13/04/2007

11:08 p.m. Home. I am going to scratch a few lines before my memory of the details, of what has been another interesting day, fades.

I dragged myself from the garden and cycled out to the boatyard. *'Where you been hiding?'* asked Martin cheerily. I boxed and tidied. I met Jim the steam, who is a clever engineer, yachtie. He has done it all and seen it all. Sceptical, cynical, critical, occasionally 'friendly'. He is embittered for some reason. He told me once that he had spent many months as a child bedridden in a Glasgow hospital recovering from tuberculosis. He is confounded, once again, as he sees that the Big Green Box 40-footer is almost packed to the roof. His attitude of cynicism to what I have been engaged in for over two years now just makes me more determined than ever to stick with my vision. I cycled back home to join the family for lunch. Johanna is ice skating with Robin over in Greenock. I sat outside in the sunshine for a while, and then set off back up the road to Port Bannatyne. I boxed more IT equipment. Nancy came by with yet another bag of new stationery – pens, notebooks etc. – that she had purchased, which is very generous and kind of her. She is a keen and long-time supporter, and fundraiser for the RNLI.

Oh! I had forgotten (this is why I try to keep some sort of a record of my fellow human beings that I meet on the road), I met Louis the builder again this morning, who comes from Barrhead and has a holiday flat in the port. He was telling me about his son's trip to Kenya and the capital city of Nairobi, where Louis's granddaughter had worked during her holidays in the sprawling community of Kabira. They had taken money from their Church of Scotland congregation – his son is raising money so that the Kenyan church community in the encampment of squatters can dig a well. Louis goes on to tell me that in spite of extreme poverty they can still worship their Lord for hours. His son and granddaughter were impressed by the GOOD

Saturday 21/04/2007

WORK being done by the people in Kabira. He is a lovely man and he said he would bring me a cd video of their trip out to Africa. He lost his wife from cancer last year and is taking a trip to Cephalonia, and mentioned that he had helped to construct the Johnston town swimming baths. I look forward to meeting him again. *How many little vignettes have you forgotten?* Too many. Like the little lad to whom you gave a book to this morning, and his mum who told me that they had visited Barbados, and so on.

I must continue to cast my books and educational resources on the seven seas and they shall return to me after many days; as I sow, so shall I reap a blessing in return or the family will. Oh! Peter the wind farm engineer, port resident, came by to offer books and Open University science and technology coursework. *'Do you just take school stuff?'* asked Peter. *'That is kind of you to make this offer, I can be fairly certain that whatever you donate will end up in appreciative hands thousands of miles from here,'* I said.

Wednesday 18/04/2007

3 p.m. Home. *'You are not a charitable trust are you?'* asked Mr Meenan.

'No, I am not. I am, for the time being, a self-funded initiative, a West Indian expatriate, now settled here, who is relying partially on pro bono, practical, in-kind assistance from the corporate commercial business sector, especially the Scottish road haulage industry, which assists me in delivering surplus educational resources and relief to the hurricane-devastated communities on the island of Grenada in the Caribbean,' I said.

Saturday 21/04/2007

9:40 p.m. Home. Earlier today Mrs Simpson arrived with her son-in law, I think he was called David, and their gift of a Singer sewing machine (vintage, in impeccable working order, and pedal driven). I invited them in after a brief chat. I then followed them out to the Caribbean Hurricane Relief Depot, where we transferred their gift to the ocean freight container. I met Mike from Aberdeen. This afternoon I cycled into the town and up to the Bush, to The Bike Shed, to leave a folder of updates and correspondence: fresh information on the progress of 'Surplus Educational Resources International'. *Are you serious are you taking the mickey?* No I am definitely not. I don't have a label for my organisation/outfit at the moment for Kevin, digital artisan, builder of web sites, to input into www.grenadarelief.org.uk

(Out of which was to grow www.haitirelief.org.uk thanks to the expertise of another digital artisan, Sam, but that would be another nine years into the future.)

We'll see what happens. Troughs and peaks, mountain tops and sloughs of despond. On that theme, I am in the doldrums at the moment. I just have to keep on going in forward gear – as long as I am moving in that direction. I have much to be thankful for, and I think much has been accomplished through the good will and practical assistance and generosity of many individuals. I owe to them to continue to drive this venture forward to a satisfactory completion. I wonder what will that look like?

Monday 07/05/2007

Home! I am working away here or trying to take my mind off what I have no control over. I am in limbo at the moment awaiting some sort of confirmation from Calliste Government School regarding their evaluation, assessment, and appreciation of the school furniture shipment that was collected from part of a donation from Fife Council on 2 December 2006 and shipped to them earlier this year. The principal of the school did call to let me know, before the Easter holidays, that the container had arrived but she had not remarked on the contents. She said that they were *'disappointed'* (her words) that they could not keep the container as they had hoped to turn it into a classroom. I told her that the container belonged to the company that had shipped it. Sorry, I am unable to please everyone and on a scale that the beneficiaries wished.

Thursday 09/05/2007

12:10 p.m. Home. I called Anna about the decanting of Midlothian Council PFI/PPP schools in August. She tells me that I will need to shift the resources in the summer. *'I am going to a meeting. Can I call you back?'* she asks. *'Most certainly,'* I said.

I called Blythswood Care, Deephaven, Ross-shire, to see if I can offload some of these large quantities of educational resources that I can no longer process/handle through 'my system.' *'You need to find customers and begin to seriously to market all those educational resources that you are being given,'* he said. *'Thanks for the advice,'* I said. But in my heart of hearts, I knew that I was in no way ready, able, let alone up-skilled enough to do either of those vital aspects if I were going to stay afloat.

Later a neighbour, who is associated with the United Kingdom's international development projects and had mentioned that she had spent time in the Sudan, came by for tea. *'You have got an expensive hobby,'* she said. I did not take kindly to that remark and let it pass. Well. Hobby. It definitely it is *not* a hobby. I would much prefer working, creating, planting, and growing stuff in what I call the garden. What are the pros and cons of becoming a social entrepreneur? How will I be able to sustain my humanitarian initiative, my vision of recycling the Scottish Local Authorities Schools fit-for-purpose, surplus to requirements, educational resources, and thereby my own shelf life for usefulness? Sustainability is the watchword as I do my bit to contribute to a zero growth economy. I begin to establish links worldwide with communities, teachers and students in the Global Village who are less favoured with educational resources, and I make arrangements to supply them with much-needed educational resources. I am doing something similar to whoever is collecting discarded tents and sleeping bags from rock concerts and mass outdoor events.

Possible connections: Oxfam; Global Hand; Library search by NGP partnerships; Ben Salinki; searching out possible synergies? Connecting people in dire need to what is available. Who needs this? There is so much in the United Kingdom's education system that is being thrown away. Surely this can't be carbon neutral and sustainable?

Friday 11/05/2007

12:10 p.m. Home. I called the office of Anna. I spoke to Matthew and left a message. I await a response.

Monday 14/05/2007

12:10 p.m. Home. I call Gillian, Property Services Fife Council, and Renwick Cowan Surveyors. I contact Edinburgh District Council.

Tuesday 15/05/2007

Where to now? Can I get premises in Midlothian rent and rates free? Who? What? Where? Problem of storage. I contact the Edinburgh Chamber of Commerce; Rotary; Midlothian Chamber of Commerce? Call Jane Crawford next week.

2:50 p.m. Call Principal Anthea Peterkin of St Paul's Government School, St George's Grenada, W. I.

Monday 21/05/2007

4:23 p.m. Home. I am sitting outside enjoying the sunshine and I get a call from Hugh, principal quantity surveyor Midlothian Council Commercial Services, who I had called last week and had left a message on his mobile. He is positive and helpful, he suggested I get in touch with Gareth.

4:30 p.m. He knows exactly what I am after. Storage capacity for the surplus resources coming out of 16 primary schools (eight schools will close). He took my telephone number and said he would ask around. I told him that Gavin had sent me the property register. I contact Kenny, Skanska, the firm that is the contractor building the eight Private Finance Initiative schools. It took me a while to finally get through to someone at the sharp end. Wait and see.

I contact Fife Council Property Services and spoke with Gillian and Renwick. I ask them if I can mention to potential landlords that I have had dealings with Fife Council Property Services. Will they give me a reference? My reach has exceeded my grasp long before now. I have become part of the problem that I had intended to solve.

(But, though I knew I was in difficulty, I kept on getting deeper into trouble and I would become almost buried under an avalanche of educational resources that I was no longer able to deliver. I had ventured off-piste and had got carried away with the excitement of just getting hold of stuff. At that point I could have loaded dozens of containers of quality fit-for-purpose resources, that was not a problem – it was storing it until I had located deserving beneficiaries, for I was unable to determine whether my potential recipients really needed, or wanted, these shipments. I was in a fantasy land dreaming of persuading the Maersk shipping company to let me have the three container ships that had been tied up in Loch Striven for months.)

Wednesday 23/05/2007

2 p.m. Home. I spoke to Rebecca, the *Glasgow Herald* journalist, and she told me to write her a letter … wait and see.

Monday 28/05/2007

8:45 a.m. Home. I called Ecosse World Express at Glasgow Airport. *'Is it Grenada? That'll be fine,'* he said. Cameron Geddes and Ross McConnell. He told me to call them at the end of the month.

1:15 p.m. I was speaking to Leanna, freelance journalist, who is going to write an article for *The Herald Supplement* for 5 June 2007 about my initiative to send educational resources to developing countries. *'You must be very proud,'* she said. *'That is kind of you to say. I would prefer to say that I am humbled, and glad at the same time, with the assistance I have had from many individuals and their firms in the business sector, that together, we have shipped three ocean freight containers loaded with educational resources to two government of Grenada primary schools, that had been devastated by Hurricane Ivan in 2004,'* I said.

Tuesday 29/05/2007

Home. My health is beginning to suffer from the stress and pressure I have brought on myself and other members of my family.

9:15 a.m. I am moving forward, as always, into the unknown. There are sharp pains at the back of my eyeballs. What sustains me is my will to do, to make and to create, so I continue my search for storage space in Midlothian. Search. Location. I was speaking to Terence at Alan Bond. Helpful. Who tells me, *'I am in the process of networking for International Development.'* I was also speaking to Amy at World Vision, who passes me on to Andy the Department for Trade and Industrial Development (DFID) Export local contact. The adviser for the Isle of Bute. No joy! *'Has Helen MacDougall of Scottish Enterprise been in touch with you?'* He asked me that twice.

They won't stop me from shipping the next container, even though right now I am barely keeping my head above water. VSO call, *'You are doing good work. Can you bare with me one moment?'* he asks. Mercy Corps: I speak with Mervyn, *'We don't ship. What do you do?'* he said. Child Hope: I am speaking to Sandra in London.

1 p.m. I am still calling up all sorts, pinning their ears back with my off-the-cuff spiel. Goal UK: I am speaking to John in London, who passes me on to Moira in Dublin. *'I'll get you to one of our senior people here,'* she said, and is going to call me back.

Here I am wheelin' an dealin'. I am leaving no stone left unturned … nothing ventured, nothing gained. I have not given up. I am going to take a break, but try and keep up the momentum somehow. Bond Directory of Members and Networks. Ernst & Young. Social Entrepreneurship. As a social entrepreneur how am I going to sustain this philanthropy/charitable foundation, expensive unilateral hobby of mine? By FAITH. *Are you seriously crazy?* No other way forward at the moment. Tomorrow I meet the *Glasgow Herald* photographer. I now need some financial support but I am reluctant to ask for it.

Wednesday 30/05/2007

8:44 p.m. Home. It is now 10:30 p.m. I have sent an email to Leanna, freelance journalist and supporter, who is writing an article for *The Herald's Society Supplement* next week and wanted to check her facts. I mentioned to her the names of some more of the supporters who have shifted, and continue to shift, fit-for-purpose, surplus-to-requirements educational resources to where they are most needed. I have been struck low again with migraine, most of this morning to early afternoon.

Gordon McFarland appeared and invited me out for a drive around the island: on through the Mount Stuart main gate and through the policies to the gate at Bruchag Farm and down to Kilchattan Bay, out round to the dead end at St Blane's Chapel, back up the hilly road and on to Ettrick Bay, and as we approached Port Bannatyne he asked me if I wanted to go through the village. I hesitated for a moment. *'Yes. Thanks for the hurl, Gordon. I'll walk back home and it will to do me good,'* I said. And he dropped me off at the boatyard. Bless him, a true friend.

Before leaving, I gave Jim the blacksmith a call on his mobile (he had given me his card some time ago), and I asked him if he would pop rivet hooks on the side of the ocean freight container for the banner that Malcom, graphic designer and multi-skilled artisan, had made for me several months ago. *'No bother. Certainly. I'll see you there at 4:30 p.m.,'* said Jim. Colin, the *Herald* photographer, is coming tomorrow and I felt it necessary that I should make the effort and take the trouble to have it up on the Big Green Box. Jim the blacksmith had had the banner in his smithy.

Issue of funding. The CEIS chappie said I would get my reward in heaven. That's all very well, but what if I have no other choice but to remain as a solo operator; fly by the seat of my breeks, ad hoc, spur of the moment decision making at the mercy of contingencies. My limitations – my skill set is modest, to say the least. On my own head, I have to make do with the opportunities, as I create them from scratch, and take the consequences of failure and the constraints on my capacity to respond timeously. This puff of national publicity, at least, must signal that I am committed and with others have achieved something of value. See Principal Thomas's letter about every item that was shipped on 1 July 2005 being used.

'You are a big show off,' said to me some time ago by one of the dogwalkers. What do you expect me to do then? Cower in the dust. Give me utterance to articulate my back story; that will be the mountain range beyond this one. *'Adam told me you were fired from the Port School,'* he said. I let the remark pass without comment. Someday I may be able to set the record straight, at the moment I am fortunate in having a vision to fulfil, and make real and meaningful work to take my mind off days that are now ancient history. The future beckons in HIS STRENGTH and we'll see what it holds.

Thursday 31/05/2007

(I had come unstuck. The cost of another commitment. I had taken my eye off what was my primary responsibility. All my own fault. I left my classroom (1992–2007) never to return. Signed off sick with benefits on half pay.)

10:30 a.m. Morning break. The children were out in the school playground, and when they saw me out beside the Big Green Box, they all started waving at me. I met Tam Boag at the bus stop and then again outside the small Co-op. *'Ah luv tae wuk. Ah luv people who stop and talk tae me. Aye may yer lum reek wi' someone else's coal,'* he said, and he always cheers me up.

I told Iain that he could have the refrigeration equipment at the back of the Stirling Yacht Services Ltd boat shed. The *Herald* photographer, who had met me earlier as I stood outside *The Buteman* in my boiler suit, drove me along to the boatyard to snap his digital pics for Leanna article for his newspaper's *Society* Tuesday supplement. He knows Andrew Parker and Magnus McFarlane-Barrow of Scottish International Relief and had been out to Bomi Liberia with them, snapping. We got along well for the brief time together. He seemed supportive of my new work. We'll see what this next bit of puff brings?

(Just that, a puff. Why should I ever bother about what others think or don't think? That lack of self-esteem has cursed me to this day.)

11:54 a.m. Home. I have just cycled back from the Little Town having been dropped off by Colin, *Herald* newspaper photographer.

Saturday 02/06/2007

8:40 a.m. Boatyard. It's damp. A thick grey blanket of cloud sits on top of me and a chill breeze is blowing in my face off Kames Bay. I have just spoken to John the yachtie from England, who was telling me about his voyage on his yacht from Poole, Dorset. Prior to that he sailed up the coast of Spain.

'You still here? My you've grown. This project of yours would have cost you thousands of pounds had you done it without help,' he said. *'Indeed it would have,'* I replied. I did not tell him that it is not only costing me financially, but had also recently cost me my teaching career.

I am now about to inventory and box a gift of educational texts that I had found on Thursday afternoon of the 30th, which came, I think, from Willa, business studies teacher at the secondary school. There were also children's hobby horses (one plastic, the other wooden), both of good quality and several bags of children's clothes. When I arrived I met Jim the blacksmith who was going to put hooks on the side of the ocean freight to which I could attach the banner. Stop ruminating and get to work.

9:50 a.m. I am onto my second box. *'What do you put in that marmalade?'* he asks. *'Do you like it?'* I ask, and I went to tell him how I made it.

10:30 a.m. I have just met Tony fae Glesga, the amateur photographer who is on his way to Australia. *'Ah see you've had* The Herald *photographer here on Thursday. I am sellin' my boats and going to*

Saturday 02/06/2007

Australia to dae a walkabout,' he said. I wished him well and gave him my card. Oh, I forgot, Andrea, Bettany's mum came by with Pepe on his leash. *'Are yah all right Mr Hanschell?'* she asks with concern. Bless them both.

11:20 a.m. Tom has just dropped off a turntable to go with the stereo set. I met Anne Shaw MBE. *'Are you here every morning?'* she asks. *'Just about,'* I reply. And later Janet and her son David stopped by to say hello. *'A lot of people are praying for you,'* she said. I was humbled. Midday I stopped to have mah piece. I met Jeffrey the jeweller, who has eyes on the small lathe which George MacKenzie had donated, and a tugging black Labrador. Then Addie and Robbie appeared. *'It was Arran who told me that you'd got fired from the port,'* he said. Nae chance of that. Adam had passed that bit of news along to Scoomba. No, I was definitely not fired.

2:20 p.m. Back home. I must believe that all things work together for good.

'The experts from Colorado State University have predicted for this season 17 named STORMS 9 of which may become hurricanes and 5 of these intense hurricanes, category three or greater,' Jeremy, coordinator of the Caribbean Disaster Emergency Response Agency asserted. CLIMATE CHANGE, sea level rise and other CHANGES in the natural domain require that we adopt innovative and aggressive measures … *'What we are saying is that it is unfortunate that we would need the events to trigger the kind of response that we are seeing. We should not see a hurricane as an outside thing. It is part of Our ENVIRONMENT and we have to live with it … As we have seen there is no state, no matter how well resourced that can meet all the NEEDS of an impacted community within a time frame that satisfies individuals.'* he said. Quote taken from the Office of Disaster Preparedness and Management (ODPM).

Another strand in my argument, to justify why I initiated what I started after learning about Hurricane Ivan's devastation of the island of Grenada, West Indies, in 2004 – see failure of the United States government to cope with the effects of Hurricane Katrina on the city of New Orleans.

6:35 p.m. Home. I forgot to note that not long after I had set to work sorting and boxing in the ocean freight container, I had noticed rust bump blisters had appeared on the outside surface, which I had thought that I had ground off. I'm told the rust process continues until 'the box' just crumbles and disintegrates. Nothing lasts, that's for sure.

Jean, who tirelessly continues to put out pot plants to beautify the port from her base in what was once the butcher shop along the road, came by pulling her smart new trolley four-wheeler. *'How are you feeling, Mr Hanschell?'* she asks me with genuine care and concern.

She proceeded to tell me that her daughter had had to leave her work for a period as a result of the work she did as a dog handler in a prison, but now she is back on her feet. I'm still on my feet, but still fragile. I am grateful for this opportunity to show the world of this island community that Mr Hanschell is not finished yet.

Tuesday 05/06/2007

Home. I sent emails to Leanna and Colin at *The Herald* to thank them for the article in today's *Glasgow Herald*, also to Alan Reid MP to thank him for his letter, and ask if he would raise the issue of recycling, reuse, refurbishment and the redirection of fit-for-purpose, surplus to requirements, educational resources to the impoverished education systems of the developing world. I left a message for Jane, Midlothian Council Development Unit and Strategic Services. I called Mr Mckenzie of New Battle Abbey

College about storage, with reference to their advertisement in the property register. *'Do you know Bob Thomson, the stonemason?'* he asked.

'Yes, by acquaintance. He lived along the road from us while his firm were doing a lot of work at Mount Stuart House, and he drove a high-powered, red, Japanese sports car. He was telling me once about the lime mortar mixes that stonemasons have used since time immemorial,' I said. Mr McKenzie said that his senior management had not replied to my request for storage, so scrub it. But I shall keep plugging away.

For 16 June I call Enda at Ernst & Young in Dublin. *'Business advice … her personal assistant is Ellen. You can tell her that you received his name and number from Maura Lennon at GOAL,'* she said. The Irish Missionary Resource Service, an umbrella organisation for missionaries, is the umbrella organisation of Irish non-governmental organisations (NGOs) involved in development and relief overseas and/or the provision of development education. T. Dochas. This information came from GOAL on 31 May 2007.

Wednesday 06/06/2007

Home. I am embarking into another day. The sun is shining brightly out of a clear blue sky. I am venturing out in weakness and frailty. For the moment I make a few telephone calls. Ernst & Young: I speak to someone who tells me that Enda and Ellen are out in the Republic of Haiti. They returned my call! Fr Sean Doggett, who is with the St Patrick's Missionary Society working in Grenada at the moment is with his sister in Dublin at Mass and will contact me. I have spoken to Eilis, Kiltegan, in Wicklow. Rose Anne will phone me later today with regard to the lease of industrial storage space in Midlothian, at a peppercorn rent. Enough of all that, I had better get outside in the sunshine or there won't be any more left for me.

Thursday 07/06/2007

1:15 p.m. Home. I have just called John. D. Russell Transport Ltd to speak to John to ask him whether or not their firm's offer to keep the container in the yard of the Hillington still stands? I speak to David at Cushman, who suggested I can't read my own hand writing. Send information about my initiative to John Ross, Kinross; I told him that I worked at Classlochie Farm on the shores of Loch Leven, down the road to Gairneybridge, for the Maclaren family during the summer of 1974. *'What was that like?'* he asks. *'Tough, but great. It was the second step that I took to establish myself in Scotland,'* I reply. I speak to Carrie at the Edinburgh Chamber of Commerce, who said she would get back to me. I'm to see her on Monday 11th June 2007 at 11:30 a.m.

(My world, my vocation and career, and almost my sanity, had come apart; I stayed off medication and out of hospital, and gave myself to continuing the task of salvaging educational resources.)

Friday 08/06/2007

6:21 a.m. I am aboard the ferry MV *Argyle*. I have a window seat, bow-wards. The sun is coming over the hills behind the coastal town of Largs. *'My, you look smart. Going somewhere?'* asks Craig, who lives along the road. I answered his question briefly and told him that the next time we met I would tell him more about what I was engaged in. Be nice tae people. I try tae onyway. Positives.

I am too polite to ask anyone what they are about. He and his family made a donation that contributed to the second shipment of resources to a government of Grenada school in 2005 and I felt it would be impolite to clam up, so I mentioned that I had been offered the surplus-to-requirements educational resources of 14 Midlothian Council Primary schools. I told him that I had an appointment with the Edinburgh Chamber of Commerce and

Friday 08/06/2007

that seemed to sharpen his query even more. The Speirin Scots. Nosey. Why couldn't he just say, *'Hi, Dave, join me for coffee and I've got some good news for you, some of my guys back in Palo Alto are going to help you with your project,'* or, *'Would you like to hear about the hospital we are building in Tanzania, we need a gung-ho go-getter like you?'* People politics is not my game. Sunlight is sparkling off the Clyde watta.

8:30 a.m. *'Welcome to the first ScotRail train to Edinburgh Waverley.'* I have not long walked up from Glasgow Central. It is a beautiful early summer's day. Glorious sunshine streams through the window.

As I was about to disembark from the boat, Craig collars me again, and continues to be curious as to where I am going. I thought that I had already told him that, so I got a copy of Leanna MacLarty's brilliant *Herald* article of the initiative and gave it to him. We travelled up from Wemyss Bay on the train together. He got off at Paisley Gilmour Street and tells me he is on his way to New York, and then out to Tanzania, East Africa, where he is supervising, I imagine, the construction of a hospital. He was giving me 'encouragement' regarding my retirement and pension rights; I could no longer pretend and I reluctantly opened up another (is it a Johari?) window into my psychodrama, long-winded, mega-pages, narrative. I divulged the reality, the truth of my current situation, when he asked me how things were at 'The School'? I was no longer there. *'Ach!'* as the Scots exclaim in disgust and exasperation. I felt as though he had removed my façade of smart attire for this new beginning, stitch by stitch. Beautiful people. I am going to enjoy the ride today. I will.

10:42 a.m. Adam the taxi driver tells me that he ran the kitchen at the Grassmarket Hotel and Blackfriars Lodging House Mission, before being made redundant. He has not long dropped me off in Festival Square. I walked across Festival Square and I am now ensconced in the foyer of the Sheraton Hotel, where I met Dirk the maître d'hôtel who asked me where I would like to sit; it must be the suit. I ordered coffee and gave the waitress a tenner. I guess if I ask for change I should not be sitting here. Capital House, where I have an appointment at 11:30 a.m. with Carrie Wilson, is just across the square.

When I walked out of Edinburgh, Waverley I swithered about getting a bus from St Andrew's Square bus station – just as well I did not. I hailed a cab from the queue on the road that goes up to the Mound, and Adam took me on the journey out to Hardinggreen Business Park. I am scribbling this, my coffee has grown cold and the waitress has brought my change (and a smile), and I indicate it's all hers. You, last of the big tippers, and I think. *'You idiot.'* Mr Bean mark 3. Great coffee, even cold. Nice view out the big bay window. I am now, after all, the CEO of Surplus Educational Supplies Foundation (www.haitirelief.org.uk). Lots of peppermint creams. I make as if 'eef', the way Trinidadians pronounce the word. *You show off.* I can pretend. Why not? Perhaps this cheery soul will remember me, should I return.

As I was saying, back at the business park I had to wait until the person I was to see had finished her cereal. I left my business card and puff article for, which many thanks to Leanna and Colin my supporters at *The Herald*. There is no point, rhyme or reason for me to take a desk in the Midlothian Enterprise Centre until I have located storage premises to store whatever surplus resources come my way. At least they have met me wearing a smart suit.

Adam the taxi driver waited for me. He had generously switched off the meter when he learned what I was all about, and brought me back into the city. I am looking up into the back end of Edinburgh Castle and across to the Royal Lyceum Theatre: the heart of the action and mischief past, present and future. Adam was telling me that his sister was a Church of Scotland missionary in Zambia during the sixties, when the Congo was

Friday 08/06/2007

ablaze. His dad had tried to send her supplies to distribute but was thwarted by officialdom.

My coffee has almost frozen. Why do I bother to scratch a few words? I'll need to have another pee soon. For a while longer I shall enjoy the ambience of this wee corner of bespoke peace and quiet. Before me there are long-stemmed white lilies in tall fluted vases filled with crushed ice. Would you believe frozen stems? I love the display of floral artistry and so would my one and only dearest sister, Diana, who was a florist and had trained in London in the early sixties, now no longer with us. And there is a single bloom of a flower that I am unable to identify in a little cuboid vase, on this round and ever so elegant table … the finer things.

11:06 a.m. I am in the office of the Edinburgh Chamber of Commerce, Capital House, Festival Square. I was temporarily, at no little cost to myself, bedazzled by the world of business, which turned out to be all smoke and mirrors, where every transaction seemed to be conducted on a nod and a wink. It was not what I and many others had achieved over the past, but who I knew, that was the thing that really mattered. I can use their logo on my website – big deal – and The Hub foyer as a meeting point.

12:52 p.m. I am now on the train for Glasgow Queen Street from Edinburgh Haymarket Station. The meeting at the Edinburgh Chamber of Commerce went well. CW was extremely helpful. Positive. Encouraging. After all, she is a sales executive and she is only doing her job, which is to sign up new members. I am a naff old sowl. We will have to wait and see whether I can network some financial support. I've signed up and paid my membership fee. 'OUCH!'

2:05 p.m. I am now on the train for Gourock and not for hanging around in Central Station to wait for a Wemyss Bay train. On the way down the road from Queen Street Station I bought a copy of

Solving the Wasteful Disposal of Educational Resources

The Big Issue, which I see has fallen out of my bag. Not tae wurry. I stopped off at Lewin's on Buchanan Street to buy a belt for my troosers. Chat, friendly salesman, he took three of my cards and a copy of the newspaper puff and said his friend was a teacher. *'Tickets please.'* Cheery.

3:15 p.m. *'Hi, good afternoon. Could you tell me when the next train for Wemyss Bay comes please? Is there is a toilet in the station?'* I ask. *'No, there is not!'* she says abruptly. Oh well, I'll have to bite the bullet and have his nibs at the hospital rejig my plumbing; he had offered on several occasions to perform an operation, if not he one of his acolytes, but no chance of that. I'm feart of surgeons, who until recently were transecting cadavers. They will not be practising on my sagging flesh. I will continue to take the two tartan tablets, which allow me to pee more frequently than I need to.

I walked back over the bridge to the other platform on the lookout for cameras. It was a case of my needs must and take the consequences. *'Sorry officer I have a medical condition.'* I walked to the far end of the platform, into the bushes under the sycamore tree and onto the privet, rhododendron and blackcurrant. What relief! I am now standing in an area of a brush and rubble clearing opposite Hoods Well, 1843. I was born a century later. Across from the railway line, the corner of Princes and John Wood Streets, where I can see all the way to the other side of the River Clyde shoreline to a patchwork quilt of fields and hydro lines on the top of the hill. Press on voyageur. A gentle breeze blows up the line, the train from the opposite direction is due any minute now. It has been a successful day, for me, at any rate.

Tuesday 12/06/2007

8:30 a.m. Home. I called Jim, deputy leader of Midlothian Council, about their donation of surplus educational resources. He told me that the five PFI/PPP new build school projects were behind schedule. *'This might work in your favour. Sorry we can't offer you any free storage space,'* he said. He took my telephone number and said he would get back to me some time.

Wednesday 13/06/2007

8 a.m. Home. It is wet and grey. I am awaiting a call from the port manager of Forth Ports Plc, Mr Gordon Clark. I called Jim of WH Malcolm Transport Ltd, responsible for container management. Called Ever Green. Stuart. *'We don't deal in containers,'* he said. I am now chasing around all over the place trying to locate a storage facility, a big secure warehouse in an industrial space. Called Andrew of Scottish International Relief. He has gone to a conference. Sustainable Partnerships, what are they, Furniture Aid? Maersk Sales I am told to speak to Stuart in the Southampton office; Maersk, Port of Felixstowe, John; Andy at Maersk in Leeds, container sales.

(Benefit of hindsight: As I read and reflect on these diary entries this afternoon [Saturday 28/02/2020)], some 14 years later, this is where I should have stopped my 'gung-ho' [Eric's phrase] and feverish collection of school furniture. But no, my pig-headed, stubborn, bulldog teeth-in-the-bone self would not let go at this point. Since Midlothian Council were not prepared to assist me to store, even on an albeit temporary basis, their 'donations' of furniture, I should have said 'no, thank you,' since I did not have the capacity to store their unwanted educational furniture at that time, and therefore I was unable to accept them. Instead, I was about to purchase another 40-foot ocean freight container. Madness. Was I bipolar? A manic depressive, self-diagnosed, borderline fruit and nut case? I call Kenny Falconer at the construction firm Skanska.)

10:11 p.m. It has been a long day here at home on my own. I have been on the phone most of the day but I have managed, I hope, to secure some storage thanks to Bryce Stuart of Colliers, who passed on my request to someone, who in turn contacted Safe Storage who have offered me SPACE, which is a big step forward: so don't weaken now!

I am no longer alone – with me are my family, who are worried greatly about my foolhardy path. Manic depressive.

I call Beth Murphy of Book Aid International. Thank-you notes to: Bryce Stuart of Colliers; Gordon Clark, port manager; Jude Ferguson, store manager, new Craighall, Fort Kinnaird; IDEAS (International Development Education Association), Scotland; Martha Ware, manager, School Aid; Ranfurly Library Trust: Caroline Simmons, Radio Forth. *'It's called hot desking,'* she said. *'In that case, this telephone and the desk, and me should have gone up in flames months ago,'* I said.

Thursday 14/06/2007

Called 'Glasgow the Caring City'; called Councillor Muirhead. No reply. I received a positive response from Kenny at Skanska, Scotland. He suggested that Midlothian Council might be willing to allow me to store their donation of surplus educational resources in one of their vacant schools due for demolition, for which his firm has been given the contract, until I am ready to load it into containers. *'It may be worth discussing with the council,'* he said; storage at no cost, a sensible and sustainable solution, is what I require. This I will do.

Friday 15/06/2007

8:50 a.m. Home. I am tired, not feeling up to much. I am waving but drowning most of the time. I am determined to hang on in there. I was listening to a Radio 4 programme about BRAC Micro Finance in Bangladesh. I contacted Professor Rosa, the George David Chair of Entrepreneurship and Family Business, and Head of Group Entrepreneurship and Innovation, William Robertson

Saturday 16/06/2007

Building, Edinburgh University. He was not forthcoming. Mince! He said a course was being offered in January 2008. Is there a demand and a market in the developing world for surplus educational resources from the United Kingdom and the rest of the EEC?

Where? And if so, how best for me to go about creating an entity that will meet and fulfil that need? What are the skills that I will need to acquire? What are the skills that I have already acquired? I have a track record of failure, have I not?

(As I go over these words this afternoon, Friday 21 January 2022, post-covid readjustment, I recall something Elon Musk said recently. 'Failure is irrelevant, unless it is catastrophic.')

1:30 p.m. I was speaking to someone at the Midlothian Council education office. Self-funded with limited potential. I have taken on an amount of educational resources that I am unable to handle.

4:30 p.m. I received an email from the principal of St Paul's Government School, The Model School, Grenada; I spoke to Stephen, janitor of RPS and gave him my card, also to Robert, principal PE teacher at the secondary school and gave him a card. I am forging a new identity for myself under the gaze of my detractors. *'You had the wind taken out of your sails,'* she said. *'Well, if that's so, then I will have to wait for the next puff of wind.'*

Saturday 16/06/2007

2:26 p.m. The Big Green Box. The Boat Yard. Grey and wet – a Scottish winter in the middle of summer. Gordon has just come by to see what he can scrounge. He has got the eyes of a magpie, yet he has been kind to me and I like him. He found a good pair of walking boots, minus the laces, from which I had scraped dried silage a while back. I had found them in a bin bag outside the depot. *'I can wear them!'* he tells me excitedly. He tries them on. They fit. Gordon has just left.

6:42 p.m. Home. Marion is in the kitchen making supper. David and Johanna are watching telly. I didn't get much done this afternoon. I put in an appearance at the Caribbean Hurricane Relief Depot, to let the passers-by know I was still in town. I spoke to Michael who works in Aberdeen, another yachtie. He helped us shift the ocean freight container back in April. There are now 119 boxes and counting.

Leyton, apprentice car mechanic in his dad's garage, and his cousin from Hamilton in Lanarkshire, came by and reappeared with some mackerel that they had caught off the end of the breakwater (that Martin is constructing for Stirling Yacht Services Ltd's. A marina, truck load of rocks by truck load of rocks from the quarry on the other side of the island, which he hauls himself), and which the generous young fishermen gave to me.

In return I said they could choose a book, instead the cousin wanted a box of new pencils. I said he could have one for every year of his age. He took 14; he didn't seem as old as that. And I gave him £3. I am now going to clean the mackerel and ice them after tea. Then Bill, driving a brand-new, box blue Ranger Rover, stopped by inquiring about the island's yacht club. I referred him to John who was working on a yacht in the boat shed, and then he came by, interested in what I was doing, and I gave him by business card and the *Herald* puff. I was impressed by his motor. I had always wanted to be among the angels, trouble is you can't read their hearts. *'Who do you think you are, David, handing out business cards, for goodness, sake? That's a good question. I think I am me. Just reinventing myself. So please back off, and leave me alone.'*

Monday 18/06/2007

7:54 p.m. Home. Yesterday afternoon the head teacher of one of the island schools called to see how I was. *'How are you, David?'* she asks. *'I am a lot better now that you have just called,'* I said. Bless her. She said that their school was disposing of a lot of school furniture and was I interested? *'Yes please. Thank you very much,'* I said.

I am not going to stop this collecting of school resources – if not, what else can I do in this place? This activity, in a curious way, in spite of the pressure, is keeping me busy and my mind free of itself and what has happened to me. She will let me know when she wants it uplifted. Second-hand containers? Pentalver. Stuart Jarvis CEO? Howard, who takes no prisoners, called and said he liked the bar of Grenada Chocolate that I sent; I called Jude, Safe Storage, Musselburgh, who will let me have some space. How much is some space? Called Councillor Muirhead's office. He might call me back; Jeff/Nigel, Blue Sky containers; SEACO Anthony Hutchins. I am attending a speed networking marathon in Edinburgh on 4 July where I might find My Team? I require business expertise, strategic planners, marketing skills, budget control spreadsheet etc. etc. Strathclyde University Business School; Heriot Watt University Business School, Jim Johnstone.

Tuesday 19/06/2007

8:35 a.m. Home. To do: see the local builders; make arrangements to collect surplus educational resources from an island school; contact Jim Clark of WH Malcolm Transport Ltd, again, who had left a message for me to call him.

I was recently inspired by The Aloha Spirit, the Hawaiian surfer who would rescue anyone in difficulty; giving without expectation of return.

9:45 a.m. I am going nowhere today. I am becalmed in the emotional and in the spiritual doldrums, entangled in the Sargasso Sea of being a nothing and going nowhere.

(Could I have told you then, I was suffering from depression or admitted to that fact? No.)

Home. Contact: Robert the haulier at 6 p.m. about containers and storage; Leanna, the journalist; Stephen, editor of the *Herald* Society Supplement; the President of the Institute of Caribbean Studies, Washington DC.

Wednesday 20/06/2007

8:40 a.m. Home. That's David and Johanna, two of my best friends, out into the pouring rain to get their bus for school. David took the two bags of kitchen waste with him to be recycled. He is taller than I am now.

I have switched on the computer. I hope to get a reply from Midlothian Council before too long. Will they help me to collect and temporarily store the fit-for-purpose educational resources that will remain in the 14 schools after their closure? I feel somewhat at a loss this morning. I want to be busy doing something useful and to be gainfully employed in meaningful work of some kind. In the spam box there was confirmation of the Edinburgh Chamber of Commerce Speed Networking session event marathon on 4 July. *'The best value membership package of any business organisation in Scotland.'*

Contact: John on 21 June regarding a loan of a Russell container; call Cameron, Ecosse World Express; call Sharon, finance manager Argyll and Bute Council, Strategic Finance, Community Services. They helped out on 11th August 2005 and contributed £1,225 towards the cost of the first shipment of educational resources, will they assist again?

Thursday 21/06/2007

Newbattle College haven't returned my call. I was speaking to Nina at Maersk regarding Pentalver. Give John at Denholm Bahr Ltd, Liverpool a call (containers – loan of them? Cheap to buy? Where? Export/import, or something: what? Finance issues. Storage issues). Call: Keith, Inverclyde Council Press; Pentalver (what's their number?); call John, Russell Transport MD; call the *Herald* about website cd and copies from editor Stephen Naysmith of journalist Leanna MacLarty's article of 5 June.

Transport? Call Denis Devlin, Frank Kay, Jimmy Hewitt, Edinburgh City Council, regarding possible help from them with the uplift of surplus resources from the 14 Midlothian Schools?. *'If all else fails, call me back,'* said James, Ben Mundell Transport Ltd, Tarbert; call the Grenada High Commission, London and Robin Swaisland, Agency for Reconstruction and Relief, Botanical Gardens, St George's Grenada; call Kenny Falconer, Skanska;

9:50 p.m. I have been speaking to Robert in Airdrie, Martin's friend. He tells me that he has an old refrigerated container. *'Are you still teaching?'* he asks. I ignore the question. Why should I bring all that up now? He delivered my first 40-foot ocean freight container to the boatyard on 25 April 2006. *'You had my number all that time?'* Yup. It's a start. Somewhere to store the next donation. Wait and see. I am now clutching at straws.

(I was to rise above my feelings of inadequacy, record of failure, and a medical condition, and become empowered for action, to make things happen when I dealt with complete strangers whose word was their bond.)

Thursday 21/06/2007

---

9 a.m. Home. *'Run out of plate,'* said John. *'What do you mean by that, John?'* I asked. *'It means that your 40-foot ocean freight* *container, which you told me you bought from Freight Container Services (Scotland) Ltd, can no long be certificated. It is no longer seaworthy,'* he said. I had called John at Denholm Bahr Ltd in Liverpool, who was cluing me in on 'boxes'. Expiry dates, marine insurance etc. *'When you buy the container, you buy it in plate. Nae use, it'll cost ya more in the long run. You don't know everything, for everything changes daily,'* said John. I am grateful to him since he talked me through part of the logistics process of shipping my first container to Grenada back on Friday 1 July 2005.

9:20 a.m. Home. I was speaking to Tom Walker, the container, boiler and tank inspector, about the plating and replating of containers so that they can be made wind, watertight and seaworthy. I then spoke to Stuart at Pentalver, Southampton, who Tom suggested I call. He in turn told me to call Andy in Leeds, who tells me that the next two containers (Maersk boxes) are mine at £700 each – two-thirds less than Freight Containers Service (Scotland) Ltd. Check The Surplus Educational Supplies Foundation business records.

I asked if he could put my payment on hold until I had paid Howard for the last one. *'No problem,'* he said.

Friday 22/06/2007

5:35 a.m. Home. I am up early. It is a beautiful morning and the birds are singing. I have created so much to do, and to think about, for myself. I am reaching way beyond my capacity. I am going to punch above my weight today; Kung Fu high kicker. I have switched on the computer. Ding dong.

9 a.m. I called Paul Fisher, managing director of Air Link, regarding the tariff on Marion's Entrepreneurs Export of Toiletries to the Bel Air Children's Home in Calliste, St George's, Grenada.

Monday 25/06/2007

10 a.m. Antonia from UNIPAC Freight Ltd called and is going to quote me a price to airfreight toiletries.

12:10 p.m. I have just spoken to Les. *'It's not my furniture ... most heavily taxed and governed country in the world.'* He said he would speak to the head teacher vis-à-vis the furniture/resources etc. that will be left at the island secondary school later this year.

1:45 p.m. I have just been speaking to Paul, Ecosse World Express. Cameron, Airlink, Inchinnan Road, Glasgow Airport, has just told me that his firm will airfreight Marion's Primary 2's Efforts in Enterprise to the Bel Air Children's Home in Grenada at a reduced cost of £120! Wonderful. Write a thank-you letter. To do: go up to St Andrews PS to collect resources; see Sam Bolton and Mr Moncrieff, the janitor and head teacher respectively. Everything is provisional, from one moment to the next, as I try to determine what resources they will or will not let my Surplus Educational Supplies have.

2 p.m. I have been speaking to the other janitor, who is going on holiday and referred me to the *other* janitor. I can't get a commitment one way or the other from these people. It is par for the course on the island, I should know that by now and not expect anything different after living here for 17 years.

Monday 25/06/2007

I worked in the garden and stayed off the telephone. Marion phoned this afternoon to tell me that an Ecosse World Express truck, along with their managing director, Paul, had come to her school to collect the 10 boxes of toiletries that her Primary 2 class had collected (with the help of other classes in Inverkip PS) and to make arrangements to forward the boxes by airfreight to the Bel Air Children's Home in Calliste. Tom Walker has agreed to inspect the container at the boatyard tomorrow. I learn it is not possible for Martin to use the crane to lift it on that day.

I received an email from Malcolm, VSO in Dublin, who is interested in my offer of educational resources. Will get back to him. Charles Cameron called at 8:44 p.m. while I was patching my trousers; email from Leanna, who had asked for my website CD not returned; Gorebridge Primary School have 1,000 items to offer. The building is due for demolition.

Terry, Midlothian Council. I had to keep on calling him, were it not for my PERSISTENCE; I called Kenny, Skanska UK, who had suggested to me that I ask Midlothian Council if the surplus resources coming from the 14 schools could be stored temporarily in one of the schools that is due for demolition. Yes! A temporary solution. Problem solved.

Wednesday 27/06/2007

7:06 a.m. Home. Cloudy sky. There are slivers of blue above my head. The uncertain expectancy of my new beckons me forward. Marion is off the island. Amy, David and Johanna are asleep: I am holding the fort for them. Call: Lorraine, Midlothian Council, Education Department. *'I will let Anna Robertson know that you still want to be kept in the loop,'* she said.

(The risks that I took during the years 2008–2017 turned out to be to my disadvantage, and I had to take the consequences – such as when a 40-foot container shipment of educational resources was stolen on delivery at the port in St Georges, Grenada in 2011 and near financial embarrassment when I was unable to pay for a container that I ordered in 2013.)

(Tuesday 03/03/2020. In the here and now? For the moment I retype, revise and reflect on the diary record of those years 2005–2017, which is enough work to keep me occupied)

2:30 p.m. Home. I called the construction site agent at the proposed new joint campus regarding the demolition of the school where I had been senior teacher from 1990 to 1991, to see what could be salvaged. *'Can I have some of it?'* was my message. He calls me back and won't give me the name of the demolition firm who have been given the contract to demolish the school; I call Robert regarding storage.

Thursday 28/06/2007

9:35 a.m. Home. I am back on the telephone. Called the Guyana High Commission, London, and left a message with their educational attaché or equivalent. No joy. Called Belize HC no answer. Called Cerio Lewis, High Commissioner to St Vincent and the Grenadines, London. *'I am also a teacher. My name is Maxwell Charles, I will speak with the High Commissioner,'* he said.

10:45 a.m. I was speaking to Hugh who is based in Motherwell and who runs a charity shop which helps and supports a school for the blind in Romania. He tells me that his charity is strapped for funds because of having to pay water rates etc. £700 per year to the council, and transport to Romania costs a fortune.

For Friday 29/06/2007: call the janitor of the secondary school. For Saturday: write to Councillor Muirhead (his catchment/bailiwick includes Gorebridge Primary School); for Guyana, Laleshwar Singh; Maxwell Charles acting HC for St Vincent and the Grenadines.

Saturday 30/06/2007

11:23 a.m. Back out in the boatyard. It is grey, cool and windy. I have been here since 9:45 a.m. Inventory and boxing a donation of surplus resources from Inverkip PS. Now.

6:05 p.m. Home. I am showered, fed, loved, helped and sheltered. I could not ask for more and I don't take any of it for granted. Roll it back: before I forget to record the end of this day I shall record the highlights of it here.

Nick accompanied by my two young friends and former pupils arrived to unload a second delivery of over 16 tables, which had to be stored outside the container. It started to drizzle. Craig and myself later managed to stack and stow all of the tables, but for three. 40-foot ocean freight container GSTU8958639 US 43101C87 is now fully loaded and ready to go, providing Tom Walker, on Monday 9 July, gives it another ISO/seaworthy inspection certificate. I got wet in the rain tidying up. I was chatting to Martin who is a brick. I cycled back home in the wind and rain. I need to get an official bill of lading and a piece list. See John, Denholm Bahr Ltd, Liverpool, call for advice. On arrival home I found a lovely card *'For You Teacher. You're the Best,'* from two of my former pupils. Bless them all. They had tooted their horn as I pedalled back along the road earlier. There was are reply to my email to Alan Reid MP.

Monday 02/07/2007

8:24 a.m. Home. I am getting ready to set out into a brand-new day. To do: post correspondence to Alan Reid MP for a supporter; to Councillor Jim Muirhead, Midlothian Council, Ward 6; to Cerio Lewis, High Commissioner for St Vincent and the Grenadines.

David, my right hand, is coming with me to the local builders' merchants to let them know that I no longer need transport to shift resources from a school, and to thank them for their kind offer, then head to the boatyard to tidy the Caribbean Hurricane Relief Depot as I had just chucked in there what I had removed from the ocean freight container on Saturday afternoon. Also, I must tidy up round the back of the boat shed.

Call the multi-skilled janitor tomorrow as he still has stuff. *'Dae yeh want it?'* he asked. *'Yes please, Billy. Thank you very much,'* I replied.

Wednesday 04/07/2007

11:03 p.m. Home. It has been a long, brilliant day, in which we have been granted journeying mercies when I was at the wheel of the car and enabled to accomplish what we had set out to do this morning. David is a great help and support to me.

While on our way over to the builders' merchants I saw his 4x4 parked at the side of the road. He's on his mobile. I wait till he has finished and he winds down the window. He stares me down. *'What are you after now?'* he asks. I gave him my 'marketing' spiel in reply. I tell him that I am looking for businesses on the island and on the mainland to sponsor the containers. *'Give me numbers. I'll think about it. Grenada is no good to me,'* he said.

I had a hot chocolate out of the machine at the builders' merchants, and went back to the post office and then along to the bank where I met Mike from England (town councillor from the south coast) and we have a chat. *'I've got Type 2 diabetes. I only believe in the now. No yesterday. No tomorrow. Only today,'* he said. A wise man. He is always smartly turned out. He thought I had handled his nibs, the aforementioned, well when I didn't quote a price for him there and then for sponsoring the Big Green Box. I tidied the depot. Home for lunch, which David cooked.

I went back out to the boatyard to start removing stuff for the municipal cowp: what the manager refers to as 'crap'. Martin, who has been very busy making pontoons for the marina, lent us the van. Home safe. I have so much to be thankful for.

Wednesday 04/07/2007

5:09 a.m. c/o The Grove, Kilbarchan, Renfrewshire – our home on the mainland. I am not just shipping containers of surplus-to-requirements educational resources, I am linking schools and communities here in Scotland to others in Blue Planet Earth Global Village; that's what I think doing. I'm currently reading *'How to change the world'* and it's giving me ideas. I am setting out later this morning for a speed networking session at The Hub (top of the Royal Mile), Castlehill, Edinburgh from 9 a.m.

Yesterday, Billy called. *'I'll see what there is in the dunny for you,'* he said. *'That's great, Billy. Many thanks.'* Later, David and I went over the school, where Billy showed us what was being flung out of the school and into the skip: more good quality school furniture. He said I could come by any morning and collect it, providing I can get the loan of the van from the boatyard. Then DA and I drove up to the Shanks & McEwen's council cowp and tipped the computers and monitors that had been expertly loaded on Monday afternoon. They had been stored behind the boatshed. He wants to put another container in the space that I have used/taken up for nearly two years now.

Then I went back into the town. I parked and collected DA's watch from McKinnon's who fixed the watch strap, no charge. Across to the Electric Bakery, purchased pies and sausage rolls. Home. Lunch with the family in the sunshine.

I am now heading into the unknown of yet another day.

Thursday 05/07/2007

5:11 p.m. Home. David and I worked to clear round the back of the Yacht Services boat shed. We made about four trips to the cowp. *'You are a man of your word,'* said Richard, who works with Robert and Peter up at the recycling centre. I had accumulated resources that I was unable to hold on to long enough, until such time as I had located deserving beneficiaries.

For tomorrow: work with Billy the janitor to lend him a hand to clear the dunny; 10:45 a.m. be at Moat Centre to collect gift of soccer balls from Jim the football coach; be at the boatyard later to complete the tidying up behind the boat shed and tidy the depot.

Friday 06/07/2007

5 p.m. Home. I set off early this morning. I was at the school by 8:30 a.m. where I met the janitor. We started clearing the basement of accumulated odds and ends. At 10:15 a.m. Billy went off to get us a bacon roll and a cup of tea each. I worked until 10:30 a.m. On the way back I met Jim who had some footballs for me. Good on him. Back here for some lunch. I received a call from Anne Marie of a sports development charity based in Loughborough who was interested in what I was doing, as she wanted to send educational resources and sports equipment worldwide. I am to contact on our return from holiday.

I set off back up the road. Just before leaving I got a call to tell me that a supporter had left a bag of shoes for me at the Caribbean Hurricane Relief Depot. *'Go for it!'* he said as I cycled past him one afternoon last year. I met George. We chatted and I tidied up a wee bit and put up the Caribbean Hurricane Relief banner. Arran, Jack and Adam, former pupils at the school, came by; they were at a loose end. I gave them a football. I called the Edinburgh Chamber of Commerce and spoke to Carrie regarding the protocols of making contact with the Grenada Chamber of Commerce and Industry. She is to call me back. I went to the bank to change funds for our family's holiday. Oh! I met Betty and Elaine from the port and her sister from Italy.

Monday 09/07/2007

9:15 p.m. Home. This morning Tom Walker called to say that he would be on the 12 o'clock boat. Sure enough. I called Martin at the boatyard to confirm that it was convenient for the inspection of the ocean freight container to take place. Marion drove me in to the ferry terminal to meet Mr and Mrs Walker. The sun was shining brightly. When we arrived at the boatyard Martin had the crane ready. *'Plenty of meat underneath,'* commented Tom when he looked under the Big Green Box. In spite of the corrosion underneath there was not enough rust to make the container unseaworthy so could get an ISC certificate. What a relief it was for me to learn that, after wondering whether or not I would be able to have the container delivered to Grenada. It weighed 11 and a half tons. We came back home for a cuppa.

Tuesday 10/07/2007

Collect money from the bank. Cheque to Ecosse World Express to pay airfreight of toiletries donation from Inverkip PS to The Bel Air Children's Home, Grenada, and make sure I have enough funds to cover Tom's inspection of container fee.

(My Bajan pride and industry. I wished to be, as far as possible, beholden to none. I would learn that operating freelance, solo, would lead me into great difficulty. Why was I a loner? An outsider for as long as I can remember? Upbringing, circumstances etc.? Where do I go from here? What do I do now, from here on, that will engage me in meaningful, constructive and a sustainable work that will remain long after I have gone?)

I met Darryl from South Africa this morning while at CBPL Ltd. He has a cynical sense of humour. A what's the point, why bother attitude? When he asked me what I was attempting to achieve he then described to me a recent project that he had been engaged in in rural Natal, a grassroots project with local farmers. This project, which had ended in failure, was showing them how they could produce methane from cattle manure. He was scathing, saying that it was hopeless and impossible to bridge the cultural divide between white and black native South Africa, where all development is politicised and is made almost impossible because of corruption; he was contemptuous of the Natal native farmers. He spoke in a strong, white South African accent. He continued with this remark, *'They don't want the White Man's cast-offs,'* referring to my, what he thought, were misguided efforts to ship surplus educational resources to the Hurricane Ivan-devastated island of Grenada in the West Indies. I called the Highlands and Islands Enterprise Board, which could be a possible source of a grant, funds, assistance and advice.

Chapter Seven

The Family Visit Grenada

Thursday 12/07/2007

3:45 p.m. (8:45 p.m. Scottish time) Grenada, West Indies. We are staying at Gaulin Cottage, Lance aux Epines, parish of St George. Breeze blowing, dogs barking. The sun is shining on the page as I write this. The Caribbean Sea is slapping Lance aux Epines beach. We arrived at Point Salines airport at around 2:45 p.m. We were through immigration and met by Joanna with a notice from Caribbean Horizon Tours, who took us out to a minibus driven by Fiona who tells me that her grandad Mr Southall is from Barbados and whose gran lives in Belize.

Well, here we all are safe and sound in Gaulin Cottage: luxurious accommodation, immaculately kept to a high housekeeping standard and a supply of groceries in the kitchen cupboards. I made a cup of tea for us all. In for a swim, but first I wet my feet and trouser bottoms along the beach with David. In for a dip. I met Paul, an informant who gave us some background on the local scene. He sits under a coconut palm tree whittling bracelets from petrified coral. The other cottages are: Frigate, Sandpiper, Osprey, Swallow, Hummingbird and Pelican. Rustling of the breeze in the coconut fronds.

We managed to make a long, nine hour journey by aircraft. I sat next to Dharaj on his way to Trinidad via Tobago. He comes originally from southern Trinidad, past the town of Siparia. His grandparents on his father's side came from India, he thinks Uttar Pradesh, as indentured labourers on the sugar, cocoa and coffee plantations. He works for a firm that teaches engineering

Thursday 12/07/2007

apprentices at the Pointe-à-Pierre oil refinery, where my Uncle Valdemar Hanschell (Wally) worked for Shell in the forties and fifties. Wally left towards the end of the latter decade to work for Texaco in Milford Haven, Pembrokeshire and lived at Pembroke Dock. The Pointe-à-Pierre and surrounding housing complex, golf course and exclusive country club, are now rebranded as Petrotin. We had a lot to chat about. He told me that his home is in Lewisham and, before leaving for the United Kingdom, he worked on his parents' smallholding during the day and went to the secondary school in Siparia, southern Trinidad, three evenings a week. He is a graduate of the University of London.

Dharaj taught science subjects at the comprehensive school and now prefers what he is doing, in a contract teaching post at the only educational institution of its kind in Trinidad, as those who wish to study engineering have to do so at the University of the West Indies at the St Augustine campus. Once upon a time the Imperial College of Tropical Agriculture. I gave him my copy of George Soros's *Age of Infallibity*. I'll have to get another copy. Well worth reading and trying to get to grip with his take on the world scene.

I have got to watch the sunlight and move back into the shade. A little red crab has not long been crawling over my bare foot.

8:40 p.m. We have just come back from The Red Crab restaurant where we had a delicious meal of Grenadian Creole cuisine. The owner comes from Inverness! Scots have flocked to the West Indies for hundreds of years. *(I was given* Blood Legacy *by Alex Renton for Christmas 2022. Scotland's power washed away historical involvement in the slave trade.)*

We walked to the restaurant and back. There is a light breeze blowing in off the sea. The sound of whistling frogs creeps into the drawing room and dining room of the palatial Gaulin Cottage. There is a flower arrangement of croton leaves, ginger lilies and strelitzias on the dining room table.

Friday 13/07/2007

8:10 a.m. The sun is coming up over the roof of Gaulin Cottage. Marion and I have walked back down the hill after going into the Prickly Bay Marina, where we were chatting to Sharon who was on duty at the security office – Grenada immigration process yachties from all over the Blue Planet. We were chatting. *'Dere's a lotta poverty in Grenada. I live up in Saint Andrew and dere is people dere, livin' below de poverty line. I no up de top, but I makes enough to live. My eldest son gotta job and the younger one he finished school and he keann get a job, but he doesn't lime about. My dream is to do animal husbandry and raise pigs. Dere is no more nutmeg trees after Hurricane Ivan in 2004,'* said Sharon, speaking from her heart.

If I continue to sit at this picnic table any longer. I am going to have to crank up the parasol or put my hat on.

8 p.m. Marion, Amy and David are reading. The fan turns slowly above my head. It's quite humid. Frogs are singing outdoors. Milo the taxi driver took us to the Grand Anse Mall where we ate food from the grill run by Syrians who have recently settled in the island. We stopped there for groceries and back 'home'.

This morning Paul was hustling his wares, making bracelets for Amy and Johanna. I met Victor, who gutted two red snappers from the huge seine net which he and his fellow fishermen spent over four hours hauling in to the beach. Poor catch for all their effort. I met Tim, the proprietor of Lance aux Epines. I pinned his ears back with my project and gave him my card. Later I met Mr Big Corporation from Toronto, a Grenadian done good in Canada, who told me that he was having a big house built on the ridge overlooking the bay. He said he was 'meetin' with Keith and Brenda next week. He had an oratorical way of speaking. He engaged me in conversation and then abruptly fobbed me off. Tomorrow is another day.

Saturday 14/07/2007

5:15 p.m. I am sitting outside at the weathered and unvarnished picnic table and I haven't put the parasol up. David is out there in the bay with snorkel, googles and flippers. Amy and Johanna have gone for a swim. Marion is getting changed.

A little while ago Milo brought us back from a marathon tour of the Isle of Spices, through all of the parishes of Grenada. He came for us at 9 a.m. We drove around and through the town of St George's and stopped at the market where folk were arriving from the airts and pairts to do their shopping. Milo manoeuvred the minibus up the narrow steep streets and parked. I bought some thyme from a vendor. On to Concord and up the narrow valley road to The Falls, where A, D and J went swimming. I met Jerry from Pittsburgh, Pennsylvania, here on the island for a short while with his international fibre-optic cable company. He told me that his sister is a teacher. Along to the coastal towns of Victoria, Grand Roy, Gouyave and St Patrick's, where we had lunch and met a Bulgarian. Onward down dale and up the hill to the rum distillery where I thought of Dad, who liked his rum punches, rum cocktails, and rum and soda water, which made me recall the unhappy memories of living in gated communities in Trinidad: Waterloo Estate, Carapachaima village and Brechin Castle, Couva town.

Next, Caroni Ltd sugar estates (a subsidiary of Tate & Lyle) and their associated sugar factories, where I saw and smelled the bagasse at this no-frills Grenadian 18th- and 19th-century artisan sugar machinery factory. I don't think the methods have changed much, or the actual fabric, in several centuries. Huge pans filled with fermenting syrup. Fletcher of Derby conveyor belt. Here can be seen the oldest waterwheel, in working order, in the Caribbean. The family directors all had a taste of white rum. I let it past my lips as a nod to all those who did and as result it led to their downfall.

From there we were driven to the Levera National Park and on through to the parish of Saint Andrew and upward into the Grand Etang National Park. David purchased Cokes and we gave two monkeys bananas and they peeled chenips 'ackies', which Milo had purchased for us on the road up to the park, with their nimble fingers. We went into the park centre which overlooked the crater lake. Back down the other side of the 'cordilliera' and up the side of Richmond Hill and 'home' to Gaulin Cottage. Safe and sound.

This morning, after ablutions, I set off to walk to Prickly Point with panoramic views up and down the indented coastline of bays and points, with the mountains to my left running up the middle of the Island of Spices, from north to south, or from south to north, from where I was standing. There were large (as far as I could see, unoccupied), palatial bungalow-type houses on either side of the road with windows tightly shuttered, from where I heard barking dogs. Coming up the road I saw a gaulin, a Caribbean heron, drinking from a pool of water on the public access road to Lance aux Epines beach. And on the way back down the road a young mum cradling her young child, a baby not many days old. I bid her a good morning as we walked past each other and she replied, *'It's good to walk.'*

On return from our tour of the island I found a note from Raymond of the St Paul's Government School PTA, who had come by here, which I followed up with a telephone call and shortly after called the principal. She hopes to come by here at 2 p.m. tomorrow. *'I don't think you are ready for the Pink House,'* she said, which is Grenada's equivalent of the Lochgilphead Hospital in Scotland, or Jenkins in Barbados.

The sun is beginning to dip over the young coconut palm trees on my right. Ground doves are cooing mournfully over my left shoulder, *'Nothing lasts, nothing lasts,'* but I will continue to make hay while the sun shines for us. The intermittent shushing of little waves on the beach.

Sunday 15/07/2007

The family got to swim at the Falls.

Sunday 15/07/2007

8:50 p.m. The frogs are singing. Overhead fan whirring above my head. David is in the lounge reading all about Harry Potter. Marion is looking for the front door key. This was the day of deputations.

The principal tells us that she is off on holiday to New York on Tuesday: she drives a 4x4 with the words 'Sexy and Black Beauty' writ large on the windscreen. *'We in de country, and we don't get nuttin' from de Ministry,'* she said. Mr Webster is the assistant principal: I managed to get him to smile and laugh, but it was tough going. He calls the shots. *'Ah tell you, I know where de next container is to go and dat's to us,'* said Claudette.

We'll see, one thing at a time. They were very interested to peruse the inventory of 212 boxes back in the seaworthy ocean freight container back in the island port village.

I am very glad now that I made the time and all-consuming effort, over many days, of itemising nearly everything I put in those boxes. Mary, one of the accompanying members of staff, was very appreciative and couldn't believe it when she learned from the editor of one the local newspapers, that a container loaded with educational resources was on its way to their school from the West of Scotland. Raymond, PTA president, gave a firm handshake and was also very appreciative of my efforts, and of all those who have helped me in this initiative back on the Isle of Bute.

We made them welcome and served juice. I let them take time to read through my project file. Transparent. All above board. They are keen to receive ocean freight container GSTU8958639 – the Big Green Box. They will call for us on Tuesday at 10 a.m. to take us up to their school, which is being rebuilt. Later, Sharon from Horizon Tours and her friend from Trinidad, business woman and industrialist, came by with a gift of Julie mangoes. Kindness. Her friend told us that her dad lived on Carmody Road, Saint Augustine, Trinidad, where we once lived! (the other Hanschell family, who came down from the Land of the Flying Fish to the Land of the Humming Bird in 1950). She told us that she had a cosmetics factory in Tacarigua, where Mum used to take our cast-offs to the orphanage and magazines further up the road for the patients at the tuberculosis sanatorium at Caura, in the foot hills of the Northern Range.

Monday 16/07/2007

It has been a long and wonderful day. I served up my fish soup, which was not popular but good enough for me. This morning Marion and I walked out on Point Drive to Prickly Point. Barking dogs behind the wrought iron gates and high walls that surrounded the properties.

Later Amy accompanied us to the Prickly Bay Marina grocery minimart, run and owned by a Devonian. I met Charles, Grenadian born yacht master, and Michael the taxi driver. Marion read and swam. I got my face burned. Amy read, swam and burned her skin. Johanna swam, read, played table tennis and watched a widescreen television. David swam, snorkelled, read and joined the latter in the Games Room. I anticipated the visitors from St Paul's, and spieled my project, sold my initiative – not yet a social entrepreneurial cash cow, more of a shallow-pocketed philanthropic adventurer with big ideas. It's not a hobby, whatever you or anyone else, or any development economist might think. It is something I have yet to do, while I can, until I have been shown otherwise.

Monday 16/07/2007

6:10 p.m. I am outside sitting at the picnic table. Quiet. The Caribbean Sea is washing the shore. I have been doing my dhobi at the kitchen sink. Everything needful is provided at Gaulin Cottage. Well founded. A and D are reading. I think J is also. It has been another wonderful day so far. I met blind Patrick. *'I'm a struggler,'* he said. Crippled and a fighter in every fibre of his being. We met him on the beach and invited him over for a herbal tea.

This morning I set off early, while everyone was still asleep, and walked up to the roundabout and then out onto the Maurice Bishop Highway to the Frequente Industrial Estate. There I met Ricardo, proprietor of the Tea Pot. I gave him my testimony and he gave me a cup of coffee. He made enquiries as to the whereabouts of the Grenada Chamber of Commerce. Unit 11, just behind his restaurant. There I met Mr De Riggs. I left my project file with him: he can read the correspondence, puff etc. He seemed to know exactly the way forward for the venture, adventure, initiative. Casual in appearance, he had not tied his tie. We exchanged business cards. He told me that he would speak to several individuals who may be in a position to move the project forward and was glad to do so. *'What you want to set up is a semi-commercial venture,'* he said, and said he would contact me on Wednesday. He's got the A to Z and I have held nothing back. I am at the crossroads.

I went paddling with Marion and Amy in the banana kayak, out to the yachts, *Beothuk* of St John, Newfoundland, and one whose name I can't remember, of the Clyde. Links. Resonances. There's a breeze blowing through the trees that survived hurricanes Ivan and Emily. The frogs have started to sing. Paul the watchie is talking away on his mobile underneath the palm hut. This morning I met Lindon and Patrick, the gardeners. Cecilia the concierge was telling me about her family, her garden and what she grew. It's great to meet and talk with island folks.

Tuesday 17/07/2007

5:30 p.m. The sun is going down, still bright and hot. I am having to lower the parasol so I am not blinded by the sunlight. It has been a busy day and I shall recount some of the events here. Samuel was left with the responsibility of taking the Famous Five out to St Paul's Government School by Principal Anthea Peterkin. He arrived at Gaulin Cottage an hour earlier than arranged.

We made him welcome. He kindly took us on another small island tour up steep winding hill and mountain and down dale, around and over and along the ridges where the houses were built on stilts on the side of the mountains, overlooking precipitous drops below. We were met at 'The Model School' by Claudette, Mary and Karen, members of staff, and their smiling, alert and friendly

Tuesday 17/07/2007

The Hanschell family visiting the construction site of the rebuild of St Paul's Government School which had been destroyed by Hurricane Ivan in 2004.

students who were attending summer school, and Raymond, PTA president, of whom they spoke highly. We were shown around 'the school', which is also the village's community centre, which they have been using for the past two and a half years. There were makeshift classrooms separated by vintage chalkboards. We were then taken to the building site where the new premises of St Paul's Government School were being constructed. We were given hard hats before entering the site, and then given a tour by the enthusiastic and diminutive clerk of works site foreman. Tradesmen and labourers, busy all over the site, appeared oblivious to our presence.

I felt out of place. Useless. I would have been happier and more comfortable in my 'whiteness' if one of the workies had shouted out, *'Hey, bro, could you help me move this wheelbarrow out the* way,' or even acknowledged us with a greeting. I'm aware of my inability to do very much and lack of importance, really, in their scheme of things, but I was glad that the family had had a first-hand look at a school that was being rebuilt from scratch, and meet Grenadians who were getting on with the demanding work of reconstruction.

Samuel then drove us back into the metropolis of St George. He declined to join us for lunch at the Nutmeg restaurant, with its view overlooking the Carenage and small container port. I saw a ship loaded with containers leaving the harbour. We dined on vegetable rotis and hamburgers. Marion, Amy and Johanna stopped off at The Art Fabrik boutique. A sympatico proprietor. The we walked along the Grand Anse Road and hailed a minibus and back 'home'. I missed doorstepping Mr Frank of the Grenada Tourist Board Public Relations office, who had said he'd help me to raise the profile of my initiative with the local press. We'll have to wait and see.

J in for a swim. I'm tired. I will wet my skin in a wee while, that's D joining them for a dip. That's a gentle breeze cooling me down. Children's voices and laughter coming from the beach. Dogs barking, and planes roaring and screaming overhead. The airport is down wind towards Calliste at Point Salines I think.

Wednesday 18/07/2007

12:01 p.m. (Reading on the microwave digital clock.) I am chatting to Cecilia, concierge extraordinaire, as she sweeps the tiled kitchen floor. She has asked me for some more of my business cards. I am running low on them. I gave her a card for Mr McQuilkin. I received a telephone call from Leonora (who had been contacted by Paul the security), who is the principal of a school who is bringing some of her prize-winners here for tea and a swim on Friday 20 July. Magic!

There is sunshine on the page as I move my words across it.

Wednesday 18/07/2007

There was a tropical downpour early this morning, like bullets on the galvanised roof, as I had my time of quiet. I went along to the minimart at the Prickly Bay Marina waterside: there I met Lindon the manager and we shot the breeze for a while. He tells me that he has relatives in Canada and finds it difficult to see them, as every time he is able to he has to go down to Trinidad to get a visa; the poor and dispossessed face stricter immigration controls in the Global Village, while wealthy North Americans, and UK and Continental Europeans are free to come and go as they wish by plane and ashore off the constantly docking cruise ships.

I was chatting to Paul and invited him in for a for a cup of tea. He comes from a close-knit community up in the hills of St Andrew parish. His mum grows a variety of food crops. Later I was talking to Patrick, one of the gardeners, who tells me, *'My destiny is to go back to school.' 'To study what Patrick?'* I ask. *'Business. I want to be a business man,'* he replied.

M, A and J have gone for a walk along the beach. David is reading, I think, indoors. I am waiting, expectantly, to meet with, or hear a word from, the head, the leader of the Grenada Chamber of Commerce. The Gatekeeper. *'He who open, or keep de doors closed.'*

No, I see David has accompanied them on their stroll. There is a cooling breeze through the coconut palm fronds. The three bairns – and the Better Half is taking a photograph of them.

7:40 p.m. (Reads the time on the digital clock.) I have just washed the dishes. The crickets and frogs are singing awa'. The fan is whirring overhead. I heard Patrick calling to me, from outside, to tell me he wanted to change a US$50 note. I took him over to meet Milo the taxi driver who had just arrived, who told me he enjoyed the Julie mangoes and that the Blind Home had run out of gas to cook with.

I returned to gazing out across the bay through the grillwork and insect mesh. Then I saw David accompanying Paul, the beach entrepreneur, who I hoped had the two petrified coral bracelets which I had paid EC$55 each for. And the Better Half said to me, as we sat together all in a state of harmony, that we should have tattooed the word 'Mug' across our foreheads; mine at any rate. Paul told us that he had been seriously ill.

Later Paul the security guard phoned to ask if there was anything apart from ginger that I wished from their garden. *'If you do good it will follow you,'* he said. *It has Paul, and will follow you and all yours as well.* A promise for this believer. He went on to tell me that there were not many nice people in his village. *'Is just me and Granny,'* he said. He went on to tell me that he had gone to school with Tim B the proprietor manager of Lance aux Epines Cottages and they had played together, but he had changed.

Thursday 19/07/2007

6 p.m. The Famous Five Fae Bonnie Scotland have been here a week this afternoon, in the lap of salubrious Caribbean bespoke comfort. D, J and A are up at the Games Room. Marion is sitting beside me eating plantain chips and drinking a cup of tea. There have been heavy tropical showers all day. It is now quiet and cool. We all went snorkelling with The Aquanauts at Flamingo Bay aboard *The Sea Wolf.* I met Jeff and Linda from Pennsylvania and their big family. *'We hired a guy from Ireland. UNISYS is right next door to us,'* he said. The small electronically interconnected world of Blue Planet Global Village. I was chatting to David the maintenance man over a cup of tea. He knows Mr Ashby the principal of the Grenada Boys Secondary School. I gave him my card.

(I was later to deliver four more 40-foot ocean freight container loads of educational resources to Grenada government schools. I did not know it then. Not including the pending shipment to St Paul's Government School later that year, I had already shipped a total of two 20-foot and one 40-foot container. Over the next nine years there would be four more 40-foot ocean freight containers of educational resources to the

following schools: Calliste Government School, St Paul's Government School, Grenada Boy's Secondary School, Samaritan Presbyterian School and Woburn Methodist School in April 2016. David, the Lance aux Epines maintenance man, thought well of the Cuban government's contribution to the overall welfare of the Grenadian Nation, which he felt was slowly being dismantled faster since Hurricane Ivan on 7 September 2004. He had not time for the present regime.)

Friday 20/07/2007

6:10 p.m. Marion is reading, David is listening to his iPod, Johanna and Amy have just come in doors. It is a quiet and peaceful afternoon, with a gentle breeze moving the young coconut palm branches. This morning, Marion and I set off at around 7:15 a.m. walking to the roundabout at the far end of Point Drive Lance aux Epines road and along the Maurice Bishop Highway to the Frequente Industrial Estate, where we chilled out under the welcome awning of the Tea Pot. Marion had juice. I had coffee. At 8:45 a.m. we walked round to the Grenada Chamber of Commerce office for my appointment with Mr De Riggs, the chief executive, who we found to be very helpful and supportive. *'You have a good spirit,'* he said and gave me a list of names to contact.

Marion and I walked back, stopping off at the Republic Bank near the roundabout to cash our Travellers' Cheques and returned to Gaulin Cottage to find The Famous Three reading out of doors. I got on the telephone. At 1 p.m. we met Leonora, a colleague, and her team of prize-winning top readers, who had arrived by hired bus at the public car park, and brought them down to Gaulin Cottage. Marion made them welcome and comfortable. Well-mannered, dear children who had come from St Mary's R. C. School and who were on a tour as a treat for their successful academic efforts. Later Robin Swaisland dropped by. The best of British expertise. I gave him my project folder to peruse over the weekend and invited him for dinner on Sunday evening.

Johanna is still reading. Bless her. The rest of this firm's directors have moved indoors. Yesterday evening Paul the security gave me a bag of nutmegs and ginger from his family's garden way up in them there hills. It was through him contacting the principal of Saint Mary's RC that the party of students were brought here this afternoon. I felt it was a privilege for us to receive them. I have an appointment at the radio station tomorrow at 8 a.m.

Monday 23/07/2007

5:54 p.m. The sun is going down over the young coconut trees on the adjacent property where the oleander is in bloom with pink blossom. It is getting dark and the dogs are barking. Watch out I don't want another migraine just yet.

There is a welcome cooling breeze. I can't rise to poetic utterance, but that doesn't stop me from experiencing these precious moments of GRACE. What have I accomplished today? I walked out the compound of these grounds, which are maintained to an immaculate standard thanks to Patrick, Lindon and Kevin. I walked up the hill and around the corner to Prickly Bay Waterside. Michael wanted to charge me EC$40, no thanks, and walked back up Point Drive. An employee of Allan (businessman and accountant, who it turns out has connections with Scottish families who own plantations on the island), wearing thick silver bracelets, stopped and gave me a lift to the small Grand Anse minimart. I then got a minibus. I met the chef of the Mona Lisa restaurant who is from Venezuela (Santa Margarita Island). Into the Careenage and got directions for the Agency of Rural Transformation on Marrast hill. It was a steep climb up a cobbled street. Barlinnie bricks. A mother hen and her brood of chicks cross my path. It's getting hot and I kept climbing. And then found the address where I met Sandra. Shrewd with a sense of humour. *'You mean you givin' dese tings to de schools free of charge?'* she asked. *'Yes,'* I replied and I no ready for de Pink House.

Monday 23/07/2007

There is a big mango tree dripping fruit outside her large office door and a flamboyant tree in full bloom in the Westmoreland School grounds. She kindly walked me up the road to show me where to take the road to the roundabout. Sympatico but not a friend of Robin. I found Hubbard's palatial new department store on the Careenage and myself in front of Alan, who was sitting behind the reception desk. I left my project dossier with him. Another doorkeeper with his hands on other doors and perhaps on levers of power. I walked through the tunnel to the post office to post some postcards and purchased some stamps. I stopped off for a stale cutter and a Coke and back through the tunnel and into the light.

Oh! I forgot. I have left out visiting the radio station where I met Claris, who introduced me to a producer who interviewed me, and I was given utterance to express what had brought me to Grenada for the second time in just over a year. I am to return at 8 a.m. for a radio show. Keep on trucking.

I walked around the Careenage where I saw a posse of workers from China, wearing large straw hats, unloading a cargo from a landing craft on to the beach. I stopped at the Lexus Café for a Coke. A brand-new hostelry with a magnificent view of the coast up to Cinnamon Hill beach. I stopped off to say hello to Mr and Mrs DeFreitas who received me with a warm welcome. They invited me in but I said I had to push on. Made it 'home' safe and sound. I went for a swim with M, A and D.

Johanna is beside me here reading *Harry Potter* – top of their list at the moment. Yesterday we went on the *Star Wind V*, which I had seen tied up at the at the Port Louis. *'We no pleased wit dat man,'* he said, referring to a gentleman I had spoken to some months ago over the telephone. I met Connor from Ireland, whose firm is building a new marina for his nibs. *'Wah you tink of dat man. I think he's full of ...'* he said. Aboard the *Star Wind V* we met Terence and Kim fellow Bajans from Barbados. *'You went to Cane Field College? So did I, man!'* Terence exclaimed. (What I referred to as the Lodge School (1955–1961), which then was surrounded by fields of sugar cane and now?)

He is a policeman and ambitious. A good arm of the law. *'Be honest and know de law,'* he said. Another passenger aboard this cruise was Andrew, who is on the Isle of Spices with a boy's cricket team from Loughborough; he works for International Development. Taciturn tight-lipped Englishman. And there has got to be a Scotsman somewhere, round the corner, hiding in the bushes, on or below deck: sure enough there was Neil from Kirkcaldy, Kingdom of Fife, who grew up in Capshard, an actuary, now based in Port of Spain, Trinidad. He has been out here for 14 years, is cruising today with his charming family, he gave me his email.

It is still light. The sun has just disappeared below the horizon. The Caribbean Sea is washing the beach shore. I have just spoken to Paul the security man. *'Ah been at hospital all day,'* he said. I felt for him. I did not wish to be nosey.

It is now dusk and I can barely read this. Crickets? Or are they frogs? Metallic chirping. Amy who joined me earlier is now down at the shore. Johanna has joined me, wearing her West Indian Cricket Team top, and is trying to read *Harry Potter* without the light on. There is a small moon way up overhead. I can hear cars driven up the road and 4x4s driven recklessly. I am on the lookout for my Evening Star. I can smell Marion's cooking. There are some yachts out on the bay, some with their top mast lights on. I found my Lone Star, its way up over my left shoulder.

Tuesday 24/07/2007

2:52 p.m. 'Home'. I have been chatting with Linda. *'I am goin' to bring some ground nut cakes for yuh,'* she said. *'Many thanks,'* I said. *'Yoh goin' back Thursday?' 'Yes, Linda. All good things come to an end. We have all had a wonderful holiday on your beautiful and friendly island,'* I replied.

Tuesday 24/07/2007

I have shifted my position under the parasol for some shade. Tim the manager comes over, ignoring me, and says brusquely to Linda. *'Will you go now and sweep the cottage as a matter of urgency.'* A rude man.

It has been a busy morning. I was up and out, leaving the family asleep. I was met by Fletcher coming out of the Calabash Hotel driveway. EC$5 into the bus station. I walked up the steep hill, past the market, along, and up along the ridge road. Constant flow of traffic hurtling perilously close to me, poor white man, as I trudge up the hill. I continued until I arrived at a dilapidated, but still functioning, broadcasting radio station building.

9 a.m. I have been up here at **GBN STUDIOS** since 8:15 a.m. I walked up the hill from the Careenage. Earlier this morning I met Fletcher who works for Alan of Hubbard's Stores: he picked me up as I walked past the Coyaba Hotel. Here I met welcoming Claris Baker, operations manager of the Grenada Broadcasting Network, who graciously invited me into his tiny office. We chatted and Gloria arrived to sit at another desk. I was waiting to be interviewed by Kenroy on his programme. Claris comes from Ealing, he tells me, and that he left Grenada for Great Britain as a young boy. *'I call it home to home,'* he said and went on to tell me that he was a musician and once upon a time had played in a band that toured the Scottish Universities circuit. A real gentleman. We chatted for a while as he worked away at his laptop, which I looked upon enviously. Then Gloria came into the reception.

Quiet of the recording studio. I was soon in conversation. Muy sympatico. I gave Gloria our address. She approves of the project. Later in the recording studio for the interview I met Kenroy, a soul brother. I then headed back down the hill, enjoying the view now largely free of traffic, for my appointment with Mr Menzies at Huggins Ltd, who couldn't see me as arranged so I hoofed it through the tunnel and along to Hubbard's Department Store to collect my file, dossier, project file from Alan, where it was returned to me by his personal assistant Lucian with no comment, which is a comment in itself, is it not? I then walked back up the road and through the tunnel and up the hill to The Huggins Ltd business office. I had a meeting with Mr Menzies the CEO. He welcomed me, gave me a cup of coffee and listened carefully to my pitch. An authentic individual. We were on the same wavelength. He comes from Guyana, or as it was in my day, British Guyana. I left my file with him. And he said he would get back to me. I was glad I made the effort to take more steps of faith to retrace my steps to his office.

I walked back out through the tunnel and out and around the Careenage and into the Port Louis Victory Bar, where I treated myself to Coke. There I met Jan, a civil engineer from Jamaica, and we had a good blether, and with my thirst quenched I walked back up the road until I came to The British High Commissioner's office, where I was well received by the welcoming receptionist who recalled my contacting the High Commissioner, Vic Wallace, last year. Further up the road I stopped for a glass of crushed ice and cane juice. What a thirst quencher. Robin Swaisland drove past me with a toot of his horn. Here I am alone and yet not alone.

Thursday 26/07/2007

I called Mr Ogilvie, the chief education officer of the government of Grenada Ministry of Education. *(I wrote him a letter on my return to Scotland.)* No reply so far? I was talking to Josepha, the house keeper, Richmond Hill, and Cecilia, House Keeper Belle Isle before we reluctantly bid the nation of great people goodbye.

Chapter Eight

I Persevere With My Project

Friday 27/07/2007

Collect surplus resources from Saint Andrews PS. For Monday 30 July: call Les, Argyll and Bute Council, Dunoon; John, Denholm Bahr Ltd, Liverpool; Stephen, ZIM Liverpool.

I left message for Terry O'Donnell: on holiday for two weeks. I was speaking to Jim, Heriot Watt School of Business, who gave me the Scottish Enterprise network link; Tom Walker phoned to let me know that he has inspected the three 40-foot ocean freight containers in the Duncan Adams Transport Ltd depot at Grange Dock, Grangemouth and that one of them can't be certificated (MAEU7412692!) See, Howard, TRIU507942 and CRXU4103197 are okay. *'Don't buy anymore containers,'* Marion pleaded with me. *(But I would not listen.)*

Tuesday 07/08/2007

10:30 a.m. Home. Tom Walker, the container surveyor, called inquiring if I had heard from Howard. I send him the payment for inspecting the box at the boatyard.

Wednesday 08/08/2007

Today I have meetings with Alan Reid MP at the Pavilion in the morning and with Jim Mather MSP for Argyll and Bute at Fyne Homes conference centre in the afternoon.

I Persevere With My Project

Monday 13/08/2007

10:15 a.m. Home. I have just received a call from Tanya of Rothesay Playgroup offering tables and chairs, which must be uplifted before Wednesday if I want them. Problem. How to collect these resources and where to store them?

3:15 p.m. Rothesay Playgroup? Furniture? They offer to contribute £10 towards cost of petrol. If I am unable to collect the furniture will go to the cowp. I arrange for the loan of a van from Chandlers Hotel.

5:50 p.m. Amy Elisabeth has just called to tell me that Alison will come by with Chandlers van at 10 a.m. tomorrow to collect the offer of furniture from Rothesay Playgroup. Transport solved. Storage for the time being will have to be at the back of Delhi Cottage.

Tuesday 14/08/2007

I had to cancel the offer from Rothesay Playgroup with regret. Not tae worry. Linda Fabiani MSP, The Scottish Parliament. Carol Anne Miller/Darren Dickson. *'That will be working through our system at the moment,'* she said.

Wednesday 15/08/2008

I speak to Terry, Midlothian Council, and Elaine *'We will see what we have to give you,'* she said. I had spoken to Donald, Director of Education, who'd suggested I meet with them. I wrote a letter to Mr Singh, High Commissioner for Guyana, indicating what educational resources my foundation had to offer.

Where does a social entrepreneur get business advice and assistance? I speak to Barbara, who put me in touch with some Glasgow solicitors, who took me for another ride.

Thursday 16/08/2007

5:45 p.m. Home. I sat and wrote letter to: Sir Tom Hunter; Jim Mather MSP; Barbara Halliday Business Adviser, AIE. I can but try. It has been a long day indoors under the skylight window, typing up my Diary of a Shipping Clerk.

I made arrangements for my meeting in Dalkeith with Midlothian Council next month. At the moment I am in a quandary. Where do I go from here? At an intuitive level, gut feeling level, I know what I need, namely, the resources, both intellectual and material, to leverage, the jargon, there's a word … my idea, initiative, project, since Hurricane Ivan on 7 September 2004 devastated the island of Grenada, to supply devastated schools with the educational resources so they can function fully and more effectively than before Hurricane Ivan struck. I need help with the business and strategic planning of this non-governmental organisation. We'll see. I am in doldrums stuck in the Sargasso Sea going nowhere, when out of the blue, I get a gust of the Trade Winds in my sails.

Thursday 16/08/2007

2:20 p.m. Home. This afternoon I received a letter dated 30 July from Mr Richard Menzies Geo. F. Huggins & Co. Ltd. He was as good as his word. He and his fellow directors have agreed to contribute US$1,000 towards defraying the cost of shipping the next ocean freight container for St Paul's Government School from Scotland to Kingston, Jamaica, and from there it would be transshipped to Grenada.

Speaking to Stephen at ZIM (Liverpool) Ltd to arrange the shipment of the container for 28 August from Grange Dock. Which terminal? I'll see if Duncan Adams Transport Ltd will meet them hauf way? I later saw Craig, editor of *The Buteman*, who will run a puff when the 40-foot ocean freight container, which has been parked up at the Port Bannatyne boatyard for more than a year, will at long last be on its way, filled with 'gifts', best of stuff, frae the Isle of Bute community. Craig was well pleased to get this fresh news.

I cycled on out to the port where I met John. *'That's my container ready to go,'* I said. He told me that he would let his dad know. On my way back along Marine Drive I stopped to tell Malcolm the news, and when I got into the wee town I saw the retired John, formerly the Hong Kong Harbour Master, and got off my bicycle to tell him that it was all systems go.

Friday 17/08/2007

8:30 a.m. Home. I called the Caledonian MacBrayne office in Dunoon to see if they will waive the ferry tariff for the ocean freight container. I speak to Alison, port manager. I left a message: reply they will not waive the fare.

I sent an email to Roland Malins-Smith about GSTU895863 if I can begin the process of shipping the container.

Saturday 18/08/2007

10:50 a.m. Home. I am calling ZIM. No answer. They don't work on Saturday. Today is the day of the Isle of Bute Highland Games. Raindrops are bouncing off the skylight window. I – the chancer, opportunist, cobbler, wheeler-dealer, born again, who feels brand new of every minute of every day should I wish to be so inclined to face the world with a beamer – am now thinking about my next move.

Monday 20/08/2007

I have booked a room at the Rosecot Guest House B&B, Bridgend Road, Dalkeith, Midlothian.

Tuesday 21/08/2007

8:45 a.m. Home. It is a beautiful summer's day. I went outside and swept the cobbles. David is up and about and Johanna is off

Tuesday 21/08/2007

to school. Amy is asleep and Marion is off across the watta; Bless them Lord. Press Release in *The Buteman*.

(I could, and should, have stopped here, but I did not. Everything up to this point had been fairly straightforward, except for the occasions recorded in this diary when it seemed that the project had come to an end. However, the real trouble that I had brought on myself lay ahead.)

I call ZIM and left a message for Stephen to call me. I called Terry, Midlothian Council, Dalkeith to confirm our meeting tomorrow, Wednesday 22 August. *'Okay pal,'* he said.

1 p.m. While I was standing in the queue waiting for the one o'clock boat, I met my premier supporter from the port, a local painter and decorator who now works on the pier for CalMac. He is one of my supporters who always greets me with the two words that lift my spirit. *'Go easy,'* he says to me.

I am back on board the one o'clock boat. I have just met Addie, former pupil, one of the All Stars. *'Is the generator still working? I didnae see the container going away,'* he said. He is travelling with his mum.

It is clouding over. It was a beautiful warm morning. Gordon came by shortly after 8:30 a.m. He told me that he was out at the boatyard to see the container being loaded. He told me that he was talking to the drivers Kenny and James. He said that he had taken digitals of the Caribbean Hurricane Relief Depot, 40-foot ocean freight container being lifted onto the trailer.

That's the paddle steamer *Waverley* steaming into the harbour with passengers fore and aft, packed shoulder to shoulder. Cool breeze picking up. I had made myself a bacon sandwich, cup of tea, piece of cheese and a few grapes.

I have personal difficulties to overcome, obstacles in my way. Ever since my days in the Big Green place 1975–1990 I have increasingly fixated on the waste of good quality fit-for-purpose, surplus to requirements, educational resources. And my pathetic efforts to salvage some of it. I am going to socialise at the Tea Bar. On the way to the ferry earlier I stopped off at Print Point to collect information that was to be faxed to Stephen (ZIM) and Ray (Denholm Bahr). Karen comes up trumps, as always, and did not charge me for sending the faxes, just a box of labels which I am to pay for later.

3:15 p.m. I am now on the bus for Edinburgh. I have not long walked up to the Buchanan Street bus station from Glasgow Central. I am now going up Cathedral Street on four wheels, where I have walked up and doon in days past.

3:45 p.m. I am sitting on a stainless-steel bench. The sun is shining brightly over my left shoulder. Platform 2 Hillington West. I am waiting for the 15:46 on-time train for Port Glasgow. The driver with John MacKirdy Transport Ltd, local haulage, has not long dropped me off outside Russell's depot in the Hillington Industrial Estate. I walked down the busy four-lane dual carriageway, turned right, up into this vast complex of industry and commerce, and here I am. Roll it back some more please.

This morning I said goodbye to David. *'Get some rolls and bacon, Dad,'* he calls out. Amy is going for a run. It is a beautiful day. The sun is cracking out of the blue. I cycled along to Print Point. They, that's Karen, Matthew and Martin were trying unsuccessfully to send my ISO certificate and information inventory to ZIM in Liverpool. It's Karen's day off I presume. The sheets of this vital information are sticking in the fax machine. Then Matt tried to send the same again to SeaFreight Agencies (Miami) and gave up not getting through. This amazing telephony makes me dizzy just thinking about it.

I met Catherine Constance (I think?) from the port, who works in the post office on a Saturday. She is a supporter and encourager

Tuesday 21/08/2007

of my efforts, from early on. We had a brief chat about how far I had got with their support. I cycled on up the High Street to CBPS Ltd to order another tin of green metallic oxide paint. No hot chocolate and no soup in the machine. My treat en route. I swithered whether to go further along up the street and into John MacKirdy Transport Ltd's yard and decided to push on home. Contingencies. *'Dad there's a message for you,'* said Johanna. I am to call John MacKirdy Transport Ltd. They tell me that they are going to move the container today. Like now, right this minute!

I cycled back to Print Point to collect the ISO certificate, which Matt had been trying to fax. I met Catherine, who was so glad to hear that the container, that had been at the port for so many months, was finally being shipped to Grenada. *'Oh good!'* she says when I her told the container was moving off the Little Island. I stopped off at CBPS Ltd to cancel the paint order, and on to MacKirdy's yard where I met young John in the office. Yes, the container was now on a trailer at the boatyard, ready to go on the one o'clock boat. I said why not drop it off in Glasgow and Duncan Adams Transport Ltd would (might) pick it up. John thought that was a good idea as they had a load to collect at Port Dundas at the drop off/pick up point depot yard. That was my suggestion in an email but he said that he had never received it. So I quickly got back on the bicycle, the trusty steed, and headed for the port.

On the way down Union Street, I saw Jim and showed him G. A Menzies letter from Huggins & Co (G'DA) Ltd. He seemed pleased. Then I stopped off at *The Buteman* to let editor Craig know that the ocean freight container at the port was at long last on its way with a cargo of Little Island gifts. Back on the bicycle and along up the Ardbeg Road. As I got past the old tram shed, now the Western Bus Co. Ltd depot, I saw the container being towed by a MacKirdy transporter coming towards me. What a sight! I was thrilled. I turned around to meet Craig in his car behind me, and I told him I would meet him at the pier.

I got the one o'clock boat. I thought I had better travel with it. For better or for worse. Pride of ownership. Later on, I joined the driver in the cab of the artic, which is fully automated. This machine almost drives itself. I met Michael and we had tea and raisin tarts. I chatted also with Elmo on the MV *Saturn*.

I just remembered – 11 a.m. on the next leg of this journey, odyssey, saga. I met Jean C of S Women's Guild in Mclean's Bakery Café en route to the boatyard. Being sidetracked again I was going off on tangents. No wonder, I met the container coming towards me! She was inquiring whether I should be at school, expressing what many would have thought. *'Why is he not at the Port School? Listen and I'll tell you why.' 'You look after yourself now,'* she said kindly. I'll try to.

4:20 p.m. Back on the rails. The sun is shining through big drawing-room-divan shaped clouds. *'We are now approaching Whin Hill. Please mind the gap when alighting from this train. This train is for Wemyss Bay,'* she said.

5:30 p.m. 'Home'. I have just called Eric at Duncan Adams Transport Ltd at Grange Dock. I need to send him a Standard Shipping Note. *'You'll need to get that from your agent before you can get it out of the Port of Grangemouth. Okay?'* he said. I was not too sure of what piece of paper he was referring to, so I'll call to find out from the freight forwarders at Denholm Bahr Ltd in the Port of Liverpool, either Stephen or John.

5:52 p.m. I called the former at ZIM no answer, their offices must be shut.

6:00 p.m. I almost called Raymond, President of the St Paul's Government School (the Model School, PTA, the consignee, beneficiary of this cargo of largesse), who had told me in a previous transatlantic conversation that he was going to look out for secure storage in the Spice Isle's city of St George's. I had suggested Frequente Industrial Estate in the capital.

He will let me know. *'I had a meetin' wid de entire staff two weeks ago and we went tru de inventory,'* he said.

7 p.m. The Cavaliere Ristorante Italiano, established 1969, Main Street, Dalkeith where I am about to have some supper. I booked into the Rosecote B&B down the hill, around the roundabout and over the road from the bridge over the river. I met Terry, the landlady's partner, who teaches sheet-metal fabrication at Telford College. He is a native of these parts and a diver in his spare time. And here I am. I ordered cream of tomato soup, a vegetarian pizza and a Coke. I called Marion. The landlord kindly let me use his mobile. A big bowl of tomato soup arrives. I had asked for mozzarella. *'You mean parmesan,'* she said. I sit corrected. I get just a grated smidgen. I can hardly see it. Get stuck in, and enjoy.

8:10 p.m. 'Home', home at last. I'm tired. The container, The Big Green Box, GSTU8958639, is now at Port Dundas, Maryhill, Glasgow, in P&H's yard. I phoned Eric earlier. Duncan Adams Transport Ltd, all being well, will collect and deliver to the Port of Grangemouth. Brilliant!

Wednesday 22/08/2007

8:45 a.m. I am travelling with Terry from Midlothian Council. We have just come from Cranston Village Primary School, where I saw a lot of fit-for-purpose, virtually new, educational resources, that appear to be left for the demolition squad. We first visit Gorebridge Primary School and a large secondary school where surplus resources were stacked up in the corridors. The car is being driven at high speed along these country roads. It is a beautiful light-filled morning.

We are now in the town of Penicuik and are about to visit Ladywood Primary School, which is to become Strathesk Primary School. There I meet the janitor, Jim, and Head Teacher Liz Barton.

I later met Jim, Newbattle Community High School, who I am to contact as soon as I have got a container to collect the resources that are surplus to their requirements. Terry then drove me all the way back to Festival Square so I could visit the Edinburgh Chamber of Commerce. No joy. An expensive membership fee for what? Bedazzled by what I imagined the business world to be like.

I walked up the road to the bottom end of Princes Street and got a taxi to Grangemouth. I have lost the plot – never again. Keith, taxi driver, will have thought that this punter has gone bananas.

3:29 p.m. I am sitting on a wooden bench on Larbert Station platform in full warm summer sunshine. I got on the wrong train from Falkirk Grahamston, where a taxi had brought me from Grangemouth town centre. 15:32. *'This train is for Glasgow Queen Street.'* The Grangemouth town centre pissoir was shut, so the kind taxi driver took me to the railway station where I could use a loo! What relief.

Well it has been all go since I bid adieu, au revoir, to the Rosecote B&B and walked back over the Lugton River Bridge, up the hill into Dalkeith town centre where I met kind, helpful taxi drivers at their rank who directed me to Fairfield House rather than take my fare as it was within a short walking distance away. I met Terry who was welcoming and drove me to collect Jim of Midlothian Council's Janitorial Services Department, the head janitor of Newbattle Community High School, and then on to visit Gorebridge Primary School where I was introduced to their janitor. A good part of the building was empty and there were lots of good surplus resources in the old junior secondary complex. It

Wednesday 22/08/2007

was then back on the road to Cranston Village Primary School, which was in an idyllic setting surrounded by fields of ripening barley. From there were views of Auld Reekie in the heat haze of urban sprawl in the south-west. The school had been abandoned. There were new resources lying about. Gym kit. You name it. I drooled. Back in the car to meet Head Teacher Liz Barton and janitor Jim at Ladywood Primary School, in Penicuik.

They were friendly. Nice. A wholesome atmosphere in that school. I shared with them my vision of what I hoped to do by attempting to salvage, and could I possibly have the resources prior to their destruction? Then Terry drove me all the way back into busy Edinburgh City Centre to Lothian Road, and dropped me off across from the Sheraton Hotel. I met the Director of the Edinburgh Chamber of Commerce, who was sceptical, unhelpful and negative: he virtually showed me the door, in spite of me being a member and the much touted, services that I would enjoy on becoming a member. I had taken myself for another ride. No further progress on that front.

I then walked up the road and took an impulsive and self-destructive taxi ride to Grange Dock, Port of Grangemouth. I had my passport with me this time round. No hassle at Forth Ports Plc Security Gate. I asked young Brian in the Duncan Adams Transport Ltd office, who I had spoken to on Monday afternoon, if he would remove the Caribbean Hurricane Relief banner off my container and send it on to me. He was very helpful and welcoming to me as ever. I met Eric out in the busy yard directing transporters coming in and going out. *'You still no got a charity yet? We like your gung-ho attitude, David, but none of us want tae see yuh end up on poverty street. And yuh only want tae move yer stuff once,'* he said. He who has my best interests to heart. *(His words were to ring in my ears for years to come.)* I walked back out the dock. A beautiful afternoon. I am satisfied that I had made the effort to remove my Caribbean Hurricane Relief Depot banner from the container before it was shipped.

3:50 p.m. Lenzie Railway Station. Pupils, Chinese and Caucasian pupils, possibly from the academy, chattering away. *'What's your star sign?'* asks one wee miss of another. Free will and determinism.

8:45 p.m. Home, home at last. It has been a long two-day jaunt across Scotland travelling by bicycle, ferry, bus, bus, car, train, on foot, bus, taxi, train, on foot, train, ferry and the trusty pleasure of my bicycle. Whew!

It's a beautiful evening. There is a harvest moon coming up down south. I am very tired at this moment. Birds are singing up there in the bushes growing out of the cliff face and in the canopy of trees at the top. There are grey-pink skies above. No gains. No pains.

(To what end? I had gone to a lot of trouble to ship those four ocean freight containers [2005–2007] to three Grenada government schools. And I was to put myself and family through a lot of worry and expense to ship over the next 10 years, seven more 40-foot ocean freight containers of educational resources to schools in Tanzania, Ghana, Liberia, Nicaragua, Jamaica, Grenada and the Republic of Haiti and Nicaragua. 'Dae yeh want a medal, David?' Jean had asked me when I told her, in answer to an earlier question, what I was doing.)

Thursday 23/08/2007

Home. Phone Stephen at ZIM to confirm that he had faxed the bill of lading inventory forms to Duncan Adams Transport Ltd. Also ask him if he would fax those same documents to Roland and Yamila at SeaFreight Agencies in Miami, Florida. Start to make contact with those who might be willing to sponsor a container, so I can begin to receive the resources from the schools that are being closed in Midlothian and in other educational authorities.

Contact Kenny at Skanksa, chief d'equipe, Midlothian Council's contractor for the PFI new build project, about temporary storage

Friday 24/08/2007

and sponsorship of a container for Ladywood Primary School. Return call to the Guyana High Commissioner. Making an issue. The negatives of the problem regarding transport etc. East West Indies Lines goes that way. Les of Argyll and Bute Council Education Department has just called to confirm I could have what was left in the island's secondary school, and to let me know that Campbell is the keyholder. Allan Reid MP had called him. Good on him! I asked for a letter of confirmation.

Contact Highland and Islands Enterprise, Lochgilphead, who tell me, *'You need to become a legal entity. Once you get the format of charitable status, it will give you credibility that as an individual you do not have.'* She suggests that my project becomes a company limited by guarantee?

(I took this advice and ended up in more of a pickle of unnecessary legal complexity and official charity status than I needed to. For my next venture, should I get the opportunity, I will stay clear of solicitors and the office of the Dundonian charity regulator. My word is my bond, what more credibility, validation do I need than that? I am not ashamed of my effort, financial commitment, and the integrity of what it took from me to deliver a dozen ocean freight containers from 2005–2017. The emotional cost it took from my dearest to achieve those shipments does, and will always, cause me regret.)

Friday 24/08/2007

Home. Call Brian at Duncan Adams Transport Ltd who tells me, *'That's the container away, half an hour after you left.' 'Thank you, for all the help and support that your family firm of Duncan Adams Transport Ltd have given me. You and your team have made this shipment to Grenada happen,'* I said.

I call Carrie at the Edinburgh Chamber of Commerce to find out where the AGM is being held? Do I really need to go? *Evening Times* article. Keith. Where to stay? Minto Street. I need a container? Howard? Ladywood PS Send an email to Roland to let him know that container GSTU8958639 USA 43101C87 for St Paul's Government School, Grenada is on its way. I called ZIM to see if I can renegotiate the £1,500 tariff.

3:45 p.m. I have been here at the desk for not a wee while. I learned from Stephen at ZIM that the tariff is still £1,500/US$2,045. I then called SeaFreight Agencies and spoke to Riberio to see if he will reduce the tariff. Nae chance. Business is business. The container is shipper owned and belongs to me. Resale of the container in Grenada is a possibility. I am now seriously in debt and out of pocket. Maxwell at the High Commission for St Vincent and The Grenadines called. He would like me to send him an inventory of my recent shipment to Grenada. He is worrying unnecessarily about transportation costs. I invited him up here to see what the surplus resources are like in the island's secondary school. *'We doan have a budget for dat,'* he said. Problem of storage. I can't keep on buying more containers but I don't listen.

Friday 25/08/2007

Find out who SeaFreight Agencies's agent is in St George's, Grenada, as they negotiate with the Port Authority there over handling charges and sale of the container. The drama teacher from Dalkeith Community High School, where Jim, head of Midlothian Council Janitorial Services, is based, left a message to say that she had seen the article in last night's *Edinburgh Evening News* and was glad that somebody was doing something about the way in which fit-for-purpose, surplus to requirements, educational resources were being disposed of and would speak to her head teacher on Monday – at least someone approves of what I am engaged in. Ideas: the staff and pupils of St Andrew's Primary School here on the island might be interested in forming a link with St. Paul's Government School in Grenada.

Tuesday 28/08/2007

2:45 p.m. I am going to check through the Edinburgh Chamber of Commerce Annual General Meeting 30 August 2007 guest list. It is a grey and wet afternoon. I had cycled in earlier to collect David Alexander's order of two Scotch pies. I will need to have my situation vis a vis my teaching post at the Port School resolved. I called Mr Mackie at the Education Institute for Scotland to arrange a meeting for 3 September. No joy.

2:57 p.m. I received a call from John, the janitor of Fairy Hill PS, Groathill Road, North Edinburgh, who had also seen the article in the *Edinburgh Evening News,* offering resources. FLOODS OF EDUCATIONAL RESOURCES COME ON STREAM AND I AM UNABLE TO HANDLE ANY OF IT.

6:05 p.m. Home. Tom Walker, independent container surveyor, has just called to let me know that the containers that I had purchased were indeed the right price and I have to take his word for it at this stage of the game. And he advised me that were I to purchase any more containers, I was to let him know and he would inspect them before I bought them to ensure that they would be given an ISO certificate. Plated.

Tuesday 28/08/2007

I called Forth Ports Plc vehicle reception at Grange Dock. The container on 27 August 2007 aboard the feeder vessel *Clonlee* to Rotterdam. The agent was Denholm Barwil Ltd. I spoke to Nick. '*We don't issue bills of lading for the short sea journey,*' he said. Home terminal for ZIM is Cartagena.

11 a.m. Home. I called Adam the journalist, to find out if he would be my guest at the ECC AGM and share a hot breakfast on 30 August 2007. '*Sorry, I am working on a deadline. Can I call you back at 12?*' he asks. '*Sure,*' I reply. I then called Elias,

International Programme Consultant, UK Sport. He said that he and the ambassador were coming north in November. Send fax to Carla Rae Briggs, editor of *The Grenada Informer*.

Wednesday 29/08/2007

5:40 p.m. Wemyss Bay Station. I am sitting in the train for Glasgow Central Station. I have just left the Sea View Café where Marion and I had supper together. I saw the 5:30 p.m. ferry leaving the pier as I waited for the green man. I am alone once more.

My mind is blank at the moment, maybe because I am bagged up with macaroni and cheese at £16.90. *'Why are you going to the AGM of the Edinburgh Chamber of Commerce?'* I ask myself. I suppose I hope to meet with people who can further the aims of what I am trying to accomplish, and who I can also assist in achieving their objectives. Quid pro quo sort of. Scratch my back and I scratch yours. In some vague way I hope to meet a business person who would be willing to help, assist me in taking the Surplus Educational Supplies project a few steps further ahead than where it is at present. I thought it might be a good place to make useful contacts. Their requirements: your job description for those with whom you wish to associate, core integrity, similar values, smarter more logical thinking, strategic thinker. Who are more able than I am with business and financial acumen, but with a sense of humour, imagination, enthusiasm, energy and fun?

7:10 p.m. I am on the bus to Edinburgh leaving Buchanan Street Bus Station. As I was about to board the bus a young student offered me her ticket since her friend was not coming. A free ride. It is a humid evening. Grey skies, but still light. Back up Cathedral Street. Into the wind and batten down the hatches. The Royal Infirmary buildings could do with a clean-up. Why did they built a place for healing adjacent to the burial ground. The Necropolis? And have they learned anything over the last century and a half when they construct the 21st-century Queen Elizabeth Hospital not far from an open sewage works? There are shrubs growing out of the pediment surrounding the clock tower. The driver is swinging the bus on to the M8. I am now looking across to Dennistoun where I sublet a flat on Garthland Drive. Continuing as ever, to move forward, not looking back, climbing upward and trying not to look down.

9:20 p.m. Euro Hostel. Kincaid Street and corner of Gulliver Street. I got off the bus on Princes Street and over and along up Jeffrey Street. Crossed over the Royal Mile, High Street down St Mary's Street and into the Cowgate, and hung a right and got lost. I asked for directions and went into the wrong hostel. I walked around in circles. Here I am in room 1/9/B on the third floor. Clean. Sounds of traffic. Let's have a look at the official tourist map of Auld Reekie.

Thursday 30/08/2007

6:15 a.m. Edinburgh International Conference Centre. I was up a lot earlier and had slept fitfully. There was a pink and orange sky behind me as I walked along the Cowgate and into the Grassmarket, past tattoo artists and second-hand antiquarian booksellers. I continued walking along to Lothian Road and Morrison Street. I was to arrive here too early so I walked back down to the Haymarket and back round, stopped at a newsagents, and bought *The Scotsman*. I can't recall the dialogue but he struck a positive note, but it's early days yet. Friendly and welcoming Edinburgh Chamber of Commerce staff. *'I've heard about all the good work you are doing,'* she said. From whom I wondered. With your help and that of many I will achieve a lot more. I am only as good as the last five minutes, riding this bicycle. I couldn't balance on a surfboard. I was soon offered a cup of coffee.

I am writing this on a glass-topped table and I am sitting in a comfortable chair in the middle of a large foyer of this modern building.

12:32 p.m. *'The next stop is Wemyss Bay, where the train will terminate.'* I am heading home on a full Scottish cooked breakfast courtesy my EEC membership fee. An expensive repast. Never mind. I showed up.

Friday 31/08/2007

9:50 a.m. Home. Cash flow concerns. I called him back to ask if Midlothian Council could contribute to the cost of the container that was to be placed at Ladywood Primary School. He said he would ask. I contacted Howard, Freight Container Services (Scotland) Ltd, regarding the ocean freight container SEAU427 2551. Eric, his partner, is on holiday and he would speak to Duncan Adams. I am not keen to renew my MasterCard. Bar selling the rest of my Barbados Shipping and Trading Ltd shares, I'll have to wait and see if I can borrow from the bank. Micro credit? *'Can ye phone me tonight. I'm kinda busy just noo,'* said Robert.

11:55 a.m. I was speaking to Lisa, Head of International Development at the Scottish Office. No joy there. Next I speak to Charles, International Officer at the Glasgow District Council, who tells me that Brian and Gillian from the council are out in Malawi 'building' an HIV clinic, and that he would pass my query as to whether they could use any of my stuff.

1 p.m. I have a meeting with Mr D. Hunter of the AIE business adviser. *'What do I need to take this project forward as a business?'* I ask. *'I'm not the best person to give you that advice,'* he replied. Exporting good quality fit-for-purpose, used classroom resources, furniture etc? The objective being to generate revenue to finance the running of my social enterprise. Suggests I set up a limited

Tuesday 03/09/2007

company so I can apply for grants. He is encouraging but not at all helpful. He tells me that I have a good-feeling promotion idea. Is this a goer, yes or no? He said he would pass my query on to someone better qualified to assist me. I am still waiting!

2:25 p.m. I have a meeting with the bank's customer adviser. I extend my loan facility. He is helpful and I get another loan and pay off the old one. Here we go again. *'I keep six honest serving men. They taught me all I knew. Their names are: What and Why, and When and How, and Where and Who.'* Rudyard Kipling.

Saturday 01/10/2007

9:50 a.m. Home. I am writing a thank-you letter to Richard GA Menzies and his fellow directors at Huggins in Grenada for their donation of US$1,000 towards defraying costs of shipping the container of educational resources from the Isle of Bute to St Paul's Government School in Grenada. I gave him Raymond's telephone number.

Tuesday 03/09/2007

Social Work Argyll and Bute Council – see Community Services. David Alexander is making lunch. I have just returned from Rothesay, Victoria Hospital, having had my hearing aid repaired, which makes my voice sound very 'RP' with gravitas. *'How are you, my dear boy?'* Contact Belcom Business Solutions, New York, about the resources being shipped to St Paul's Government School in Grenada. Speak to Carla, editor of *The Grenada Informer*.

9:57 a.m. Home. As I was answering an urgent call of nature, I received a phone call out of the blue from Mungo, an associate of Petr of Argyll Wind Farms Ltd, to tell me that his firm was offering me the office furniture in a property at 250 Seaward Street in

Glasgow and was I interested? Yes, but I have nowhere to store these resources at present, let alone being able to collect them. He told me I was to call Colliers, the real estate people, and speak to a Ian, the director, during the week to get a key to view and to call if I was going to accept their 'donation' (get stuff moved and it doesn't cost them anything).

More high hopes and expectations. I should have said there and then. *'I AM NO LONGER ACCEPTING ANY MORE STUFF. THANK YOU.'* Find out from Glasgow District Council what it cost to have these resources removed from these premises. Asked Mungo for directions to Seaward Street? Come out Central Station, walk down to Argyle Street. Walk over George IV Bridge, follow the River Clyde bank down the river, under the Kingston Bridge, over to Paisley Road West, past Watt Street and turn left to Seaward Street into the business park.

'Essentially, we are looking for people who have real drive and ambition. People who are building companies of substance and scale in Scotland. ... You have to be prepared to step up to the mark, be passionate about what you do and surround yourself with people who know more than you if you if you want to succeed ... nobody is going to look after you and there isn't a job for life. There will be multiple jobs,' said Sir Tom Hunter. Article. 'Up close and personal with Scotland's entrepreneurs.' He never replied to my letter.

2:30 p.m. I was speaking with Chris who said he would let his counterpart in Dunoon know that I was looking for volunteers to assist in removing resources from the island's secondary school.

Monday 10/09/2007

9:31 a.m. Home. I am feeling awful. There are splitting pains behind my eyes as I am about to make this call. The gentleman I wish to speak with is on holiday till the 13th. *'I will get one of his* *colleagues to give you a call,'* she said. I am to meet Fraser of Colliers at 250 Seaward Street on 11 September at 10:30 a.m. *'I hope it's a productive journey for you,'* he said. I hope so to. Mungo said, *'Don't push your luck. I used to work for them. Mention that it was Argyll Wind Farms Ltd that are donating the furniture.'*

Tuesday 11/09/2007

9:40 a.m. 250 Seaward Street. I got the train up to Central Station where I spent 20p. I withdrew £50 and bought an A to Z Map of Glasgow City. I walked out the station down the road. Waiting for the green man.

Over the Bridge past Graham's Construction site where they were driving piles into the Clyde river bank. Along and under the Kingston Bridge and found the street. Had stopped to buy a coffee and a roll and sausage. Here I am with no expectations and presumptions. Mr Duguid said he'd meet me here at 10:30 a.m. I am always early, I am. Quiet. Grey. It has been sprinkling a little rain. Marlow Street. Facing railway line into Central.

11:50 a.m. *'This train is for Wemyss Bay.'* I met Fraser who was late, at 10:50 a.m., who apologised, and who was young enough to be my great-grandson. He took me on a quick tour round an industrial unit in the dark. What's left? Most of the furniture appears to have been sold and removed. Filing cabinets. A few filing cabinets. Where to store them? Fraser is a pleasant lad and smartly dressed, comes from Motherwell, and who remembers using Strathclyde Regional Council jotters – so do I. He said that Colliers would give me a month's storage.

Monday 17/09/2007

Home. Contact Campbell, janitor of the island's secondary school to see what resources are still available in the old building that is due to be demolished so I can take an inventory. Book an appointment with the dentist.

Send an email to Wilson James Security, Jamie MacPherson. We met at a speed networking session on 4 July, and he told me to drop him an email, as did a few others. No reply? Call Adam the journalist to see if he'll post me a copy of his article in the *Evening News* for 24 August 2007, and if he will also email me a copy. Contact Howard to see if Freight Container Services (Scotland) Ltd will sponsor two containers: one for the island's secondary school and the other for Ladywood Primary School in Penicuik. Call Gillian at Lofthus Signs, who I met at the Edinburgh Chamber of Commerce Speed Networking session.

Wednesday 19/09/2007

Frank, community services officer, Dalkeith, called to offer help with a team of young offenders with the shifting of resources from schools. I told him that I would get back to him as soon as I have containers on site. Call Jim the Janny to see where he wants the container parked. Call Terry to let him know that the container that I will purchase has to have an ISO certificate.

2 p.m. Home. I left a message with Linda, MSP office secretary. They have been away on a junket. No joy whatsoever from that quarter; it must be nice tae travel aboot. Called Jim, head janny based at Dalkeith Community High School, about the offer of 'helpers' from Community Services. I sent faxes to Elias from Zimbabwe at UK Sport Relief and Carla, editor of *The Grenada Informer*. I must make arrangements to have a container at Ladywood Primary School. Call Jim to let him know when it is going to be delivered. I called Howard who asked me to ask Tom Walker, the container inspector, to call him. *'We have an ally,'* he said. I then called Tom, who said, *'Call me later I am on the motorway.'*

Thursday 20/09/2007

8:30 p.m. Home. I have been down in the dumps, shrouded by a grey and overcast sky. I have a sore gum where a tooth was extracted from last week. I came to the computer this afternoon and found an email from Howard, which encouraged me, and I made some more telephone calls, contacts. My efforts of will to achieve something of worth, in my eyes at any rate; there is no one else I can rely on to act on my behalf. However, I have just received another email from Howard suggesting I move my containers from Duncan Adams Transport Ltd yard at Grange Dock. I can no longer keep them there. I have overstayed my welcome. Where to now? Problems *'What's your business model? Do you have access to credit? Accountability counts. Incentives matter. Global poverty. Is it just Africa? What about Grenada WI? Viable systems on the ground.'* A load of gobbledygook!

Call Suzanne (Pearson Longman USA surplus stock) 5 October 2007. Out-of-date textbooks, CXC'S. I am looking at the Sabre Foundation website. You match up what schools want with what you have available. Calculate overall costs of collecting, storage and shipping. Your ethos. My ethos. Donors. Demand driven? Transparency? There is an abundance of surplus and lack of it abroad in the developing world. How can I get books from publishers? Ask! If they would donate their new inventory to my public charity (BOOK DUMPING). Get priority listings from partners? Their list of priority areas (DATA BASE). Match priority areas with my database. *'So they don't get what they don't need.'* For Friday 21 September 2007 – fax bills of lading to all and sundry. They want originals? Contact webhosts regarding missing images on site. See Kevin, the digital artisan. Speaking to Will at the British Council in Edinburgh who took my details but did not call me back. I guess because I am too far down the food chain. Call Robert. *'I'll try and get one of they certificated ones,'* he said.

I Persevere With My Project

Friday 21/09/2007

4:05 p.m. Home. I am alone. Marion and Johanna are off up to Kilbarchan, off to Mum Gran's birthday celebrations. David and Amy are working at Chandler's Hotel.

4:55 p.m. Off the phone to Marion. Awaiting her and Johanna coming off the ferry. This afternoon I spoke to Jim of WH Malcolm Ltd, Grangemouth, who told me that I can store my three ocean freight containers, currently at Duncan Adams Transport Ltd Grange Dock yard, at their Foul Dubs Grangemouth yard. Brilliant! I owe so much gratitude to so many firms in the Scottish road haulage industry. I called Howard who had suggested in an email that I move them. He will let Eric know that he might not mind me moving my ocean freight containers from Duncan Adams Transport Ltd depot up the road to Fould Dums yard. Howard always sounds so glad to hear from me. An encouragement always. I am a good customer, that's why. *Don't be cynical.* I sent faxes this morning to SeaFreight Agencies, W. E. Julien & Co Ltd, Christopher De Riggs, and Richard (GA) Menzies.

10:45 p.m. Amy and David are home from their shift at Chandlers Hotel and I shall now turn in. This afternoon one of the people I called was Adam Morris, journalist with the *Edinburgh Evening News*, who wrote an article for his paper on 24 September about my efforts. He told me that he had been away from his desk for a while and he had been at a meeting where he had met Tanya, journalist with the *Fife Free Press*, who had written the break through article for her paper on 2 December 2006, 'puffing' my initial foray into the Kingdom of Fife, to collect, salvage, surplus school resources from Capshard and North Kirkcaldy primary schools, which was accomplished with the help of the gallus jannies and team from Warehousing Co. Ltd. He said he would run another story. I called SeaFreight Agencies (Miami, Fla) and left a message on Novaldo's voicemail who hasn't called me back. Has he left the company?

Monday 24/09/2007

Home. Send Eric an email regarding the removal of my containers from their yard at Grange Dock to WH Malcolm Transport Ltd yard at Foul Dubs in Grangemouth. Containers: GSTU8958639 left Port Bannatyne for Grange Dock 21 August en route to St Paul's Government School, Grenada; MAEU7412692 failed inspection; CRXU4103197; TRIU5079422; SEAU4272551. Bob Tannahill called to let me know I can store containers at Foul Dubs Yard in Grangemouth.

(One of the premier Scottish road haulage firms whose team of stalwarts in the office at head office in Linwood, the container base, and on the road, were to enable the Shipping Clerk to make more shipments possible.)

Tuesday 25/09/2007

I spoke to Andy, Pentalver Container Sales Ltd (Maersk), Leeds, who tells me that I have paid more for the containers than I should have. Call Jim at WH Malcolm Transport Ltd to let him know that my containers can remain for the time being at Duncan Adams Transport Ltd, Grange Dock yard. Call Howard to let him know that Eric says it is okay for me to keep my containers where they are at the present time. Done. '*It's a crisp blue sky,*' he tells me and that he had asked Eric if they could remain there for the time being. Why then did he email me suggesting I move them from the Grange Dock depot in the first place? I sent faxes: information regarding shipment to St Paul's Government School to the Grenada High Commissioner in London.

I Persevere With My Project

Wednesday 26/09/2007

9:55 a.m. The Island Academy (old building circa 1935) to meet Campbell, the key holder, Argyll and Bute Council joiner, up at the island secondary school to take an inventory of resources in the old building. He has just shown me around. Classrooms. What's on offer. Mostly classroom furniture and a lot of it. I am now going to inventory, get a rough idea of what is in each classroom.

I am at present in a music room with instruments scattered throughout. It is a beautiful sun-filled morning. Blue skies and puffy clouds. I drove round the island and got here at 9:20 a.m. I was chatting to Campbell and then Mr Moncrieff, the head teacher, appeared. I will need at least two containers to start with. I will call Andy later. I called Robert. *'I've got a container,'* he tells me. He has to find out whether it's certificated, shippable.

12:15 p.m. I am to pick up Johanna in the carpark opposite the creamery.

1:40 p.m. I meet Ivor at Saint Ninian's Church, Ardbeg at 4 p.m. to collect. *'I've got Bibles and hymn books for you.'*

4:25 p.m. Home. Roll it back.

I spent most of this morning inventorying classroom furniture in the academy old building (what was once the old primary school). Using the car. I left at midday. I stopped off at Cowal Builders' Supplies for a paper cup full of soup from the machine and collected my Surplus Educational Supplies poster from Duncan. I met Christian and Ronny and then drove up the High Street to meet Johanna, who was waiting for me in the Flexi Tech car park. Then it was back doon the road and I dropped her off at the Electric Bakery shop and then drove on home for a fried egg sandwich and a mug of coffee, and sat outside in the sunshine.

Thursday 27/09/2007

I received a call from Ivor to say that he had boxes for me. I called Robert to arrange for the collection of a container. Back to the Toon. Parked. Walked to *The Buteman* office at 2:15 p.m. I was eating a Cox's Pippin when I met Mike, journalist and photographer, and then it was back up to the academy where Campbell gave me the swipe card. Back up the steep brae and into the solid 70-year-old building to tour classrooms and to show the local Fourth Estate what was on 'offer'. He showed me Room 36, which was his dad's classroom. We toured and chatted until 4 p.m. I then set off up the Ardbeg Road to Saint Ninian's Church, where there was a skip on the road outside the kirk. Ivor said I could come later this afternoon to make a start at collecting the boxes. Here I am catching my breath, drinking a cup of tea in the sunshine, getting cooler before I drive back to meet Marion and Johanna off the ferry DV.

10:15 p.m. I have just received a telephone call from Raymond, President of St Paul's Government School PTA to tell me that WE Julien & Co Ltd don't have the invoice for the shipment. I told him that I had faxed all the necessary paperwork.

Thursday 27/09/2007

Call Ivor to cancel collection of furniture remaining in Saint Ninian's Church Hall as I have nowhere to store it on the island, furthermore I can no longer presume on Martin's goodwill at the boatyard.

9:20 a.m. Home. I have just been speaking to Gillian the marketing and operations manager at Lofthus Signs, West Shore Trading Estate, Granton, who has spoken to her managing director and they have kindly offered to put signage on container SEAU4272551 gratis. Pro bono. Brilliant! The container will be delivered to Ladywood Primary School, Penicuik, Midlothian on 15 October. I have called Douglas, EIS representative, and left a message on his mobile regarding my return to full-time employment and make an appointment with my 'line manager' in Dunoon.

Send faxes to GA Menzies; WE Julien Ltd; The Honourable Claris Charles; Christopher De Riggs; Carla Rae Briggs; Roland Malins-Smith RCS

11:45 a.m. Home. A beautiful blue sky sunlight-filled morning, but becoming cooler. Crisp. *'That's what I do to moles,'* said Howard, who was answering my call in his garden before I set off for the Little Town Post Office. He told me to send Tom Walker his fee for inspection of container SEAU4272551.

Up to the bank and then back down Victoria Street, turned right at the lights and parked the bicycle against the railings before the moat of the castle. Into the Clydesdale Bank, deposited £180, and up the High Street around the old Sheriff Court and whizzed down the Watergate and into Print Point. Karen as cheerful and helpful as always. I sent faxes to all and sundry. I bought a copy of *The Wealth of Nations* by Adam Smith, former resident of Kirkcaldy, and now I have to read this weighty tome. Hopefully it will teach me something about economics and the way the business world works that I can apply to my project. Then it was along to the Co-op where I purchased fixings for supper: chops, strawberries and tomatoes.

12:10 p.m. Home. I called Kenny, honcho with Skanska Construction. *'It was only a suggestion,'* he said, but it led to Midlothian Council storing surplus educational resources in an empty school building, from where it could be loaded into one of Surplus Educational Supplies 40-foot ocean freight containers. He said that he had contacted Mrs Adams about the flooring.

I stopped off at The Pier at Craigmore Café to ask Jean if she could put me in touch with someone with the expertise to put my project on a commercial, quasi-charitable, and legal footing. She gave me a warm welcome. Greets me with a hug. Her hands covered with flour. And later serves me up a freshly baked scone. Bless her. I am always looking for affirmation, which does wonders for my morale. I tell her about recent developments in the life of a Shipping Clerk's Apprentice. *'That's marvellous! See what happens when you encourage and nurture entrepreneurs. It's better than you weaving baskets in Lochgilphead,'* said Councillor Jean.

I can't get an internet connection. I am trying to contact Eric to see if I can come to the depot in Grange Dock and put a lick of paint on SEAU4272551, and whether Lofthus Signs Ltd can come into the yard to put signage on it. My 'commercial livery.'

12:55 p.m. I called Stephen at ZIM. I was speaking to Patricia, PA to Mr GA Menzies, CEO, Geo F. Huggins & Co (G'DA), Grenada, who has asked me to write a covering note. I am now going to cycle into the Little Town for the third time and see if I can fax my note, bill of lading, and invoice once more as it wouldn't go this morning.

Snatches of remembered dialogue: *'Don't turn the pages so fast,'* he said as we worked our way along the raspberry bushes at Classlochie Farm, Loch Leven Gairneybridge, Kinrosshire, summer 1974. Kitchen porter, berry picker, tattie howker and redeemed vagabond, made brand-new in Scotia Land.

Friday 28/09/2007

7:30 a.m. Home. I sent an email to Eric to ask him if it's okay for me to come across to bram up the container to be delivered to Ladywood Primary School, Penicuik on 15 October.

12:45 p.m. I cycled out and into the town. Great to get some fresh air in my lungs. On and up Bishop Street. Call Katherine, Community Services, regarding 'conscripts' and helpers. Social

I Persevere With My Project

A 40-foot ocean freight container shipment of educational resources from Rothesay Academy.

Work. Call as soon as container comes. Send an email to COSLA with an up to date of my NGO initiative. Make it for the attention of Penny Curtis.

Monday 01/10/2007

9:30 a.m. Home. *'What do we get out of helping you? What's in it for me, for you?'* she asked. Speaking to Cara at *Free Press*, Kirkcaldy. Could you please pass message on to Tanya and Adam I don't want to keep flogging a dead horse, but maybe it is worthwhile to keep on 'puffing' the pro bono help that I have received from the Scottish road haulage industry. *'You only want to move it once. We will take your containers to any port in the United Kingdom. You find the shipping line and we will deliver your containers to any port in the United Kingdom,'* said Eric of Duncan Adams Transport Ltd to me that Saturday afternoon of 16 December 2006.

Tuesday 02/10/2007

10:55 a.m. I have just had a call from haulier Robert who tells me that Tom Walker, was going to look at the container in Shotts.

12:20 p.m. I called the Grenada High Commission and spoke to Cathy at reception. Mr Sandy and Mr Charter are not in the office. They have my faxes. This morning I had met Nan the neighbour in the post office. *'Are you not working? Is it something serious? I didn't mean to be rude,'* she said. Methinks I am working through a self-directed programme of intense creative and useful work therapy.

12:45 p.m. I called the *Fife Free Press* and spoke to Tanya and brought her up to date on developments since her article 1 December 2006.

1:15 p.m. I spoke with Vicky *'Victoria is my Sunday name.'* Gillian of Lofthus Signs was not in and left a message to hang fire on their offer to put some signage on SEAU427 2551.

Tuesday 02/10/2007

9:30 a.m. Home. Tom Walker calls to say he can't drive the forklift to lift the container in Shotts and that there is a lock on the door. Okay, scrub it. He doesn't sound as if he thinks much of the state of it. I then call Robert, who is annoyed that Tom wouldn't make an attempt to drive the forklift. *'Leave it wi' me. Nothing is never easy,'* he said.

The container at Shotts is not in a fit state. Robert is keen to have Tom inspect it, in spite of what the latter thinks. Do containers have a resale value? Is there a markup? Yoh no gonnae tell me. I call Container Sales Ltd in Rutherglen and I speak with Pauline who tells me that Keith is on holiday. There has been no official response from Calliste Government School.

12:15 p.m. Home. It is getting cooler. The leaves are beginning to shrivel. I am slowing down. I am trying to move beyond my limitations. But how? That's David off into the town for an appointment.

6:30 p.m. I have been typing out my notes taken over these many months and weeks. I am not feeling too good. David has gone off to work at Chandlers Hotel at Ascog. Johanna has set the table for supper. Marion is on her way home.

8:30 p.m. I received a call from Raymond. More hassle. They need the invoice. I tell him that it has been sent. I call Stephen at ZIM to get proof of payment. Fax invoice and bill of lading again. Why do they make it so difficult? Wee bits of paper.

Wednesday 03/10/2007

7:45 a.m. Home. It is grey and drizzling. Marion has left with David, who is off on his own to see a GP in Greenock for his Clyde Marine medical. Johanna has gone into the shower. I force myself to keep moving in front of the monitor.

8:25 a.m. That's Johanna left for school in the bucketing rain. She asked me if Granny Hanschell was a Catholic. *'No,'* I say, *'She was a Christian.'*

10:15 a.m. I received a call from Rebecca, the *Herald* journalist. Would I be interested in being nominated for The Eco Trust Award? This news takes me by surprise. I tell her that I would, most certainly, and thank you very much. An encouragement, which has come from out of the blue.

I have just been speaking to Tom Walker who tells me that he has 'certificated' INBU4702128 in Brian Cardiff's yard. Then I call Robert. *'Ah, see whit ah kan dae for ye,'* he said.

Friday 05/10/2007

11:20 a.m. I call The Edinburgh Chamber of Commerce International Trade section. I was told to call Murdo. Call Maersk, based in the Port of Felixstowe. Call Maersk Southampton, speak to Stuart. They have a monopoly on 'boxes' *'He operates in that end of the market,'* he said. Now learn.

Friday 05/10/2007

9:30 a.m. Home. I called John, managing director of Russell in Hillington. *'I'll let you have a couple of containers out of the yard here,'* he said. High hopes. *(It was too good to be true as I learned to my cost, they were pin-holed and only fit for scrap.)*

10:30 a.m. I called ZIM regarding the release of the container. I spoke to Dave.

11:30 a.m. Called Fraser at Colliers Surveyors about the office furniture offer from Peter Blacker at 250 Seaward Street and to make arrangements for its collection and storage in containers in Russell Transport's depot in Hillington. Catherine has just called asking how I was and wanted to know when I was going to collect the stuff that I had left in the St Andrew's Primary School basement, and if I did not want it would I help their janitor shift the stuff to the cowp.

That was Alastair, a big supporter of SESF from the early days, from DC Murray Ltd the local painting and decorator firm, who has dropped in to see how much paint I will need to paint the house.

3:50 p.m. That was Sam who works for Shanks, the waste disposal firm, to tell me that I can park containers up at their recycling centre. The cowp. Stephen from ZIM had spoken to Andrew at W. E. Julien Ltd.

5:40 p.m. Home. David has just asked me, *'Are you pleased the way your "business" is going?'* Yes! Slow, but sure. In fits and starts. Forward one step, back two. I am moving forward one container shipment of educational resources at a time.

Saturday 06/10/2007

9 a.m. Home. I called Sam at Shanks about the demolition of Dunoon Grammar School. He is to call me back. Receptive. Marion is off up to Glasgow to meet chums. Amy is working, D and J are asleep. I called Tom Walker to see if he could have a look at the two containers in Russell's yard in Hillington on Monday.

10:45 a.m. Mr Bulloch of Rothesay Academy has just dropped off a box of English (American) texts, reading scheme and comprehension exercises. Someone, somewhere, I hope, will get the good out of it. *'Just throw it out. I cannae be bothered with it.'* Attitudes to useful waste with a shelf life.

THE LORD'S DAY 07/10/2007

9:30 p.m. (4:30 p.m. Grenada time) Raymond called to say customs need the original invoice. I told him that I would contact ZIM once again tomorrow. *'Drink a coconut water for me,'* I tell him. *'I hear you. I know Azam,'* he replied. For tomorrow, Monday 8 October: resale of containers. Send an email to Christopher De Riggs to let him know that I had approached Spice Isle Retreaders Ltd about the purchase of containers.

Monday 08/10/2007

'With the greatest of respect, David. I've just had a director in the office and I have had to take your call. What is on the commercial invoice? The problem is at your end, and it is to do with the documentation.' I

Monday 08/10/2007

was speaking to John, the freight forwarder at Denholm Bahr Ltd in Liverpool, hoping that he'll be able to give me some advice as to the reason for the hold up in Grenada.

11 a.m. Home. My self-belief, confidence, is wearing thin. Can I stay the course? I sent an email to Julie Anne, personal assistant to Sir Tom Hunter who had not replied to my letter. Thanks to Evelyn at Ayr Chamber of Commerce.

12:05 p.m. Home. That was Tom Walker saying that he had been round to Russell's yard in Hillington, but they did not have the units ready and he will have to go back there tomorrow. It was good of him to call me and take the trouble to inspect these containers. It has been a wet, grey, damp and miserable morning. I am making my own sunshine. Johanna is off to work at Paula's Café or is it Margaret Zavaroni's? David is up to the health centre. Marion and Amy left me in bed this morning. I was up most of the night.

4:30 p.m. I was speaking to Charles, transatlantic, my mentor on Social Edge. *'Be careful you don't miss someone who is talking to you,'* he said. Called Charles, Argyll and Bute Council, Lochgilphead. Shanks will provide me with storage. Wait and see.

8 p.m. I have just called Campbell (Dunoon Argyll and Bute Council joiner and key holder), who they had told me was in hospital, to see how he was. He told me that he had to have his gall bladder removed and he will be recuperating for the next three to four weeks.

8:42 p.m. The printer is out of action, which has brought my efforts to present these rough notes in a more legible form to a standstill.

I Persevere With My Project

Tuesday 09/10/2007

9:15 a.m. Saint Andrew's Primary School, Gowanfield Terrace. It is a damp, cool and grey morning. I am impatiently awaiting the arrival of Billy, the mobile janitor. I have come up here to give him a hand and collect some resources that I said I would be glad to receive way back in July, and help him take stuff from the dunny to the dump, cowp, recycling centre. And he's not here. I can feel the eyes on me from behind binoculars in front rooms across in the Bush.

Thoughts, intentions, plans and ideas forming: to set up a company and bid for surplus to requirements educational resources, essential kit that would otherwise be crushed, dumped, jettisoned, wasted in landfill. I said I would be back with the car at 1 p.m. Is there a market with a profit somewhere to be made from these resources? Can I turn a profit to cover and exceed the COSTS of marketing, collecting, storing, sorting, packing, transporting and shipping?

9:50 a.m. There is no one here. I am pushing off, whizzing doon the brae. I meet Billy as I turn roon the roundabout on Victoria Street, so I follow him back up the road.

10:25 a.m. I stopped off at *The Buteman* and touched bases with Craig, my friend, number one ally and supporter. He is keen to run a story about the irresponsible, unsustainable and profligate waste of educational resources from the PFI/PPP schemes. Mike the journalist is in California. He likes the pictures he took. *'Just think of what they are throwing out in the other schools,'* he said. Yes. I light a candle better than to curse the darkness. You'll get your reward in heaven.

10:40 a.m. I have spoken to Sam, Shanks's operative in Argyll, who says his firm will support my effort and total commitment. Shanks will provide storage (somewhere to park containers) on the island and elsewhere.

Wednesday 10/10/2007

10:55 a.m. That was Tom Walker. It was indeed too good to be true to tell me about his inspection of the containers that John Russell Transport Ltd said I could use for storage. *'I've got bad news for you. I would not put my name on any of them,'* he said. *'Are they any good for storage though?'* I asked. *'No, they they've got holes in the roof,'* he replied. These are the containers which Russell, Hillingdon Industrial Estate said I could have. Ach well, keep on looking and asking.

11:10 a.m. I called Pentalver. Stuart is on holiday. I called John at Geest in Portsmouth, who mentioned Alastair with Hubbards, who are the Geest Agents in St George's in Grenada. They want US$2,000. *'Empty containers are at a premium,'* he said.

I called Container Services Ltd, Sales to speak to Keith, who was on holiday. I spoke to Pauline, sales agent, partner, colleague. They keep their containers at Cardiff Brothers in Rutherglen. *'We have a good relationship with Maersk,'* she said. Good will? May waive price. Nae chance, Cyril! £1,000 for a 40-foot rusty box. I called Bob Baxter at EWL of Felixstowe; Olympia; Adaptainer Container Sales.

'It would be a commercial decision, but he looks favourably on these things,' he said. I was talking to Iain, Denholm Barwil Ltd, Ocean Terminal, Greenock who is going to speak to Hugh the port manager.

5:10 p.m. Ask John, managing director Russell, to call me back about the container purchase.

Wednesday 10/10/2007

10:30 a.m. I don't feel up to scratch. There are sharp pains, aches and pressure behind my eyeballs as I type out these rough notes. I just have to keep moving forward, if only ever so slowly.

Call Les when he returns from holiday about the educational

resources remaining in the Lochgilphead High School, having spoken to Dalgarno Platt.

11:10 a.m. I called Jim, chief janitor Midlothian Council, to make arrangements for collection on 15 October and a PIECE LIST for SEAU4272551. Called Douglas, EIS representative who had sent an email to Carol Walker. No reply. He will get back to me. I called Lucy at ZIM – did not get my email, will fax. Called Terry to confirm for the 15 October loading of SEAU4272551. I suggested he contact Eric. Yvonne at Eldapoint, Grangemouth: container £1,116.25. Too much and cost to transport here. COSLA David Kennedy. Penny Curtis. Nancy, business trainer, Boulder, Colorado USA.

Craigiebield Hotel, 50 Bog Road, Penicuik. A number 37A/47 bus from Edinburgh stops outside the hotel. I booked a room for 14 October 2007.

Sunday 14/10/2007

9:25 p.m. Here I am in Room 12. Marion drove me in to catch the 4 o'clock boat. The train got as far as Paisley Gilmour Street and bussed to Central Station. I walked up to Buchanan Street Bus Station and got the 6 p.m. National Express bus to Edinburgh. Into the St James Centre and had to walk all the way back to Princes Street and the Bridges to get a no. 37 bus to Penicuik. I didn't wait long. I'd still be walking to get here. You get what you pay for.

John from Kirkcaldy, the receptionist with impassive staring eyes booked me in. *'Can I get a sandwich?'* I ask. He calls the chef in the kitchen. No problem. I put my gear in the room. Jolomo print on the wall. Luxurious accommodation. I open the window. Quiet and comfortable. I should have the family in here with me. Back downstairs to the dining room-cum-conservatory. Tickety-boo. Grated cheese sandwich, salad bowl of chips and a pot of tea.

Monday 15/10/2007

Young waitress. No money in my wallet for a tip. Will remedy tomorrow. I will find out where Ladywood Primary School is in relation to here for 1 p.m. tomorrow.

Here I am, feeling very much on my own, out on a limb once more. Nothing else for it but to make the most of what I have set in motion. I journey by FAITH. Many imponderables. *'Be it on your own head,'* he said to me as I stood at the door of the kirk that Sunday morning handing out hymn books way back in 1982. Not much help you were, I guess you were being cruel to be kind, to let me go my own way at no little cost. Yes.

I had a brief chat with John as he polished the cutlery and set the dining tables. He tells me that his sister visits Goa on holiday and takes the biggest suitcase she can find and fills most of it with T-shirts and toys, *'fur the kiddies.'* Good aid in action right enough.

Monday 15/10/2007

11:30 a.m. I have just met Jim, the janitor, who has allowed me in to Ladywood Primary School to stow my gear and now I am going to take an inventory of what resources are going to be loaded into SEAU4272551. INVENTORY: Chairs, plastic, assorted colours (28 blue, 9 light blue, 29 green, 6 light green, 4 yellow, 25 red); 15 desks; 5 round tables; 6 square tables; 8 language resource cupboards; 7 chalkboards; 18 cupboards with shelving; 5 filing cabinets.

12:20 p.m. Ladywood Primary School, East Field Farm Road, Penicuik. I am sitting in the teachers' common room. Jim the janitor said that he would put the *'biler oan fur tea.'* I've helped myself. Scoffed a cheese and tomato sandwich and quaffed a bottle of Tropicana orange juice purchased from the big Tesco back up the road, where I had also purchased a copy of *The Big Issue* from a seller at the door.

I Persevere With My Project

I am alone in the staff room. Teachers and their pupils are away for their October break, also known as the 'Teachers Rest.' They will not be tattie howkin' I wager. I am waiting for the arrival of my container SEAU4275551. I went back over to the Skanska Construction site office where the new PFI/PPP school is being built and left more information about my initiative, 'The Project', for Kenny the site manager, having left my business card earlier.

Roll it back. I walked out from the Craigiebield Hotel after a breakfast of prunes (*'They are like missionaries, they go into the interior and do good work,'* said once upon a time by Father Humphrey Whistler of the SPCG, Codrington College, St John, Barbados, to my sister Diana who was a termly boarder at the Codrington High School for Girls), scrambled egg, toast and coffee. I walked across the rugby pitches and along the main road past Tesco and got lost in the Ladywood housing scheme. A kind mechanic gave me lift to the school where Jim the janitor met me with a warm welcome. I was a bit early. The container is not due until after midday.

I walked back to the hotel and left more of my publicity for the Rotary, who meet there for lunch tomorrow. The sun shone brightly on my path. And back along the main road.

12:45 p.m. I am standing at the school entrance awaiting the arrival of the container. I have just phoned Duncan Adams Transport Ltd to let them know I am here. *'Eric has his hands dirty. The container is on its way,'* he said was the message for me.

The janitors from schools in the authority have arrived to help load the container. I don my boiler suit and climb up into the container and am kept busy. There is still plenty of room in the container for more educational resources. We have loaded what was donated. Thank you all very much.

I get a lift back to Grange Dock with driver James, who tells me that he is satisfied with his current work and has had at least a hundred jobs before this one. We drove back through the Grangemouth Refinery. Eric has a staff member bring me a coffee and makes arrangements for me to get a lift back to Glasgow. I meet Duncan and Elisabeth and, surprise, surprise, Mick in the office, who was working with Freightliner Roadways Logistics Coatbridge in 2005. He had arranged for the second container, that was shipped to Grand Roy Government School, to be delivered to the Port of Felixstowe. The firm of Freightliner Roadways Logistics Ltd had waived the £500 charge, which had encouraged me to purchase my first ocean freight container.

I was dropped off on Saint Vincent Street across from George Square. My heart was full of gratitude for all who had cut me slack over the last 48 hours. On my return home I get a call from the Honourable Mr Joseph Charter High Commissioner for Grenada in London, giving me the names of five schools on the Island of Carriacou that he would like educational resources sent to (Harvey Vale Government School, Lesterre Rosary School, Mount Pleasant Government School, Hillsborough School, and Petit Martinque School) and would I send the resources care of another Honourable, Mr Elvin Nimrod the Minister for Foreign Affairs. Yes, of course, but will the government of Grenada provide the means to enable me to ship these resources?

Tuesday 16/10/2007

3:45 p.m. Home. Call from Iain at Ocean Terminal, Greenock who suggested Eldapoint, he at Denholm Barwil Ltd has nothing else to offer.

Monday 22/10/2007

Email from Anne (Balfour) *Herald* journalist about schools in Kenya who need school resources.

Tuesday 23/10/2007

Call Azam, managing director of Spice Isle Retreaders Ltd, Frequente Industrial Estate, off the Maurice Bishop Highway, Grenada. He has not returned my call.

Wednesday 24/10/2007

3:16 p.m. Home. It is a beautiful late autumn, early winter day. Clear blue sky with just a smidgen of cloud through the skylight window above my head. I have just come back from a cycle into the town to stop off at Print Point where Karen was helpful, cheerful, positive, kind and supportive as ever. When she asked me how I was, I said not too good and she said, *'David you should get a wee job out of doors, and you should go and see Jan De Vries.'*

Karen was faxing details of container purchases and newspaper puff publicity articles about my project for me to Azam. I had said I would send him some information about my initiative. He had said that he would buy the containers for US$1,000. We will have to wait and see how the sale of GSTU895863 goes. This morning I was up the road to the health centre for 9:20 a.m. for an appointment with Dr Clark, who I found to be sympathetic, and who signed me off sick for the next 13 weeks. He offered me medication, which I declined, choosing to try and keep my mind occupied with my project.

Thursday 25/10/2007

Home. I call John managing director Russell Transport Ltd depot, Hillington Industrial Estate. Fraser at Colliers CRE wants the donated furniture and stuff remaining at 250 Seaward Street shifted as soon as possible. The pressure and incumbent stress on me is being turned up. Will Russell store it for me?

Friday 26/10/2007

10 a.m. I have been given the contact of a solicitor, Simon in Stornoway, in the Western Isles, who is familiar with the legislation regarding social enterprise and social entrepreneurship. *'I'll get Simon to phone you,'* she said.

David's left for keep-fit class up at Rothesay Baths. I have just eaten my marmalade and toast and am going to type these scribbled notes.

10:30 a.m. I called Councillor Jim Muirhead. *'He's in a meetin,'* she said. I called Robert. *'Who is it? I am in Amsterdam,'* he said.

I then called Keith, Container Sales Ltd. *'I'm on the other line. Can I take your number? We have a good relationship with Maersk when they are sold into the second-hand market. Eric Adams is a good guy,'* he said. I think he doesn't want me to queer their pitch and corner their the market for one-way shippers.

Friday 26/10/2007

I call Stephen, Glasgow solicitor, and make an appointment to see him on 29 October at 3 p.m., Burness, Glasgow. It is now after 12 p.m. Simon, the other legal, has not returned my call after several attempts to speak to him. I called Anthea Peterkin Principal St Paul's Government School. Write letters to be faxed to Hon Elvin Nimrod, Ministry of Carriacou and Petit Martinque, Beausejour, Carriacou, Grenada. Permanent Secretary Bernadette Lindore.

5:30 p.m. Talking to Diana at SeaFreight Agencies in Miami, thanking them for shipping GSTU8958639 from Kingston, Jamaica, to Grenada pro bono, gratis. I can't complain. I am so grateful with the assistance from many quarters to deliver these precious educational resources.

I Persevere With My Project

Monday 29/10/2007

7:50 a.m. I can't remember the login name or password to the Social Edge website: If you have forgotten your password click here to retrieve it. *'Welcome you are now logged in.'*

2:20 p.m. Burness office, 9th floor. Beautiful afternoon. I am early. Floor-to-ceiling window. Another new office block going up on Bothwell Street. Tall cranes moving loads into position and another building being demolished.

Who is he? *'Brilliant lawyer whose approachability and extensive knowledge serves as a magnet for clients.'* Chambers UK. I meet himself and his young assistant Inez. They are welcoming and appear supportive. There was filter coffee and bowls of peanuts. I was smitten.

Tuesday 30/10/2007

Home. As I was lying on my bed, chilling, not feeling too great, David Alexander calls me to tell me that there was someone on the phone wishing to speak to me. Brian of Fife Council, who tells me that there are resources to be collected at Dunshalt Village Primary School that are going to be crushed and the school must be emptied by the end of November. Immediately I think, *'here are the resources for some of the schools in Carriacou and Petit Martinque.'*

'I have a contract to have this lot crushed. Ah'll take some digital foties an' send it tae yuh,' he said. I had better get crackin', tae the rescue. Here we go again. Salvagei. I make yet another call to the supportive press, the *North East Fife Herald*.

11:30 a.m. I call the Fife Warehousing Co. Ltd. Would they be willing to assist me once more with removal and storage? I speak to Sharon at reception who is always helpful.

Tuesday 30/10/2007

11:45 a.m. I was speaking with Liz, journalist and reporter at the *Fife Herald*, who is sympatico and said she will write an article for her paper drumming up support for the community of Dunshalt Village who do not want to lose their school. I gave her Brian's telephone number with regard to Dunshalt Village Primary School, and also that of Tanya Scoon at *the Fife Free Press*.

12:30 p.m. I call Brian. *'That'll cost you a fortune to get a crane to lift the container into the school playground,'* he said. Problems always. Obstacles, never solutions. *(Community Services and their teams with transport, were to come to the rescue.)*

The issue is the wasteful disposal of fit-for-purpose educational resources from schools and colleges across Scotland that are flooding into the waste stream. Who cares? Difficulties of transport to Uganda, Malawi etc. Remote areas. Problems of logistics. Non-existent national governance and endemic state corruption at the consignee end. I was speaking to Sonia at Build Africa. Feeder vessels from the Port of Felixstowe. Call office of Ministry of Education and Labour, Grenada government. Hon. Claris Charles. I have been speaking to the chief education officer and got nowhere. He has not replied to my letter.

(My long-distance telephone bill was astronomical. I did not count the cost. 'Do you want your money back?' *Iain, Irvine businessman had asked me that bright morning, many months later, as he sat behind the wheel of his Rolls Bentley Sport, and asked me for the second time* 'Do you want your money back?' *I replied,* 'Yes, Mr Murray, I know my family would want me to recover much of what it had cost them.' 'Well then, I might be able to help you, providing you send me an audited account of every penny you have spent on your project,' *he said. This I was able to do thanks to the pro bono assistance of Ross & Company, the local accountancy*

firm who were able to prepare an audited account from the haphazard invoices and finances that I had kept since 2005.)

4 p.m. I call Pauline, who has offered me chairs from the Dunshalt Village Hall. The community were most unhappy about the decision of Fife Council to close their village primary school. Children from Dunshalt will now attend Auchtermuchty Primary School.

Wednesday 31/10/2007

11:20 a.m. I call Avril, Fife Council Education Department, to call back. Call Social Security Office.

4 p.m. I called Burness, spoke to Inez. They are going to draft a document of incorporation. What is that?

(You will end up paying for it.)

I called Chantal, who had been speaking to Mott, the cocoa farmer and chocolatier, who tells me his neighbour has links with Carriacou. Removal van supplied by community helpers to collect resources from Dunshalt PS. It has been a busy day. I'm going to fry some fish for family supper.

9:25 p.m. I've just stopped filing and tidying my files. I still haven't done the dishes.

Thursday 01/11/2007

9:32 a.m. I called the Fife Group and spoke to Douglas. Brian is in a meeting. They can't help me this year.
   Soap Box Marketing? Tae Glasgow by taxi to the SECC. The nitty gritty of it all. It was boring but necessary in order to accomplish my goal.

Friday 02/11/2007

9 a.m. I called Eric about the collection of boxes of hymn books and crockery from Kilchattan Bay C of S Church. Called John at Russell's. They can store the stuff from 250 Seaward Street in the two leaky ocean freight containers that I will cover with tarpaulins. I will need to arrange my own transport.

5:45 p.m. Called Mr Fleming of Fleming Removals. '*We have laid off 10 men this* afternoon,' he said. I am to call him back when I have somewhere to store the educational resources from Dunshalt Primary School.

Monday 05/11/2007

Midday. I am calling Sam at Shanks Waste Solutions and Brian at Fife Council. I called Robert at the Archbishop of York's office. Spoke to Harriet. Call Edinburgh Chamber of Commerce. Received a call from Paul, managing director of Air Link Ecosse World Express, acknowledging the bar of Grenada Chocolate I sent him. He told me to call on him next time I am in Glasgow. *'You have to keep up the momentum of what you are doing,'* he said.

Tuesday 06/11/2007

10:25 a.m. Home. At the desk. *'The number you have called is busy.'* High Commissioner for St Vincent and the Grenadines. I called John at Ogilvie Ross in Kinross, a haulier.

Kinross. Gairneybridge, Classlochie Farm, Summer 1974, I recall kindness from farmers, Mr and Mrs MacClaren, Alastair, Jane and Linda, who celebrated my 31st year with birthday cake in their kitchen, and not least Norman and Susan who lived at the toll house on the main road into the town.

I Persevere With My Project

11:30 a.m. Both Chambers of Commerce down south have received my requests, my queries. Now I await the result of those enquiries. CRXU4103197 (262 chairs, 184 tables). I called Jim of Rotary at Craigiebield Hotel, Penicuik. Wrote another letter to Niall, managing director of Denholm Barwil Ltd, Southampton. Called Rod, managing director East West Indies Lines Ltd, Port of Felixstowe. Called Keith, North East, Sunderland. Called Stuart, Pentalver Maersk. He told me to call him after Christmas. They can offer me a much better deal on containers! Barry, Port of Felixstowe. Geest Line, Fareham, Portsmouth. DHL Port of Felixstowe, Nick, depot manager – tight for space. Steve, P&O Logistics.

5:45 p.m. Sam calls me back and mentions ORIN? This firm in Fife might be somewhere where I can park my containers.

6:10 p.m. I call Jim, Rotary in Penicuik.

(I would like to acknowledge the firms that have contributed to my efforts to deliver a dozen ocean freight containers of educational resources in the words I am typing here for the Diary of A Shipping Clerk, *who by donating their time, storage and transport, free of charge, made these shipments possible.)*

Get in touch with the Scottish Road Haulage Association.

Wednesday 07/11/2007

1:30 p.m. Home. *'I'll put you on hold and talk to my boss for a moment,'* said Lorraine at Sharkey in Edinburgh. Go for it! Barry at the Port of Felixstowe suggested I contact Nick, manager for property, Port of Felixstowe. He is to call me back. *'We own the Port of Dar Es Salaam,'* he tells me. Hutchinson Whampoa. He suggests I try the area around Barking for storage of containers

– would be more convenient. CEVA Logistics, Laurence to call back if Nick doesn't get through to me. Get in touch with him.

Thursday 08/11/2007

9:30 a.m. Home. Down to work on the phone. *'Welcome you've got mail.'* Spam. I spoke to someone in the Archbishop of York's office who suggests I speak to Neil, chief executive of Thorpe Kilworth in Corby. *'I'll give you his mobile,'* he said. See the work being done by this charity Education For All.

Friday 09/11/2007

9:40 a.m. Home. Another day in Paradise.

I called the Honourable Mr Joseph Charter. *'I called you yesterday, but you were having lunch at the House of Commons,'* I said. Received messages yesterday from Nick of Port of Felixstowe management.

CV Logistics: speak to Laurence Tucker. Call Gillian, estates surveyor, Fife Council, Glenrothes, and Renwick Cowan, estates surveyor. Friends of the Earth Scotland. Duncan MacLaren? *'This is a goer,'* he said, for whom I wonder? *'The mobile number you have called is switched off.'*

12:45 p.m. Gillian returned my call. She is very helpful.

1:35 p.m. I call Brian, Fife Council. He has not sent, as he promised he would, photographs/digitals of the educational resources in storage at Dunshalt Primary School. I called Liz, reporter at *Fife Herald* news line.

Call the Barbados National Bank and spoke to Olivia: send BCSD form and copy of my passport etc. Call Azam, managing director, Spice Isle Retreaders Ltd. *'He's in Trinidad right now,'* he said. Call again tomorrow at 3:15 p.m. *'I have a meeting with the minister,'* he said. Which one? Barbados *Nation* newspaper, Richard Hoad journalist.

I have woken up to the fact that my project is in conflict with commercial interests of the waste collection, demolition and crusher contractors. If muggins collects the resources before disposal and truck to landfill, they lose out. And contracts are awarded to the sectors in this industry. It's a case of the crushers versus the recyclers. This recycler is heading for poverty street.

Call Reverend Canon Paterson, Bishopthorpe Palace, York. Link with Thorpe Kilworth, Corby, Neil Logue, Jon Wragg. Who are these people? I am now clutching at straws in the wind. And Archbishop John Sentamu is the patron of their charity, Education For All.

2:30 p.m. I call Scott, at Andrew Wishart & Sons Ltd who were in Kirkcaldy, now in Rosyth. Call Mr Charter the High Commissioner. Call Azam at 3:15 p.m. Call Neil Logue at Thorpe Kilworth.

Fortres Mutual Fund, Barbados, Barbados Stock Exchange. To sell or not to sell BS&T Shares?

5:40 p.m. Home. Speaking to Scott, who is always approachable and positive, at Andrew Wishart & Sons Ltd. *'I'll speak to the powers that be,'* he said.

Saturday 10/11/2007

This morning I got a call from Mchima Trust, Bapepa Thylo Craft Centre in Southern Malawi.

Monday 12/11/2007

9:50 a.m. Home. Called Neil Logue, who said he would call me sometime? Why do I have to make such a nuisance of myself?

Tuesday 13/11/2007

Karen his personal assistant, has passed on my message. Received email from Azam. Fresh news. We'll see. Called Fraser, surveyor with Colliers CRE, Glasgow. He will get the lights switched on at 250 Seaward Street. I mentioned to him that I still had not been able to source transport, but I was working on it, and I had arranged for the storage of the resources in two 40-foot derelict ocean freight containers at John G Russell Transport Ltd depot in the Hillington Industrial Estate.

I sent a faxed document regarding donation of resources from Dunshalt Village Primary School to the Minister for Foreign Affairs, Ministry for Carriacou and Petit Martinque, Grenada.

7:45 p.m. Speaking to Jon of the firm Thorpe Kilworth, who is off to South Africa where their charity, Education For All, has re-equipped a large number of schools. He said he would call me when he comes up to Scotland in December to see David of ESA McIntosh in Kirkcaldy. Links and connections.

I called Charles to put him in good heart. Trevor Huddleston, of the book *Nought For Your Comfort,* of The Mirfield Fathers, was his mentor and was also Archbishop Desmond Tutu's mentor: trying to cheer him up. He had introduced me to the Social Edge Community on the internet. Short-lived dialogue. I had high hopes for this link.

Willa, neighbour along the road, called offering boxes of resources stuff from the island secondary school, which are in her garage and she wants me to go round there on Wednesday after tea to collect.

Tuesday 13/11/2007

9 a.m. I am sitting in the REAL cafeteria of Glasgow Caledonian University eating my apple, tangerine and most of a squashed banana, and supping an aerated-with-steam hot chocolate, which is now lukewarm. Scroll it back as always.

I was up at 5 a.m. I lay abed for a while, conscious, catatonic, inert, and had to fight my way off the bed. Energised. Kissed my best friend adieu and told David to hold the fort and answer the phone. Dry and damp morning. The stars were still out. Into the town, the road to myself. I cycled round the prefab ferry office. I was shouted at by one of the pier men, *'Ye cannae put yer bike there.'* Okay, okay, dinnae lose your hard hat. So at that moment in time I decided to take the bike onto the ferry. Whizzed around on to the car deck. No sooner had I parked my bicycle than one of the lady ticket agents stormed down the ramp. *'Oi there. Who do you think you are? You just can't cycle onto the ferry.'* Sorry. Don't lose your shirt. And I walked back up to the ticket office. Got my free ticket. Pensioner perk.

I returned to where I had the bike and trotted up the steps. I bought a coffee and went and sat with Robert who was the joiner who, along with his team, were repairing the ancient fabric of Delhi Cottage when we arrived in 1990, and for some time after. Hanschell Plc had to remortgage the bothy so we could repair a section of the roof. He told me that he was working for Barr Construction Ltd on a PFI/PPP school overlooking Port Glasgow. He told me he remembered using a chalk and slate at the main island primary school in 1962.

As I cycled off the ferry on arrival at Wemyss Bay the chappie at the other side, pleasant, said I had the wrong ticket. So I cycled up and into Wemyss Bay Station and down the wooden-planked pier as half-asleep foot passengers were walking up the other side. Hairy-eyeball glances. There goes that nutter. No one shouted at me, *'Hi, Dave, waur yer off to today!'* There were more pleasant ticket ladies this side of the watta. I had to pay for my bike and left them with some Surplus Educational Supplies publicity. I cycled back up the pier to the station platform to board, just in time, the 7:15 a.m. train. I was chatting to Scott who was asking after Amy. He now has an apprenticeship with

Tuesday 13/11/2007

the same company that Ted (Iain's dad) works for. Pleasant. I waited until all the commuters had got off the train and pushed the bike through Glasgow Central Station. I cycled up West Nile Street. Here I am, scribbling, going to attend a social enterprise conference: 'Make A Difference'.

9:45 a.m. I met Thomas from Cumbernauld, Scotland Unlimited Development manager. *'Unlimited's mission is to reach out and unleash the energies of people who can transform the world in which they live. We call these people Social Entrepreneurs.'* Later I met Naomi, executive director First Port, 'Doing Good Business'.

Transport assistance that I have been favoured to receive so far: John MacKirdy and Son (The Island); Fife Warehousing Co. Ltd (Dysart); Duncan Adams Transport Ltd (Grange Dock); Pentalver Transport Ltd (Southampton); John G Russell Ltd (Coatbridge and Hillington); Shanks Waste Management (Grantham); Sterling Furniture (Auchtermuchty).

4:35 p.m. Home. *'We are all part of a chain,'* said Canon Pat McInally, who Fife Councillor Fiona Grant suggested I get in touch with. He has just called me back, to tell me that he is going out to Uganda and that he has been given 35 microscopes by a private school in St Andrews and wants to know who to donate them to. I spoke to Forbes, assistant to the Midlothian Council's Director of Education, who has been off work. I was to contact Anna about Midlothian Council's surplus schools furniture offer. Contact Keith at Maersk in Southampton. *'We will make a space for you. I'll find space for you at the Western Docks,'* he said. Brill! I had contacted Keith about acquiring containers at cost. He then suggested I speak to Carl. *'It's their shout,'* he said. I speak to Karl at Pentalver Transport Ltd. Contact WH Malcolm Transport Ltd. Speak to Jim Clark and Bob Tannahill and also Gavin Brown at their Muirhouse Depot.

Wednesday 14/11/2007

Home. Contact Renwick, Fife Council estates surveyor, and Gillian, and Avril, Fife Council's education department coordinator. Fife Council Estates Department have spoken to her and she now understands the situation at Dunshalt Village Primary School. *'It's okay ... as usual Gillian is ahead of the game,'* said Avril. I must make arrangements to have these resources uplifted, stored, inventoried and shipped soon.

10:20 a.m. I call Azam, Zaid Spice Isle Retreaders Ltd.; call Principal Rosetta Brathwaite, St George's Anglican Junior School; call Gerry, Just Grenada ; call Avril, Fife Council; Peter at John G Russell, Mossend, Coatbridge.

Thursday 15/11/2007

Home. Call John, managing director, Russell's depot, to make an appointment. Russell's depot in Hillington. Receive directions to their depot. *'When you get to the Innovation Centre turn near the burger van, beside the building with the purple trim, and be there for 4:30 p.m,'* he said. I am always pushing the envelope and I ask him if they have any spare containers, bearing in mind that what his firm are giving me are only fit for scrap. But I reckon I can cover them with tarpaulins, and I now have use of a site where I can park a serviceable container as and when. Don't look a gift horse in the mouth, or whether a container is seaworthy or not. I sought his advice and discussed with him the delivering of containers of surplus educational resources to the developing world, and the logistics of storing and shipping ocean freight containers. Called Sharkey about premises in Glasgow for the 250 Seaward Street office furniture. Called AB Containers Ltd, Hull. Thanks to Angie who gave me this contact. Call bank regarding cheque that was deposited in Educational Resources account. They were unable to tell me.

Friday 16/11/2007

Call Colliers CRE to arrange to have electricity switched on at 250 Seaward Street. Call Salvation Army office in Glasgow to see if they can provide transport to shift furniture from 250 Seaward Street out to Deanside Road in Hillington. Call Ben Mundell Transport Ltd (Tarbert Argyll). Call Andrew Wishart & Sons Ltd (Rosyth). I spoke to Anton who will speak to Scott. *'He's loading a trailer just now,'* he said. He told me to call again this afternoon. He had told me last week that he would speak to the powers that be. Call Fleming Removals Ltd (Inverkeithing Fife).

Friday 16/11/2007

I am having a meeting with John, managing director of John G Russell Transport Ltd, off Ainslie Drive, Hillington, today. He mentioned St Modwen Properties Ltd, Warrington, who have bought an ex-Rolls Royce factory warehouse at Hillington and have refurbished units on that site, and said to speak to Joan. Colin is the site manager. John gave me the time of day. Helpful, and told me to get in touch with the former. Later I called Trump Developments, Edison Street, Glasgow, and I spoke to Jonathan.

'We can't offer you anything,' he said.

1:15 p.m. Home. I am just in from Wemyss Bay. David Alexander has just handed me cup of tea.

1:35 p.m. Speaking to Stuart at Pentalver Maersk, Southampton *'You'll be able to sell 'em to you for £500 and you can get your money back.'* Some good news for a change.

3 p.m. I received a call from the Honourable Mr Joseph Charter telling me to get in contact directly with Honourable Elvin Nimrod *'Ah gie anoder nomba foh him,'* he said.

I Persevere With My Project

Monday 19/11/2007

11:45 a.m. Call from LEWA about schools in Kenya interested in obtaining surplus educational resources. Problems with shipping and transportation. Port of Mombasa – ships queuing up to unload cargo.

I received a call from Douglas, EIS representative for teachers who work for Argyll and Bute Council. He tells me that they will extend my half pay until I am 65 and I will receive a letter from Carol to confirm. I am a late entrant to the teaching career. I am in a limbo, a parallel universe world, feeling that I am living in now. Here I am trying to reconstruct, reinvent myself, with a sense of purpose beyond my capacity, enabled by my pride and innate capacity for enthusiasm as a do-gooder, charity worker, and social entrepreneur. I will have to keep going on, one day at a time.

Call from Nick about property in the South East, who suggests the Essex, Kent, Medway, Barking area. Helpful and approachable. Barry and Stuart. Pentalver links. Another container? £500?

Call LINK about the salmon farm site. Spoke to Alice, who is helpful and suggested I contact Arron Forsyth in Scoraig which I did. Call Friends of the Earth and speak to Claire Symonds.

Thursday 22/11/2007

3:15 p.m. Home. Called Carla, editor of *The Grenada Informer*, who said she was running an article next week: she is supportive of SESF efforts to a certain extent. I have to keep badgering these indifferent, self-sufficient people for the sake of the voiceless. Call Peggy, who is an insider in the government of Grenada, who Azam has mentioned several times as being able to facilitate the shipment and delivery of resources. She has never replied and yet I keep leaving polite, deferential, messages.

Monday 26/11/2007

4:15 p.m. Home. I called Brian about Dunshalt Village Primary School. *'Ah'll get the digital foties tae ye this week.'* Promises, promises. I need them for Hon. Elvin Nimrod, Ministry of Carriacou, to show him the resources that are here on offer for schools in Carriacou and Petit Martinque. Call Grenada Boys Secondary School and speak to Mrs Lord, the school secretary. Call Marvin, President, Grenada Union of Teachers. Acting Permanent Secretary, Martin Baptiste. Commercial integrity in Scotland? How many families, members of the landed gentry, companies, individuals, and charitable trusts had, or still have, interests in Grenada when it was just another slave colony in the Caribbean?

Tuesday 27/11/2007

Home. I called Jim of the Rotary that meets in the Craigiebield Hotel at 6:30 p.m. He never replied.

Wednesday 28/11/2007

3:35 p.m. Home. I received a call from Ian from Suffolk, who I met at the Malawi Scotland Trade Exhibition at the SECC in November 2006, who has just returned from Africa. I put him in touch with Education For All, Thorpe Kilworth, and also Elias of Sport for All. Email from the Principal of Bishops College, Hillsborough, Carriacou indicating that they were keen to receive the resources currently in storage at Dunshalt Village Primary School. She told me that she had had good reports about the educational resources that I had sent to the four schools on the neighbouring island of Grenada. Replied and filed.

This morning I faxed my dossier to Dr Friday, managing director of Glenelg Spring Water, high-flying Grenada government representative in New York. Good, assuring talker but nothing forthcoming in terms of support. I am still awaiting a response from the Hon. Elvin Nimrod. I called Liz, journalist reporter with the *Fife Herald,* who is helpful and supportive, who said she would run an article on Dunshalt Village Primary School about my attempts to ship the educational resources in the school to deserving recipients in the Caribbean, and hopefully soften the blow to that community on the closure by Fife Council of their village school. She said she would send some photographs of the school, which I will send on to the ministry in Carriacou.

Thursday 29/11/2007

I received emails from Adaptainer Ltd's Ipswich office.

Friday 30/11/2007

I called Stuart, Pentalver Transport Ltd. Could the container go to Russell's at Hillington? Call John Hume to see if this possible. Call Liz Rougvie. I call the High Commissioner for Grenada, to let him know that I have established a contact with a school in Carriacou.

11:49 a.m. Back home on the bike through the gentle rain. It is pelting down now. Chat over a good coffee at The Musicker on the High Street with Jim, who was telling me about his early days of tenement life growing up in Cowcaddens, Glasgow. Earlier I had a chat with Sue, a sympathetic soul. Then it was along to collect my prescriptions: migraine pain killer, heart circulation, aspirin and prostate shrinking tablets.

I am now checking emails in an empty hoose, beautiful bothy, converted van shed. David Alexander is off the island today to help a local builder, Sam, load tiles. Johanna is at school all day. Amy is studying at University and Marion is at work. Oh forgot! After collection prescription from the chemists I withdrew £100

Saturday 01/12/2007

and deposited in account at Clydesdale Bank, while there I met Mrs Jardine, mother of two former pupils and chatted briefly. '... *but the children miss yeh,*' she said. '*I miss them too,*' I replied.

'*You are an old man,*' he says to me in conversation, after I had picked him up in the car for a lift along the road from to his office in the town. With friends like that, who needs enemies. That remark of his stung. I didn't need anyone to tell me that. Who said the last time, after I been excitedly telling him about the progress of my project, *'Aye but will you have any money left?'*

4:30 p.m. For next Friday: collect football kit from Jim, Scottish Football Association coach at the Moat Centre.

Saturday 01/12/2007

11:20 a.m. Home. A pause for reflection. Where do I go from here?

'What's next?' Eric asked me that afternoon as I stood in the queue of truck drivers handing in their tachographs at Duncan Adams Transport Ltd office. Way back on that late Friday afternoon of 16 December 2006. I am awaiting replies to letters I have written, emails and faxes sent. To achieve these goals before the end of the month:

1. Collect, and ship to Grenadian schools, the educational resources donated by Argyll and Bute Council in the former local secondary school. Hanschell Freight Plc. Are You Joking? No. I am serious.

(I was delusional. See those words which I chalked on the side of my first container before I painted it. I had big ideas. Maersk had four container ships mothballed in Loch Striven.)

2. Collect and ship to Carriacou schools the resources donated by Fife Council that are currently in storage in the now derelict Dunshalt Village Primary School.

11:35 a.m. I've just called Robert, the farmer haulier in Airdrie, who says he's on the lookout for a container for me. He will let me know as soon as one comes into the container base at Coatbridge. *'Ah've got your number in my book.'*

Bless him. He brought my first container down from Coatbridge gratis to the port boatyard on 25 April 2006. Thanks to Martin who had called him up at 8 a.m. the morning before. When Robert climbed out of the cab he asked me, that bright sunshine-filled spring morning, *'Are you a born again?' 'I try to be BORN AGAIN every day,'* I replied.

I have got to get a breakthrough sooner or later. I keep hanging on. Critical mass. The tipping point. The Break Point. I am interested in building ongoing relationships with the beneficiaries of these shipments of educational resources. Why? It's more than just things I am sending: they are items of great value and usefulness to me, who happens to be an education professional —it's just not stuff to be passed on, got out of the way, otherwise I would not be going to all this trouble and personal expense to collect, store and ship them to where it will be valued and appreciated.

11:45 a.m. I thought I would make one more telephone call and I finally got to speak with Neil, of Thorpe Kilworth in Corby, who is switched on. I said I would write to him. *'You have to persist,'* he said. Right enough, I sure do that. I can but continue to try, wait and see.

4 p.m. I cycled into the town post office at Guildford Square with letter and enclosed documents in the dossier file of Surplus Educational Supplies Foundation.

I chatted with Mrs Donald the postmistress as she sold me stamps and weighed the envelope prior to handing it over to the postman just before he was about to drive off. She is always an encouragement to me to keep going on. I cycled back up the road and stopped off at The Pier at Craigmore and The Tea Room,

Monday 03/12/2007

where I received a warm welcome from Keira's mum and Jean, who wouldn't let me pay for my pot of tea and lemon slices. I perused *The Buteman* and *The Piers and Harbours of Bute* by Ian McLagan. I called George, HGV driver and bus driver, who on Saturday 9 December 2006 drove a 40-foot artic and curtain-sider trailer up from Duncan Adams Transport Ltd depot at Grange Dock, accompanied by young Kenneth, truck garage mechanic's apprentice, and who drove all the way from the Port of Grangemouth to meet me in the Inverkeithen town centre to assist in the collection of donated educational resources from what was the former Inverkeithen Primary School that I was rescuing and salvaging from the crusher. It was a beautiful morning. They picked me up in front of the Volunteer Arms pub and drove on to the school. I also phoned Linda and Harry in Kirkcaldy (I stayed at their B&B on Friday 1 December 2006 when I went over to collect school furniture that had been stored at Capshard Primary School and North Kirkcaldy Primary School).

For Monday call: Rod, managing director EWL, Port of Felixstowe, regarding information of shipping of container from that port to Kingston Jamaica. Tariff reduction? Duncan Adams Transport Ltd will deliver my container to the Port of Felixstowe. Call/email Roland Malins-Smith regarding his offer that his firm, SeaFreight Agencies, will take the container from Kingston, Jamaica, to St George's, Grenada, gratis. I call Stuart, Pentalver Maersk Transport Ltd, about purchase of containers and delivery to John G Russell Transport Ltd depots in Coatbridge and Hillington. Call Gina at Adaptainer Ltd about their quote.

Monday 03/12/2007

11:50 a.m. I was speaking to Stuart about the container for storage and shipment of educational resources from Dunshalt Primary School. He told me to ring and ask for Sam. Helpful and supportive. Call Keith Wilson or Phil? Call Tom at Maersk.

Called Adaptainer – Gina away on business. From where can I obtain a container and have it delivered so that it will be near enough to Dunshalt PS? Call Brian Schultz. Problem of storing containers where ports are already congested. I called EWL, Port of Felixstowe and spoke to Roger, who was very helpful and informative about the logistics and problems associated with seaborne transportation. *'Costs are going through the roof,'* he said. He talks about niche feeders, mentioned Geest at Fareham in Portsmouth and gives me the name of Jim, their freight commercial manager. I then call him, just before he leaves the office for a holiday on the Isle of Islay.

He said that Geest might waive handling charges on my shipment.

I called David, development director at ESA McIntosh, Kirkaldy and left a message on his answering machine. Called John and Alan of Fleming Removals, Inverkeithing, Fife: call back at 6 p.m. Called Joyce at Fife Group. Iain Paterson: call if and when I am ready to put the container in place. Send email to Diane, Southampton Port Information Network. Write letter to Piers, Public Relations, Associated British Ports, Southampton. Make arrangements to collect donated office furniture from Seaward Street. Obtain/rent transport from Boulevard Self-Drive. Called John regarding storage in containers at Russell in Hillington. *'You can do what you like with them,'* he said.

(I should have taken him at his word and sold them for scrap. This was where I should have called this collection off, but I did not.)

I called Colliers CRE, George Square, Glasgow, spoke to Fraser who tells me that I must make arrangements to remove the resources from 250 Seaward Street. Call on Tuesday. *'You never stop do you?'* said Derek. No, I don't know when to quit. The pressure and stress I have brought on myself and the rest of the family is taking its toll.

3:50 p.m. I have been speaking with Yamila at SeaFreight Agencies Miami. They will ship the container to Grenada free of charge. Magic!

Wednesday 05/12/2007

Call *The Fife Herald.* Speaking with Simon, who tells me, *'P&O has been bought out by Maersk. I have known Stuart Jarvis for a long time.'* I thought Dubai Ports had bought P&O. They can't keep containers and have no lifting capacity. He suggested I contact Pentalver Transport Ltd, which I do and speak to Stuart, who says they may give me some space. Call Fraser Duguid, Liz Rougvie and John Hume to let him know what is happening.

Thursday 06/12/2007

Home. Call Eldapoint at Grangemouth for the price of their containers. David, managing director at Bishops Move, can give me six weeks of storage in wooden boxes.

11:30 a.m. I call Catherine, Community Services Criminal Justice Department, Dunoon, who is always positive, to see if they will supply a team of Community Payback Scheme helpers for the uplift of resources from 250 Seaward Street. She gives me a long list of addresses and telephone numbers out of the Criminal Justice Address Book and tells me, *'You are up for it. I think it is a great idea.'* Encouragement, just when I needed it, and I think to myself, *'You would be a washout were it not for all the help and goodwill you are receiving.'* She tells me that the community services takes a variety of forms. *'What service do I want?'*

2:12 p.m. I call Community Services Criminal Justice, Possil Park office. I speak with Callum, social worker who is very helpful. *'We are not looking for any placements. We are quite stressed at the* moment. *We have similar arrangements with Scottish International Relief,*' he said. He then gives me contacts for the majority of Scotland. *'The manager will call you back, okay,'* he said.

Call Joan, surveyor, regarding lease or rent of Rolls Royce industrial unit out at Hillington. For Friday: call Peter, Community Services Criminal Justice Department, regarding a team for removal of resources at 250 Seaward Street. CRXU4103197 will be delivered to the Grenada Boy's Secondary School. I called Mrs Lord, the school secretary, this afternoon.

Friday 07/12/2007

9:50 a.m. Home. I was speaking to Kelly, who is very helpful. I had been referred to their firm by Yvonne at Eldapoint. I try to contact Gilly Drummond, the Deputy Lieutenant of Hampshire, who had mentioned to me that she was friendly with Geoffrey Stirling, the former chairman of P&O, who way back in 2005 told me to get in touch.

11:50 a.m. I am about to speak with the High Commissioner for Grenada in London. *'All dat is possible. Ah goin' to call him right now,'* said Mr Charter. I think in the vernacular, *'Ah is still waitin' for sometin' tae happen man. What rong wit you people?'*

Monday 10/12/2007

8:25 a.m. Johanna left for school. There is a pale blue sky with orange-streaked clouds hanging above the Isle of Cumbrae. David is getting ready for work at a house down the road at Ascog. I received a call from Jake, Community Services, Hillington Criminal Justice System Services. *'I'll run it past my manager,'* he said. Call him on Tuesday next week. *'He's travelling. I'll put you through to the human relations department.'* Who are they and

Tuesday 11/12/2007

how best to contact them directly? Bruce Lucas, V.Ships? A global player. Follow this up.

I call Andrew at Bidwells in Perth, the estate agents who have had an advertisement in *The Buteman* regarding the sale of the 1938 local secondary school building to build 24 new homes. Confusion. The building is supposed to belong to the Argyll and Bute Council and Fyne Homes are negotiating to buy both buildings. He's very approachable and has seen the resources that have been left behind in the old building.

No they can't sponsor a container, but he is prepared to discuss the issue of profligate and unsustainable waste of educational resources. Keep him informed.

Tuesday 11/12/2007

11:20 a.m. Home. I called Sam at Pentalver Transport Ltd. If you don't ask you don't get.

11:22 a.m. *'You wanna give Keith a call. He is one of our traders. Send him an email,'* he said. I did as he suggested and sent Keith an email.

Shanks Waste Management (Grantham Depot) in Lincolnshire: they can bring a container up from there, which is a most generous offer. I now have to source from that neck of the woods. Call Sleaford Chamber of Commerce. I called making enquiries about the purchase of a container, which Shanks & Mcewan Southern Waste Services Ltd will support in my social enterprise venture. I will bring up the container from their depot in Grantham: a generous offer from Sam Grant who is one of their managers. He is always supportive.

Call Grantham Vehicles, Hessle, Hull and Lincolnshire Enterprise, Grantham. WONDERFUL SUPPORT! Call Jake at East Renfrewshire Community Services to make arrangements for a squad of helpers to uplift resources from the industrial units at

250 Seaward Street. *'Give me a wee second and I'll get in touch with my line manager,'* he said. Call Jake tomorrow and he'll put me through to Jackie, senior social worker. *(I wrote a letter 12 December: no reply.)*

Wednesday 12/12/2007

Home. I call *The Grantham Journal*, which is owned by Johnston Press, possible patron owners of *The Buteman*. I am on another wild goose chase. I can try to continue and leave no stone unturned.

(The task before me, during these days of a global pandemic and self-enforced locked down since March 2020, is to write and rewrite this Diary of a Shipping Clerk 2005–2017. It's all water under the bridge now. Negativity, nihilism, zeitgeist rules the 21st century. Nothing matters. Why persevere, since it has been three years since my last shipment went to the Republic of Haiti in April 2017? Why not shred these diaries and voluminous records of all the work, expense, worry and heartache that I invested in The Surplus Educational Supplies Foundation. If it was indeed a pointless exercise, why should I not walk down the driveway, cross the road, walk to the shore and step into the Firth of Clyde and start swimming? Why not?

Well, I wish to acknowledge and celebrate, and show my debt of gratitude to, all those individuals, or as many of them as possible in these pages, who assisted me in making my vision, however flawed, a reality for many students and their teachers in places like Grenada, Ghana, Tanzania, Nicaragua, Jamaica, Liberia, and Haiti. I also wish to show that although there were many times when I could have given up, I am glad that I did not. In spite of the problems there was success and much to celebrate, and more good outcomes that will be recorded in succeeding pages of my story. A way opened up through the many difficulties, by operating as I did, which was dependent on my own efforts, limited funds and the pro bono assistance of the corporate sector.)

Thursday 13/12/2007

Home. Calling Trump Developments, Edison Street, Glasgow. Speaking to Jonathan, who has possibly the largest property portfolio in Scotland. Try and locate a large central location for storage. Speak to landlords and landladies directly.

12:50 p.m. *'I'll have a ring around and see what I can come up with,'* said a helpful soul in Hull at Neill & Brown Global Logistics. Call AB Containers Ltd, Hull. I speak to Eddie who tells me the cost of one ocean freight container is £900 plus VAT, that's £1,057.50; Ship managers (V.Ships) – the owners. Contact them.

4:50 p.m. After weeks and months of trying to contact the Minister of Carriacou and Petit Martinque and Joint Portfolio Minister for Foreign Affairs, the High Commissioner for Grenada in London, has finally got around to giving me his number. *'We are at de end of de financial year. De budget prepared already. I'll speak to de government,'* was all he could say. I am getting nowhere on the government of Grenada.

Wednesday 19/12/2007

Home. I called Raymond, PTA President of St Paul's Government School. He tells me that an article will appear in *The Grenada Informer* newspaper. They move into the new building in January 2008.

Thursday 20/12/2007

10:27 a.m. Home. I called Pat of The Scottish Road Haulage Association, to whom I had sent an email to some weeks ago, and spoke to Phil who said they will do something in the New Year. *'Someone is looking at it, we'll see what we can do,'* he said. I am still waiting for a constructive response. I would like them to give a puff to all those firms, especially all the transport firms in Scotland that made each shipment possible.

Saturday 29/12/2007

Home. This morning, as I was coming out of the Gallowgate Post Office, I hailed Richard QC as he sailed past me on his bicycle. He crosses the road to speak with me and tells me that he was defending a ships officer. *'I was defending a ships officer from Maersk. Is it like a black cloud, David?'* referring to my state of depression. He said I could call on him at his chambers if ever I was in London and gave me his telephone number.

'Hey, my bruder, how ya doin' man?' asked the Honourable Mr Joseph Charter. The Surplus Educational Supplies Foundation is my passion and is not a hobby; call me a social entrepreneur on a learning curve and a shoogly peg, if you will. I will define myself and what I do thank you.

(The bairns were studying and working at part-time jobs. I had to set them some sort of an example through my own work in this project, which was another reason for me to have kept going on with it.)

Thursday 03/01/2008

Home. Publicity, marketing, public relations. I call Scottish Road Haulage and speak to Phil about a publicity article for their journal and on their website. I mention to him that I had forgotten to acknowledge the help that I had received from Freightliner Ltd Roadways Logistics, Coatbridge, who had waived the charges for delivering my container of educational resources from Coatbridge Container Terminal to the Port of Felixstowe. *(And were to continue to do so until 2016.)*

I need to rectify these omissions from the website, so contact webmaster, and digital artisan, Kevin. *'If you want to go fast, go alone. If you want to go far, go together.'* Who is coming with me? I called Donald McKay's office about the acknowledgement from Midlothian Council regarding the successful uplift of school furniture and resources from Ladywood Primary School, Penicuik in November 2007. They are not replying. Called Rachel Jackson, Corporate Affairs, at Hutchinson Ports, Felixstowe. I have been down with migraine all day.

Tuesday 15/01/2008

Home. Collect keys for 250 Seaward Street from Colliers. Call Fraser Duguid; call John Hume on Thursday 18 January; call Jackie MacRae about the team from Community Services, Renfrewshire to assist in the uplift of resources from 250 Seaward Street. She called me this morning; Mike, ABSEN Argyll and Bute Social Enterprise Network, called. I have been down with migraine all day.

Thursday 17/01/2008.

Home. Call John Hume. Call Jake, team leader, Community Services, Renfrewshire for Monday 21 January at 10 a.m.

First thing, collect keys for 250 Seaward Street from Colliers. *'Our greatest glory is not in never falling but in rising every time we fall,'* Confucius.

Monday 21/01/2008

8:45 a.m. Café Prima, Trongate, Glasgow. Corner café. High ceiling, bright and airy. Spacious, comfortable ambience. No pretensions. Traffic rushing past in all four directions. I am chilling out here for a little while. Nae worry huv a curry. I had to come in here to spend more than a penny. *'Can I have some tea and toast please?'* while I headed quickly to the gentleman's to make a deposit.

I Persevere With My Project

I have just walked over the River Clyde from the Glasgow Nautical College to drop off the young merchant navy cadet's college uniform of black jacket an' trousers. On arrival at Central Station I got a taxi over to the college. It is a grey, wet morning. I am on my way up the High Street and along to Colliers CRE, the surveyors at 9 George's Square, to collect the keys for the industrial units at 250 Seaward Street. On the way up the road I met Jim on his way to his current Glasgow City Council post at 20 Trongate as purchasing manager for the 2012 Commonwealth Games. He was formerly the purchasing agent manager with Rolls Royce out at Hillington Industrial Park. He had given the time of the morning when we met on the 7 a.m. train from Wemyss Bay last Easter holidays as I was heading over to Duncan Adams Transport Ltd, Grange Dock depot to 'bram' up one of my containers.

And over these many months of travelling up from Wemyss Bay on the train we have become friends. Enough of the provenance of this present connection. *'I retire this year,'* said Jim. *'You are not the only one,'* I think. He asks me what I am doing and I tell him briefly. *'It'll keep the marbles moving, David,'* he said. You bet it does, referring to my current preoccupation. Later he graciously introduced me to his fellow travelling chums, David and Anne, who he meets regularly when they get on the train on their way up the line, heading to their varied employments in the city. His son is a ship's engineer on a cruise ship based in Florida. *'This friend of mine is passionate about Uganda,'* said fellow traveller David when he learns what I am about.

(The encouragement for my efforts that came from strangers on my road when they learned about where I was going and what I hoped to achieve, just fuelled my faltering steps to power on. A bumper-sticker-length title that sums up my project in 2–12 words. My track record to date: To supply fit-for-purpose, surplus to requirements, educational resources at points of need in the world.

Here is the form of words from the Glasgow solicitors that was to establish my project as a legal entity and registered Scottish charity. Here is my manifesto for The Surplus Educational Supplies Foundation. 'To advance education through supplying schools and other educational establishments in disadvantaged communities in any part of the world and/or pupils, students, children attending any such establishments, with furniture, equipment, books and/or other resources to improve the quality and/or scope of the educational services which are provided, and the ability of the pupils, students, children, to benefit fully from such educational services. To advance environmental protection and in particular protect the natural environment from further damage caused by the proliferation of landfill sites by redistributing furniture and/or other surplus resources to educational establishments as Referred to in paragraph (1), which would otherwise be sent to landfill sites.' *Thanks to Inez and Stephen at Burness who drafted these words. Give credit where it is due.)*

Wednesday 23/01/2008

6:36 p.m. I am on board the MV *Argyle* heading homeward. Well what of today? I will roll it back and capture some of the moments.

I saw Dr Clark up at the health centre at 9:40 a.m. He has signed me off for another 13 weeks. I got the 10 o'clock boat. I met Mr and Mrs Paton. He is the trainee Minister of the Baptist Church on the island. We chatted on our way over to the mainland. They were telling me about the work of the Bethany Trust and helping to run one of their charity shops in Edinburgh. This work began when the founder, Mr Berry, took a homeless man into his home. This charity now has over 20 shops, a farm and a respite centre for burned out Christians. I got the train, intending to get off at Hillington East. Chatted to Jim, SFA coach and community worker, or rather listened to Jim, who was telling me about how he had run away to sea, aboard a ship (he found work on board the ship in the laundry room) and about his National

Service in REME. I missed my stop and the train went all the way into Central Station. I remained cool and at peace, and I had to await the next train back up the line.

I got off at Hillington East and cycled over to the Jewson hardware store and purchased two 10x4 metre tarpaulins, broom, locks and a tuke, which I loaded on the back of the bicycle and pushed from there all the way through to the Hillington Industrial Park estate, to the Russell's Deanside Road depot just off the M8, and got stuck in. The two 40-foot ocean freight containers had 'SCRAP' chalked on them and are leaking like sieves. It was tough going but I was not deterred. There was a strong wind blowing in from the south-west across the Renfrewshire plain, which was attempting to blow off the top of the containers. I struggled to open out the tarpaulins and spread them over the top of the containers until Kenny the Manitou driver appeared from nowhere and was very helpful. I shall always be grateful to him. He brought pallets over and used the forklift on the vehicle to lift them up to me to weigh down the tarpaulins. I required a dozen or so to weight them down as the wind snapped away at me. I managed to temporarily reduce the rain dripping into the containers.

I felt it was a job well done under the circumstances. My mend and make do method will keep some of the rain out and it will have to suffice for the time being. Homeward bound!

Thursday 24/01/2008

10:28 a.m. Home. I call Pentalver Transport Ltd. *'Long time no speak, mate. Speak to you soon my friend,'* said Andy. I then speak to Julie in the office and send a cheque for their attention of £450 plus VAT (£528.75) to Pentalver Transport Ltd, Leeds. I call Sam, who Stuart had told me to speak to. I then call John G Russell Transport Ltd at Mossend to let them know that my next container is coming their way. I speak to Janice in the office, who tells me that I must give the release reference number to the driver (Release reference SU 04339 MAEU6085656 DK 4310).

Friday 25/01/2008

I call Russell Transport at Gartcosh by mistake and speak to Linda. Then I spoke to Tom, the welder. I ask him if he can patch up the leaking containers at their depot in Hillington. *'It's just heavy kit I have, nae portable stuff,'* he said. I then call Russell Transport at Mossend and I speak to Mark, who is the transport manager in the depot, and who is helpful and supportive. He tells me I have to speak to Graham Russell about permission to loan me a trailer, a skelly. I then call Peter, the Russell Transport manager at Hillington depot. *'What's the bottom line?'* I ask. *'He does have your number,'* he said. I am to call again on 27 January to see if they will loan me a trailer. *Buy one!* Not yet!

10:38 a.m. I am on board the MV *Bute* en route for Wemyss Bay. I set off from hame with a strong north-west wind trying to blaw me backwards. I kept on pressing forward on the pedals ever so slowly.

I thought (or rather Marion did, bless her, who phoned to advise me) to get the 10 o'clock boat, as there may not be another one at 1 p.m. on account of the weather. I had called Peter, Transport Manager at Russell's depot in Hillington, who told me that they did not have any spare trailers, or trailers to spare. I kept pressing, pushing the envelope. Is that the expression? I then asked him if I could get a temporary loan of one. I told him that Freightliner Ltd at Coatbridge Container Terminal would take my container, as and when, down to Southampton Docks, and Maersk would allow me to unload it at their depot, so that I could then load a Geest trailer from Portsmouth with pallets. I also mentioned that I had purchased another container and it was going to be delivered to their base at Mossend. He told me to speak to Graham on Monday and mention to him that I had heard that Russell Transport were keen to work with Maersk.

I then called Russell's at Mossend at spoke to James and gave him the container number and release reference numbers. He told me that the container had been offloaded from the trailer. He sounded helpful and I told him I would be speaking to the boss. Well here I am, for the third time this week, crossing the watta. Step by step. Sailing and moving. I huvnae a clue as to what happens next. However, I do know where and what I am heading for in a temporal sense.

2:25 p.m. I am back at the Café Prima, 3 Trongate, Glasgow. I have not long been pushing the bike through the merchant city having come from 9 George's Square. I met Fraser, the surveyor, just after introducing myself to the receptionist concierge, who took me directly up to Colliers CRE office. He gave me the bunches of keys for the vacated industrial units at 250 Seaward Street.

Saturday 26/01/2008

6:20 a.m. Here I am now, with construction of the new pier site generators humming. I am sitting on a bench outside the ferry terminal building. I am too early. I roused myself into conscious awareness from an exhausted slumber with migraine pains nipping their tingling way along to the nerves into my right eyeball. I swallowed two pain killers (Co-codamol) and set off pedalling into a strong wind, which is still blowing strong as I sit here. I am very tired and I am forcing myself forward because I am totally committed to meeting the next squad of helpers from the Community Services Criminal Justice Department, Renfrewshire Council, for 10 a.m. at 250 Seaward Street.

I am whacked. Exhausted. It wasn't until after 2:30 a.m. that I fell asleep, only to awake a few hours later. Not feeling too good right now. I am here too early. Better than miss the ferry

Monday 21/01/2008

because of a few extra hours of sleep – at least I have got a bench to sit on.

7:30 a.m. I am now sitting inside the ferry terminal waiting room. I have bought a return ticket to Glasgow Central Station. I have just met Graeme who used to be a painter and decorator and works at the pier, who always has a cheery hello for me. *'You are doing something worthwhile,'* he said. I now have a squeezing, nipping, migraine aching pain behind my right eye. I don't want to take any more painkillers. It's warm in here. I am grateful for small mercies.

8:40 a.m. I have just boarded the train for Central Station. The Jackies, the croaking craws, are echoing along the station platform.

On the way over I met Isabel and Robert Rich's son; he's off on a book makers course in Glasgow. He has always been friendly towards me. I feel physically fragile, but I will just have to keep moving.

10:05 a.m. I am now outside 250 Seaward Street, the former premises of ADS Sign & Light Visual Ltd. I wonder if this firm have gone bust. I got a taxi over from Central Station. It's dry, but there is a chill wind blowing in from the north-west from away over the tops of the Campsie Fells. I have the keys to units, 250, 248, 246, 244 and 242.

Monday 21/01/2008

We made a start on industrial units 250 and 248. I will see how much more of value can be collected today. 'To let Industrial Unit. 1134.94 square metres. 12,216 square feet. All enquiries Colliers CRE. Jones La Salle.'

3:30 p.m. I am now on the train for Gourock. Lindsay, the team leader, gave me a lift to Paisley Gilmour Street Station. He, his assistant Archie, and their teams arrived at 10 a.m. We all worked steadily and made four trips out to the leaky containers at Russell Transport, Deanside Road depot. A lot of good furniture, electrical fittings and bits and bobs. *'We are now approaching Langbank. Please mind the gap when alighting from the train,'* she said.

I have been working alongside young offenders who were doing this type of work in lieu of a prison sentence. I have just had a hot chocolate and a raisin bun doughnut from the AMT Fair Trade Espresso bar, which is a long overdue and welcome addition to the Paisley Gilmour Street Station platform. I am whacked and still feeling fragile, but the migraine pain has gone. I have accomplished what I set out to do, and take some satisfaction from that achievement, bearing in mind all of the telephone calls (local and transatlantic) and arrangements over many weeks that went into making this current shipment and uplift possible. Who gives a monkeys? I do GIVE A MONKEYS. I am bothered enough to be bothered.

Sundy 27/01/2008

8:05 a.m. I have just met Frank the musician from Dundee who was once the manager of the Dundee University bookstore. He donated stacks of jigsaws for the shipment of educational resources that went out to St Paul's Government School last year. And earlier I met Victor from the Lucky Box shop at the front. All aboard the MV *Argyle*. I am heading back up to Glasgow and over to Seaward Street, hopefully to collect several truckloads of what may be useful and much appreciated resources for the consignee.

I cycled into a cool, refreshing wind leaving home and my best friends, who were sound asleep.

(Little did I know then that I was unable to keep all those precious fit-for-purpose resources for which I had gone to all that monumental

amount of trouble to collect, salvage, and transport, for want of a convenient storage centre in the vicinity of the Hillington Industrial Estate. One of the many failures SNAFU's. The COST of my EFFORT. I won't get or go anywhere without it. Would that I had started earlier in my life with that attitude of determination, but that's another story.)

No looking back now. As Frank, resident of Ardbeg, Isle of Bute, said to me as I cycled past him along the Ardbeg Road. '*Go for it!*' He was one of the early encouragers.

10 a.m. 250 Seaward Street steps. There is a cold wind blowing across the Clyde Valley. I have not long been dropped off here by taxi. I travelled up with Tricia from the Boat Pub. She comes from Bridgeton, where I once taught at Dalmarnock Primary School. Her brother Michael is a Jesuit priest working in Kenya and trained at a seminary in Valladolid Spain. I am now going to enjoy a Cornish pasty that has gone cold and quaff a bottle of mango juice.

3 p.m. I am now aboard the train for Wemyss Bay and have just munched a turkey and cranberry sandwich washed down wi' a cup o' tea. David of Monarch Security has kindly given me a lift up to Central Station. He is concerned about a damaged roller-door of the industrial unit at the back entrance of 250 Seaward Street. He thinks that perhaps some of 'the helpers', conscripts from the Monday and Saturday teams or their chums, may have returned to uplift some of the stuff they fancied that I did not take.

I left a trolley on the back of Archie's lorry. I must try and get it back somehow. It has been a very long day chivvying, cajoling, encouraging and supporting this squad. I am grateful to each of them and all the other lads who came yesterday and on Monday. I am trying to remember names. Motivational leadership is simple. I will lead my team as I would wish to be lead. What's that? '*The gemme's a bogie.*'

I Persevere With My Project

Monday 28/01/2008

8:55 a.m. Home. I am now going to call Graham of John G Russell Transport Ltd regarding the loan of a trailer (or what they call in the industry, a skelly) for the ocean freight container.

9:50 a.m. I am now sitting in the ferry terminal waiting room. Where to next? Squeaking doors, coughing, muffled voices. I stopped off earlier in Guildford Square Post Office and sent the signed 'Articles' for Companies House and the Office of The Scottish Charities Regulator, OSCR. I registered the documents special delivery to Stephen, solicitor, word engineer at Burness. *(More pains, much cost and, as I was to discover almost eight years later, no gain whatsoever.)* Before I left home, I got a call from Fraser, the Colliers CRE surveyor, concerned about what appeared to be a possible break-in through the roller shutter door at 250 Seaward Street. He told me that he'd had a call from the Monarch security manager. I told him who it was that he should get in touch with himself. I said it was possible that it was one of the squads over Monday and Saturday and yesterday who could have been responsible. *'Or one of their pals,'* I said. I told him that I was on my way up with the keys.

10:55 a.m. Rolling forward on the train from Wemyss Bay to Glasgow. When I arrived at Central Station there was nowhere to tether my bike. *'The next stop is Bishopton,'* she said.

'Those are not strelitzias, they are heliconias,' she said. *'Do you have any long-lasting flowers?'* I walked across to Marks & Spencer and saw orchids on display. They always remind me of gardens in Trinidad, and the ones that Dad and Mum grew on the stumps of coconut palm trees in the Caroni Ltd Brechin Castle gated-community garden. I got a white one £7.99, bags of Fair Trade tea and coffee, and a bag of humbugs.

I took the bag of 'minders' along to Colliers CRE with the keys

Monday 28/01/2008

from 250 Seaward Street to meet Fraser, and I told him about the apparent break in. I also met Iain. Nothing to offer. They represent owners of property. The landlords.

'My favourite sweet. All that was not necessary,' said the receptionist, which was true. My gratuitous, impulsive, and over the top generosity. A weakness that has dogged my heels for as long as I can remember. That little errand of acknowledgement didn't take long. I am pushing the bicycle along pavements and dodging people and traffic. On the train I met a mum with a wee one, who told me that she was studying for a PhD in psycholinguistics. Mainly hand signals. They got off at Cardonald. *'NIGHT TIME ORPHAN.'* Graffiti spray painted on the wall of the derelict warehouse which was soon to be demolished. We are all cosmic orphans. Wall art graffiti on the underpass. The train is rolling, rumbling and grinding its way along.

2 p.m. I am now sitting in the Cal Mac Gourock to Dunoon ferry terminal waiting room. I have come off the mobile payphone. I have been speaking to someone in the Russell Transport Ltd office HQ in Hillington. He has tried to get in touch with Graham Russell for me. I gave him my details and request to loan a skelly/trailer from their firm and said he would pass on it on for me. He was helpful. I told him that I had already spoken to Peter, transport manager at their Coatbridge office, who had suggested I speak directly to Mr Russell. I gave him Duncan and John as references and said that James at Mossend (Coatbridge) had said that I would have to speak to the boss. *'That's no bother,'* he said.

I am looking out onto the watta of Gourock Harbour. There is a container ship cargo vessel coming round the point at Fort Matilda. Doors are squeaking and more sneezing.

9:50 p.m. Room 30 of The Cottage, Royal Marine Hotel, Hunter's Quay, Cowal Peninsula which overlooks the Holy Loch. I have not long had a delicious meal of asparagus soup, vegetable lasagne, cheesecake and coffee. I called Marion. All is well on the home front. I now have to prepare my, or rather her, talk, spiel, elevator pitch for 'The Dragon's Den' type presentation either for tomorrow or the next day. It's tomorrow, 2:45 p.m. to 3:45 p.m. and 4 p.m. to 6 p.m. I'll try and give it my best shot.

REWIND. I got the MV *Jupiter*, once a familiar vessel, which seems so much smaller now.

2:15 p.m. Arrived in Dunoon. Great to be on the bicycle. Up the main street and stopped off at Bookpoint and got some reading material. *The World is Flat* by Thomas Friedman, *Shaping the Entrepreneurial Company* by McKeran & Flannagan, and *My Life* by Fidel Castro with Ignacio Ramonet.

I then cycled out of the town and up a long stretch of gradually steepening brae and then whizzed into Sandbank Village scheme. I took a short cut onto Ferry Road, past the war memorial overlooking the loch, cycling on the pavement as the road gave me no room for pedalling. I received a welcome from Michael. *'Go and have a shower and relax,'* he said. Grateful for the luxury. I am here to make another effort, that will move my initiative, project, social enterprise, The Surplus Educational Supplies Foundation (Registered Scottish Charity SCO 39331 and Registered Scottish Company No337348) up a notch.

Tuesday 29/01/2008

10:05 a.m. Kintyre Room. Marketing workshop. I have just met Frank of Argyll Training. Marketing for Social Enterprises. 'Marketing is more than selling and advertising, it is a mixture of six core activities. Product, Place, Prices, Promotion, People, Planning.'

I will need employer's liability insurance. How do you present what it is that I am doing? What am I doing, and doing well. *'It's the little things that count,'* said Mr Harkins. *'What is my core competence, Dingo Dave, that is unique to me?'* What difference will my project make?

1:45 p.m. The Stewart Room. Afternoon session. I meet John who is a motivational speaker trainer. What are my overall goals? They were to build a school from recyclable building materials and deliver it to a community that does not have a school building, and to continue to supply natural or man-made disaster communities with fit-for-purpose educational resources.

Wednesday 30/01/2008

9:30 a.m. The hotel's dining room. I am in with Brian of the McSence Group for another lesson in social enterprise. I am sitting next to Frank of Argyll Training, who tells me that he knows the Parlane Family. Mr Parlane was my head teacher at Sandbank Primary School 1991–1992. So far, I have found the experience of this course a worthwhile two days.

3 p.m. Station Café, Wemyss Bay Railway Station. I am not long in here having pushed my bicycle from the Western Ferries terminus outside Gourock. The wind was against me all the way here and it was raining heavily. My cussed determination in the face of the elements. There is nothing else fur it, right enough.

Thursday 31/01/2008

9:40 a.m. I have just called Graham of Russell Transport Ltd and left a message. I have made repeated phone calls to him and he has not replied. When will I ever learn to just back off and leave well enough alone?

Friday 01/02/2008

9:50 a.m. I am chasing up the Scottish Road Haulage Association for a copy of an article from their in-house magazine, which mentioned the firms who have assisted me in collecting, storing and delivering surplus educational resources.

Monday 04/02/2008

9:40 a.m. *'Edinburgh is awash with books,'* said Sandra, librarian, to me some years ago when I was introduced to her mum, Betty, Port community activist.

I am sitting in at 39 Café and Deli on Argyle Place, Edinburgh. I have just walked across The Meadows. It is a beautiful spring morning. I ordered a cappuccino, which came in a huge bowl. I need to spring a leak soon, but not yet. These pairts are 'Morningside Maisie the Cat' territory, and where my mum, who was living in army quarters with my sister at Redford Barracks, would bring me on a Saturday morning for a treat, circa 1980.

I got the Edinburgh Express bus from Glasgow Buchanan Street Bus Station and it dropped me off on Princes Street. I then walked on through the Edinburgh University campus where my dad, David Manning Hanschell, was a student in the 1930s. Georgian residences of a former day, now university offices for the schools of various academic study. School of Celtic and Scottish Studies. I thought of dropping in on John Bannerman, lecturer at the School of Scottish Studies, a distant cousin on the Mundell line and Miss Garry Middleton of Meggetland's lodger: she, who had gone to a lot of trouble to research and prepare the Mundell family tree from records in Registry House after her retirement from the Astley Ainslie Hospital. But I thought better of it: I don't think he's the type to welcome a hail fellow well met Caribbean colonial out of the blue. It is a beautiful day with the sun coming up over the Pentland Hills. Roll it back.

Tuesday 05/02/2008

I got an Arriva bus from The Grove, Kilbarchan, Renfrewshire at 6:10 a.m., arrived in midtown Glasgow, walked up to Buchanan Street Bus Station, and eventually here I am. I am going to walk over to the Morningside Library to meet Sandra and her team of librarians at the library. Sandra had called me on Saturday morning to tell me that they had 29 boxes of books for The Surplus Educational Supplies Foundation.

12:45 p.m. Grosvenor Hilton Hotel, Grosvenor Crescent. First turn on the left of the Bean Scene Café. Ryan from Korea and Taiwan has signed me in. I am now ensconced and sitting at a table near the bar of this up-market hostelry. He has reappeared to tell me that I have not paid. What's up? I gave him my reservation number, which I had booked through Luis, from Puerto Rico, some weeks ago. Incidentally, that is where my great-grandmother Julia Celia McCormick on the Hanschell line comes from. I have not paid twice, I hope. I have a pot of tea and a toasted cheese and tomato sandwich to deal with, which has been served by Noah, who has not told me where he hails from. I did not hear what he said. I get chatting with Phil the concierge and porter from Brisbane.

Tuesday 05/02/2008

3:10 p.m. Rolling on the rails again for Glasgow Queen Street Station. I have made another big effort in attending another social enterprise conference (and not to mention the cost).

(It may only have been seen to have been worthwhile in days to come. From it I gained more confidence to present and express myself among strangers in such a quasi-corporate milieu.)

'You talk volubly,' said Buzzy, conference organiser. Yes, I know I do, that's because I am deaf as a post. Well nothing ventured and nothing gained.

I Persevere With My Project

Tuesday 19/02/2008

Home. I am making some progress in fits and starts.

3 p.m. I called Sam of Shanks Waste Management and left a message. I continue to clutch at straws and I am carried forward in this initiative by the momentum of my sheer cussed determination to see that these 40-foot ocean freight containers loaded with fit-for-purpose educational resources, which I at no little personal cost have collected over the past two years, are delivered to worthwhile and deserving recipients.

Thursday 21/02/2008

5:45 p.m. Sam Grant has returned my call to tell me that, all being well, my 40-foot ocean freight container MAEU6085656 will be brought over to the island of Bute by George, next week, 27 February. I call Geest Line for quotes to ship the container to Grenada.

Friday 22/02/2008

12:55 p.m. I call Brian of Fife Council, who has the responsibility for disposing of the educational resources that remain in Dunshalt Village Primary School. He has never sent me the digital pics of resources as promised. *'Are you still going aboot?'* he asks. You betcha. I am still very much alive and kicking. I still have those resources in that school to collect, store, sort, inventory and deliver to schools on the islands of Carriacou and Petite Martinique in the West Indies.

I am on the phone again to Pentalver Transport Ltd, a Maersk subsidiary, Western Docks, Southampton. *'He has meetings all day today. He will call you tomorrow,'* he said. I call, yet again, Graham of Russell Transport Ltd, Hillington and speak with his secretary.

Wednesday 27/02/2008

I finally get through to Mr Russell who said he would speak with Sam of Shanks Waste Management.

I am spending a fortune on telephone calls to Carriacou. There is apathy and indifference. Do they want surplus educational resources for their island schools or not? I have called the Minister for Carriacou and Petit Martinque numerous times with no result. Will the business community there spread the cost of shipment?

Wednesday 27/02/2008

9:30 a.m. The sun is shining bright from a clear blue sky after many days of rain, gusting wind, more rain and ferry cancellations. The first call I received this morning was from Sam Lowry to let me know that George was on his way to collect container MAEU608565 (release reference SU043399).

I called Les of Argyll and Bute Council in Dunoon to confirm whether or not SESF could still have the rest of the resources that remain in the former Rothesay Academy building, which is due for demolition and which is now a Bute Estates property. He will call me back.

I have not had my breakfast of porridge yet, just coffee, toast and marmalade. George, the Shanks Waste Management artic driver, has called me to say that Russell Transport Ltd depot at Mossend, Coatbridge, did not know that he was coming to pick up the SESF container, and since they hadn't dug the box out from their container base, he was not going to wait around for two hours until they did. I asked him if he could just hang around for another 10 minutes while I called the Russell Transport manager Mark. He was helpful and said he would try and get the container out to the transporter as soon as possible. SOLUTION. Problem solved.

1:25 p.m. I get on my bicycle and stop off at The Bike Shed on my way into town and see David, who gives me the name of Phil Kirkham, who is multi-talented when it comes to things to do with digital media and is also a signwriter.

1:45 p.m. I meet George, who is here at last, off the ferry with MAEU608565. I am to send him the photograph from *The Buteman*. The container must be ready to go as soon as possible, and I am to call Sam and he will return to pick it up. My next big box is due to leave for Grenada, which makes me happy, and to know that all that valuable stuff would be soon loaded into it, makes me even happier.

I cycled down Ballochgoy Hill on wings of exhilaration and accomplishment. Just past the faux cheese factory across from Rothesay motors I stopped to speak to Neville, ship's chef, who told me that he had passed his fire-fighting test after the fifth attempt. He asked kindly after the Young David, and then I was on up the High Street to the local Argyll and Bute Council office and there left a message for Mr Reynolds and his team. I then called Mr Gillies to get the keys for the academy annex, who tells me that Louis, the plumber, has them!

Thursday 28/02/2008

9:35 a.m. I call Gillian, Fife Council estates surveyor, to discuss making arrangements to collect the educational resources from the Dunshalt Village Primary School and leave a message.

11:30 a.m. I have just had a call from Gillian to tell me that she has seen all of the resources at Dunshalt Village PS and that they are all there for the asking. She tells me that I must have them uplifted as soon as possible, so they can put the building on the market. I told her that I would get over there next week to take an inventory of what is on offer and see if I can drum up some sponsorship from the local community to raise funds for their collection, storage and transportation to the island schools of Carriacou and Petite Martinique. I've got high hopes. I will give her a call next week. I will be on my way across Scotland to return to the Kingdom of Fife.

3:14 p.m. Home. George Reynolds called just now to tell me that he will call me on Monday with an employability team to help me shift the resources from the former Rothesay Academy building. He told me that Mr Mellish has the key. No one knows who is now responsible for that building.

4:44 p.m. It has been a busy day. I have been working non-stop all day. Maria at the Bute Estate office at Mount Stuart called to say that Mr Mellish, the factor, will drop off the keys to me! I am so grateful. This beggar has to be. I have no other option but to be one since I am unable to command assistance.

5:45 p.m. Canon Pat McInally, the Cupar and Auchtermuchty parish priest who is well known in the area apparently, has not long returned from Uganda. He wants to send a container of educational resources. *'How do we overcome the problems?'* he asks. I tell him he must try and source the best carrier at the cheapest rate to deliver to East Africa: one with a social conscience and disposed to assisting social entrepreneurial do-gooders. I am to call him whenever I am able to get over to the Kingdom of Fife.

7 p.m. I call Campbell, who will call for me tomorrow on his return from Dunoon and will run me up to the former academy building and show me which keys are which.

Friday 29/02/2008

12:30 a.m. Home. Remember to collect inner tubes for the two barras for the employability team. I have just switched on the computer. I see there are five emails. I wonder who they are from?

3 p.m. I have just had a call from Tayside recyclers in Dundee and was speaking to Doug, who has given me the name of Pete, an executive with Dundee Council's Waste Management Department, sited at an old jute mill with a fancy chimney, who may be prepared to offer SESF storage capacity for the educational resources school furniture etc. from Dunshalt Village Primary School. I am to call him when I get over to Fife.

5 p.m. Home. I have just returned from having been collected earlier by Campbell, the Argyll and Bute Council's island joiner with whom I had made arrangements to show me which keys opened which doors up at the former 1938 academy building. Unfortunately, there is a large quantity of educational resources missing from what I had inventoried back in September 2007. There are still enough educational resources of quality, in my view, to load another 40-foot ocean freight container. Sadly, the buildings are slowly being destroyed through neglect and vandalism. I pray that the SESF container and the trailer on which it sits will be left alone.

Saturday 01/03/2008

12:40 p.m. Marion and I have just returned from taking two carloads of boxes (crockery, hymn books – a gift from the Kilchattan Bay Church of Scotland Women's Guild and from St Ninians Church of Scotland kirk in Ardbeg – and secretarial studies textbooks thanks to Willa Stewart, Business Studies teacher at the academy) to MAEU6085656 for a shipment to the GBBS Secondary School.

3:15 p.m. On the way up the High Street to see John MacKirdy and Son, I saw young John driving towards me and I flagged him down. He stopped outside the wee paper shop and I asked him if he wouldn't mind looking through the up-to-date Surplus Educational Supplies Foundation file that I was bringing up to their depot. Their island-based storage and haulage distribution firm have already collected four pallet loads of library books from the Stirling Council libraries, made several collections of books from the Morningside Library in Edinburgh, and transported the first 40-foot container shipment from the boatyard at the port to Port Dundas in Glasgow, where it was picked up by Duncan Adams Transport Ltd who took it across to the Port of Grangemouth on 21 August 2007. All of this assistance is absolutely great of them and I can't expect them to do much more, however, if they can offer any advice regarding the logistics of this SESF initiative it would be invaluable.

Monday 03/03/2008

9:16 a.m. I have not long arrived here on my bike and am sitting on the front steps of the 1938 former academy building overlooking the town. My pinkies are starting to freeze off, so I'll try and continue this scribble later. The employability team and George, the gaffer, helped me to load the container today. Many, many, thanks lads.

5 p.m. Home. I have seen John MacKirdy Junior of John MacKirdy Transport Ltd and they have kindly agreed to take the container up to Russell Transport depot at Mossend Coatbridge tomorrow.

Tuesday 04/03/2008

10:35 a.m. Kenny has driven off with the container. The sun is shining brightly as I sit here on the stone balustrade/banister of the front steps to the 1938 building. I am looking out over Rothesay

Bay and over to the hills of the Cowal Peninsula. I drove around the shore earlier with John, up Canada Hill and down to Eastfield on the Serpentine to collect a donation of two computers from Mrs Hanson. I hope now that all this joint collaborative effort, against the current tide of indifference, apathy and cannae be bothered cynicism, towards the goal of reducing the amount of fit-for-purpose educational resources that are being disposed of into landfill, will have proved worthwhile to the beneficiaries of this shipment.

Call Mark at Russell Transport Ltd, Mossend, to let him know that MAEU6085656 is now on its way to their depot and would it be possible to stow the box so it is readily accessible as and when the time comes to ship it.

I could sit here all day and admire this magnificent view of the bay, which is like a mill pond today with the ferry MV *Bute,* or is it MV *Argyle,* making its way into its berth at the pier. I look across to see the Cowal Hills, which are blanketed with snow. I pray for all the pupils who have left this now derelict building holding so many memories, that they will be blessed.

1:36 p.m. Home. Mark has called to say that the container had arrived and they would keep it on trailer SK183 for the time being. Wonderful! Call Sam to let him know that the container is off the island and back at Mossend, and thank him and Shanks Waste Management for making this collection and delivery possible. I call Danny to let him know that I am interested in attending the 'free' Financial Management for Social Enterprise course to be held at the Royal Marine Hotel, Hunter's Quay, Dunoon on 14 March 2008. Return keys to the Bute Estate factor.

Wednesday 05/03/2008

I get a call from Gary, the panel beater, offering books from his deceased neighbour's library, which I gratefully accept. Try and see if I get the donation of library books from the Morningside

Library shifted to the container now at the Mossend depot. I call Graham to thank him for the loan of the trailer and temporary storage of the container. I speak to his secretary. I call Jimmy at City of Edinburgh Council to cancel the pre-arranged movement of 50 plus boxes of children's books from the Morningside Library all the way out to Duncan Adams Transport Ltd depot at Grange Dock, Grangemouth.

As each member of his team on that collection must have photographic identification for the Forth Ports security hopefully this will not be a hassle for the Edinburgh Community Transport team members. I thanked him for all the assistance that they have given to The Surplus Educational Supplies Foundation.

Thursday 06/03/2008

6:33 a.m. The engines of the MV *Argyle* are thrumming away beneath my seat, or are those the generators? I did not give myself enough time to tether my bike at the Albert Pier bicycle rail and had to move quickly through the green light. I purchased a return ticket on the train to Glasgow and then I will be on another train to Edinburgh. I don't feel confident about leaving my bicycle in Central Station. We'll see.

I have made arrangements to meet Jimmy and the Edinburgh Community Transport Team at the Morningside Library to collect 30 boxes of books. He and his team have kindly offered to store them at the Muirhouse Depot, Unit 4C, Elizafield, Newhaven Road, Edinburgh until such time as I can arrange to have them uplifted out to one of the SESF containers at Duncan Adams Transport Ltd depot at Grange Dock.

(Little did I know then that these boxes of books would be in Edinburgh for many months until I made arrangements to have them shipped out to schools in Bluefields, Costa Caribena, Nicaragua, Meso America.)

7:10 a.m. Some motor on the train/carriage is clicking away. I was last to leave the ferry, up the wee brae and around to Wemyss Bay Station heralded by scraping raucous caws of the jackdaws. That's another electric motor humming away. That's the station master's whistle, a hiss and the doors shut and we are on our way back on the iron rails. Clickety clack, clickety clack. I need to pee again. I'll need tae haud ma watta.

8 a.m. I just managed to board the train at Queen Street Station for Edinburgh. I pushed my bike up from Central Station. I had to stop off at Bishopton Station. *'Is there no a toilet here?'* I said. *'No. The community centre might be open,'* he replied. *'Where's that?'* I asked. I pedalled past the secure 1930s suburb. The lights were on, but the large glassed-in front doors were locked. I chapped the door loudly. Come on. Hurry up, will you? *'Could I use your toilet please?'* I asked. *'No. We are shut and do not open until 9 o'clock,'* he said with a scowly face. *'I can see that you are shut, but they told me at the station I might be able to use your facilities,'* I said, barely able to keep myself from an accident. *'Okay, then. Make it quick,'* he said.

8:45 a.m. Here I am back on the train, humming, rolling forward and feeling a lot better after that embarrassing interruption to my journeying. I am an aspiring homme d'affaire these days, aware that I fall far short of any grip on the skills that go with that title. I am just trying to accomplish something which I believe to be worthwhile.

'Is that you retired now?' asked the scaffie binman as he was about to empty the bins at the end of the driveway yesterday afternoon. *'I guess so, but not quite. I am trying to build another life and career for myself,'* I replied … in the process of reinventing myself. It's a reconstruction process of self-renewal that goes in fits and starts.

10:30 a.m. I am now sitting in The Hub, foyer, lounge of the

Thursday 06/03/2008

Edinburgh Chamber of Commerce. Carrie, who signed me up at some cost last year, has just come through the door to speak to me, has poured me a welcome cup of coffee and handed me a copy of *The Scotsman*. Gracious soul. Bless her. I brought her up to date with SESF developments since the last time I was here, or I should say on my first visit (when I was across the square at the Sheraton: my little fling at luxury.) This is cheaper coffee and more suitable. I will chill here for a few minutes and enjoy this welcome respite.

11:30 a.m. It is a beautiful day. I cycled up Lothian Road, across part of The Meadows, and pushed the bike where cycling is forbidden. I am always trying to be a good lad and eager to please. I cycled down the hill into Morningside where I received a warm welcome from Jane, and later Sandra, who arrived on her bicycle – a Brompton, which collapses and folds into itself. Brilliant British engineering. Very helpful all of them. There were 36 boxes of books all labelled for me c/o The Surplus Educational Supplies Foundation. Seeing these boxes of salvaged books, all of top quality, made me very happy.

I went across the road to Café Nero for a mug of tea and a tuna fish and brown bread sandwich, and to await the arrival of Edinburgh Community Transport. I waited and waited. I finally called Jimmy, who told me that, yes, they were on their way but had stopped for lunch, and at around 1:45 p.m. they eventually appeared. I helped them to load the boxes into a City of Edinburgh Council van, put my bicycle in the back of the van and off we went across the city to the Muirhouse Social Work Centre. We stopped off at an industrial estate and unloaded the 36 boxes of books, which they will store temporarily for me. I said give me five weeks.

(As it turned out they were going to hang on to those boxes for much longer than that.)

I got chatting to Craig. *'I'm a chef,'* he tells me and describes to me how he cooks duck and makes confit. *'Are you bipolar too?'* he asks. *'I guess so. I go up and down in my moods,'* I reply. *'You are sensitive too, then?'* he asks. *'Aye, too much for my own good,'* I reply.

2:25 p.m. I have just boarded the train at Edinburgh Haymarket Station. Craig, one of the team leaders at Edinburgh Community Transport, kindly dropped me off at the top end of George Street and St Andrew's Square, and I turned around and pedalled over the cobbles back doon the road. Waiting for the green man.

It's been a long day. Home. It's now after 10 p.m. I am whacked.

Friday 07/03/2008

7:25 a.m. Rolling, swaying along on the rails once again and there's something squeaking under the carriage. Here I am travelling ever hopefully forward to what was once the Dunshalt Village Primary School. I haven't got a clue where it is. North-west corner of the Kingdom of Fife in the vicinity of the village of Auchtermuchty. There I have an appointment to meet Gillian, estates surveyor of the Property Services, Asset and Facilities Management, Fife Council, who at 12 noon will show me the educational resources that have been left behind in the former village primary school. Nothing ventured nothing gained; what goes around comes around, so they tell me.

I was chatting to Mary and John coming over on the ferry. The former is a supporter from the early days of this project.

8:50 a.m. Sunshine is beaming into my face as I stand here in the Glasgow Buchanan Street bus station en route for Perth via Stirling, Dunblane and Gleneagles.

1:20 p.m. Sterling Furniture Company Ltd Depot and Warehouse,

Friday 07/03/2008

Auchtermuchty. I was welcomed by the office staff, who made me a coffee and let me use their photocopier. There I met Mr Macdonald who worked with TDG at Grangemouth and knows Eric Adams. I left SESF information for Mr Patterson, who Brian at the Fife Warehousing Company Ltd had suggested I contact. This firm have kindly offered to let me park a container in their yard and may be able to supply a team from their depot to assist in the uplift of educational resources from the Dunshalt Village school building, which is just down the road and where earlier I had met Gillian and Brian. This small, one-roomed village school is crammed with first-class quality educational resources. Problem: how to collect, store and deliver these educational resources to the schools on the islands of Carriacou and Petite Martinique as soon as possible? These resources, I was told, must be uplifted from the building within the next fortnight. I keep my skates on.

10:20 p.m. The Wood House Hotel, Largs, Ayrshire, Room 7. I am ensconced. I chatted with the landlord at the bar with my cup of tea, having had a fish supper wi' mushie peas. I journeyed all the way down to find that I had missed the ferry. It had left at 7:33 p.m. I arrived off the train shortly after. Nothing else fur it but to find a place for the nicht.

I set off from Wemyss Bay in the drizzle and stopped at the bus stop in front of the Skelmorelie Parish Kirk, where I stood for a while. Taxi coming up the road. I flagged it and we headed back doon the road to Largs. The ABC taxi driver was helpful and dropped me aff here, which beats sleeping rough on the shore. Run it. Roll it back a little.

The office staff at Sterling Furniture Ltd could not have been more helpful to me. '*Would you like a taxi?*' she asked cheerily. '*Yes please,*' I said. '*It will take you to Ladybank where you can catch the train for Dundee,*' she said. The taxi driver said I could get the bus at 2:02 p.m. On arrival at the bus station; it was a dreich afternoon. I crossed the road to a call box and called Pete, the

Dundee Council waste management manager. He ran me up the Law to proudly show me his city. Bonnie Dundee. Home of Oor Wullie, Desperate Dan, jute and marmalade. Panoramic views of the Howes of Fife, River Tay, the Bridges etc. And then over to his office where he introduced me to assembled staff having their tea break in their 'bothy'. His workmate and long-time chum 'Deck' was telling me about his dad's visit to Cuba in the sixties with a Scottish Trade Union delegation and who, on his return, was hassled by MI5/6 for doing so. *'The most dangerous man in Britain,'* commented Deck.

They heard my patter, which went on for longer than I had intended, only to give Deck the opportunity to poke a little fun at my determined efforts to salvage educational resources. Water off this duck's back.

Pete then drove me back to the train station, offering more than once to put me up if I could not get back to the island. But instead, hoping against hope that I might make the ferry, I declined his kind offer of hospitality.

Journeying mercies have prevailed on my behalf throughout this day. I just miss very much the other four parts of my life.

Saturday 8/03/2008

9:35 a.m. Aboard the MV *Coriusk*. Wind and lashing rain blowing up from the south-west. Gulls facing into the wind. Here I am, after a full Scottish breakfast, journeying home. The prospect beckons.

Monday 10/03/2008

Social Enterprise Academy, Financial Management Course. *'Go for it,'* Methinks. To be held at the Royal Marine Hotel ABSEN, 14 March 2008. The facilitators are Udday Thakar and Keith Jones. Bring a calculator. I call GBBS.

Tuesday 11/03/2008

4:30 p.m. Home. I was speaking to John of WH Malcolm Transport Ltd. He said he would call me back. Still waiting. I need transport from Dunshalt Village Primary School to an industrial unit. I am to contact Renwick Cowan, estates surveyor. I received a reply to my call earlier to the Hon. Mr Joseph Charter, High Commissioner in London for the government of Grenada. *'De minister has given me power of attorney,'* he said. What does that mean? Stalling. Sweet words. Grenadians tell you what you want to hear. Delivering nothing so far, no commitment on their part to assist me after all that I have managed to do for four of the schools over the last three years. I am the biggest doing-good mug on Blue Planet. I am unable to step back from the precipice having accumulated container loads of educational resources, and more to come, out of the waste stream. Why press on? Because of the helpful human beings I encountered who affirmed my flaky self-worth.

(My initiative [see haitirelief.org.uk] and the hours spent on typing out the diary is a tribute to the help they gave me.)

Wednesday 12/03/2008

I am to meet Johanna Louise at 12:30 p.m. at Flexi Tech Creamery car park. We are travelling up to Inverclyde Infirmary. *You've got three saved messages*: 12:06 p.m. Geoffrey Cave; 4:35 p.m. Buzzy Murray, Edinburgh Chamber of Commerce; 4:34 p.m. Ken Johnston, Criminal Justice and Community Services, Perth.

Thursday 13/03/2008

9:50 a.m. I have learned that MSC Mediterranean Shipping Company sail from the Port of Grangemouth direct to St George's,

Grenada. I was speaking to Emma in their office. I call Archie, Fife Council Criminal Justice and Community Services, regarding the supply of one of their teams to assist in the removal of resources from Dunshalt Village Primary School. They can do it. A positive development. Wonderful!

Friday 14/03/2008

MV *Argyle*. I have just bought a coffee. *'White coffee?' 'Yes please.'* I am en route for the Social Enterprise Academy financial management course being held today at the Royal Marine Hotel, Hunter's Quay, Dunoon.

It's a beautiful morning, washed clean with all the rain this week. I spoke to Robin Swaisland last night – long-distance Atlantic call. All of these calls will have cost a fortune. He said he would try and chivvy Azam of Spice Isle Retreaders, along with the payment he owes me for the container I shipped out to St Paul Government School, the Model School, in August last year. Robin said he knew Valentino, the broker in St George's. *'Just leave every ting wid me,'* he said. Robin Swaisland, DFID supremo in charge of the Agency For Reconstruction post Hurricane Ivan, had assured me that what I was doing was worthwhile, and the pending shipment of resources were very much needed and I should continue, in spite of the difficulties.

Yesterday, James in the Denholm Bahr Ltd freight forwarders office in the Epoch building, Grangemouth, gave me the following contacts of three shipping companies: Martin at CSAV Albert Drive G41, Hugh McGraw at CMA, Victoria Crescent Road G40; Doreen Hendry, Hapag Lloyd, Mercantile Chambers, Bothwell Street. It's now almost 10 a.m. and I am going to call them up. I need a vessel to take a container to Kingston Jamaica. I am told that CSAV operate from the Port of Tilbury. CMA were helpful and suggested I write to her and will forward my letter. She took umbrage when I mentioned a rival firm. *'Wash yur mooth oot. They are our competition,'* she said. No reply received so I called her up again. Always approachable but no result.

10:30 a.m. I shan't bore you, reader, with lecture notes should you have journeyed with me thus far.

10:45 a.m. I am going to do a practical exercise. Prepare a budget.

Thursday 24/04/2008

8:45 a.m. Home. It is raining heavily. Grey. I am down in the dumps. Is it worth the candle? I have to persist. I am about to give some time and attention to the tour operators and hotel owners in Grenada, Carraiacou, and Petit Martinque, using a Grenada Tourist Board list. Some of whom may prove to be a possible source of funding for a social enterprise initiative that may assist in defraying the cost of transport of the next container shipment.

11:45 a.m. I have not long spoken to First Port in Edinburgh, and to Kim, who comes across as encouraging. I told her about my SESF 'social enterprise'. Tighnabruaich. I will leave it with her. *'What media coverage have you had?'* she asks. I have had plenty. And I told her about the recent article *'Dunshalt Furniture on its way to Grenada'* by Liz Rougvie and Liz Howie, *Fife Herald*, Friday, 28 March, 2008. I then mentioned to her that I had met Naomi Johnson in a meeting at a Glasgow Caledonian social enterprise conference, ABSEN Dunoon and at an Edinburgh Chamber of Commerce social enterprise conference at the Grosvenor Hilton Hotel.

Friday 25/04/2008

12:15 p.m. Home. I am back in the doldrums. It is a time of waiting again. I am going to heat up some of my soup. It is grey and wet out of doors. The sun shone through a while earlier.

Friday 02/05/2008

9:20 a.m. Home. I was speaking to Norman of First Port in Edinburgh. He tells me that I need to 'validate' my business model. What does that mean? He suggests 'tapping' into councils? Not helpful. I want action and 'deliverables'. *'I have come from the commercial sector,'* he tells me, and goes on to mention, *'common forms of evaluation of outcomes.'* I am baffled by that phrase.

Wednesday 07/05/2008

11:10 a.m. Home. *'All decals must be removed from the containers,'* said Stuart, CEO of Pentalver Transport Ltd, Southampton. I was speaking to him about a 40-foot ocean freight container that I have recently purchased which, all being well, will be delivered to The Food and Business Centre, Unit 3, Glenrothes. Fife. I am now going to write to him.

Monday 19/05/2008

11:30 a.m. I had to drag myself off the bed. I am now calling architectural firms that are, or maybe, or intend to be, involved in the Scottish Executive's PFI/PPP schemes. Possible sponsors of my foundation. No chance. I must be daft.

Why on earth should I, at this stage, want to accumulate more surplus educational resources than I can cope with?

* * *

'Life can only be understood backwards but it must be lived forwards.'

Soren Kierkegaard

'You cannot leap a chasm in two bounds.'

Chinese Proverb

Hurricane Ivan struck the island of Grenada, West Indies on Tuesday, 7 September 2004. The previous 363 entries of Volume One of the *Diary of a Shipping Clerk* give a brief account of how I, along with many individuals, was able to deliver four ocean freight containers of salvaged, fit-for-purpose, surplus to requirements educational resources to three Grenada Government Schools (Grand Roy, Calliste and St Paul's), that had been devastated by the hurricane; from the two visits that I made to the island, in 2006 and 2007, I knew that this was just a tiny drop in the bucket of need, and so I was determined to see if I could organise some more shipments to the island schools.

* * *

Acknowledgements

There are so many to thank for the crucial assistance they gave me:-

Jerry Copsey, Just Grenada • The Barns, Frome, Somerset • Cameron Geddes, General Manager, Ecosse World Express Ltd, Airlink, Glasgow Airport • Craig Boreland, Editor, *The Buteman* • Martin Stirling, The Boat Yard and Marina, Port Bannatyne • David Kilpatrick, The Bike Shed, Rothesay, Isle of Bute • Kevin Sayers • Tom Walker Container Surveyor, Chryston, Glasgow • Fraser Russell, Account Manager, Freightliner Ltd, Eurocentral Freight Terminal, Coatbridge • John Sas, Ligentia, National Commercial Manager • Brian Munro and Team Operations Director, Fife Warehousing Co. Ltd, Kirkcaldy • Duncan and Elisabeth Adams, Eric Adams and their Team at Duncan Adams Transport Ltd, Grangemouth • Roland Malins-Smith and his Team, Sea Freight Agencies/Crowley Inc, Miami, USA • Mr John MacKirdy and his Team at John MacKirdy Ltd, Rothesay, Isle of Bute • John G. Russell • Graeme Russell • Mark Furmage at John G. Russell Transport Ltd • Peter McGarry, Transport Manager, Container Base, Coatbridge • Peter and Tish Timms, Ascog, Isle of Bute • John Hume, General Manager, John G. Russell Transport Ltd, Hillington • William McCord • Jimmy Hewitt, Community Payback Work Officer, City of Edinburgh • Katherine McNiven, Community Services, Dunoon • Archie Melville, Senior Project Officer, Craig Pearson, Community Services Social Work, Glenrothes • Andrew Malcolm, John Murray, Gavin Brown, Jim Clark, Bob Tannahill, John Boal, John Morrison, W H Malcolm Transport Ltd, Brookfield House, Linwood • Brian Kreslins, Hugh Carroll, Frank Berrie, W. H. Malcolm Transport Ltd, Container Base, Elderslie • Alan Nicoll, General Manager Port and Property Services, Babcock International Group, Marine Division, Rosyth • Brian Herron, Community Services Edinburgh City Council • Hugh Hardie, Operations Manager, Clydeport, Ocean Terminal, Greenock • Andrew Hemphill • Derek

ACKNOWLEDGEMENTS

Knox, Port Manager, Forth Ports, Port of Grangemouth • The Team at Edinburgh Community Transport, • Howard Clack Freight Container Services (Scotland) Ltd, Littlecarlton, Newark • Renwick Cowan, Estates Surveyor and Gillian Bobby, Estates Surveyor, Fife Council • Sam Baggley, Pentalver Transport Ltd, Container Sales, Southampton • Andy Rushton, Pentalver Transport Ltd, Stourton, Leeds • Colin Todd, Marine Surveyor, Prestwick • Bill Williamson, MSL Associates • Paul Fisher • Alan Galt and Team, Alan Galt Transport Ltd, Dumbarton • Shona Guthrie, Human Resources and Team, James Walker DeVol, Gourock • J. Michel Guite, Greenwich, USA • Liz Rougvie, Reporter, *Fife Herald*, Cupar • Danny, HGV driver; Agnes and Andrew, Traffic Office, FreightLiner Co. Ltd, Coatbridge • Tanya Scoon, *The Fife Free Press*, Kirkcaldy • Barry L Ayre, Social Enterprise Academy, Edinburgh • Lesley Paul and her Team, One2One Accountancy Services, Isle of Bute • James R. B. Ross, Chartered Accountant and his Team, Dunoon • The Journalists, Simon Bain, Rebecca McQuillan, Leanna McLarty and Stephen Naysmith, *The Herald*, Glasgow • Kenneth Brodie, Regional Manager Scotland, Advantage Worldwide, Renfrew • John Morrison, Carson Lifting and Transport Solutions Ltd, Cumbernauld • Anne I. McIntyre Campbell, Caribbean Horizon Tours and Services, Grenada, West Indies • Stevie Cameron, HGV Driver, and son Daniel, Duncan Adams Transport Ltd, Port of Grangemouth • Jane Harris, Group Commercial Director, J & J Denholm Ltd, Glasgow • Ray Perkins, Denholm Forwarding Ltd, Liverpool • Alan Ewing and his Team, Haulier, Ardbeg, Isle of Bute • George Flatters, HGV Driver, Shanks, Nottingham • Robert Hyslop, Haulier, Airdrie • Ricky Henderson, Edinburgh City Councillor, Pentland Hills • Phil and Anne Kirkham, Picture Bute • Ioannis Kottoris, Freight Forwarder, Noble Global Logistics UK Ltd, Manchester Airport • Murray McGilchrist, Commercial Representative, Forth Ports Ltd, Port of Grangemouth • Nina McElroy, Estates Manager, Waterfront Edinburgh Ltd, Madelvic House, Granton • George McGroarty, HGV Driver, Duncan Adams Transport Ltd • Colin McDonald, Operations Manager, Jennifer Blackwood, Texas Instruments, Greenock • Stephen Phillips, Solicitor, Burness, Glasgow • Ronnie McEwen, Mhairi Anderson, Joan Kildae and Teams, Pickfords Glasgow and Motherwell • Euan Burns, Storage Advisor, Pickfords Self-Store, Granton • Philip

ACKNOWLEDGEMENTS

Turley, Willmot Dixon Construction Ltd, Hitchin, Herts • Ian Steel, Managing Director, J. A. Steel & Son, Enfield • Stuart Schap, HGV Driver, Duncan Adams Transport Ltd • Sam Tweedlie, Digital Artisan, Isle of Bute • Karen, Matt and Martin, Print Point, Rothesay.

I think these are all – or practically all – of the individuals and firms I wish to acknowledge who made it possible for me to ship worldwide over a dozen ocean-freight containers of fit for purpose surplus to requirements educational resources.

www.ingramcontent.com/pod-product-compliance
Lightning Source LLC
Chambersburg PA
CBHW070458120526
44590CB00013B/682